Internet
ANNOYANCES™

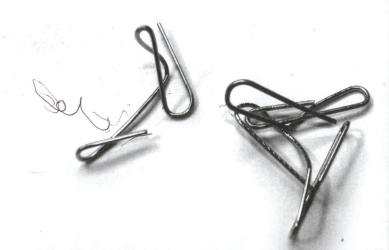

Internet ANNOYANCES™

How to Fix the Most ANNOYING Things About Going Online

Preston Gralla

O REILLY®

Beijing • Cambridge • Farnham • Köln • Paris • Sebastopol • Taipei • Tokyo

Internet Annoyances™
How to Fix the Most Annoying Things About Going Online

by Preston Gralla

Published by O'Reilly Media, Inc., 1005 Gravenstein Highway North, Sebastopol, CA 95472.

O'Reilly books may be purchased for educational, business, or sales promotional use. Online editions are also available for most titles *(safari.oreilly.com)*. For more information, contact our corporate/institutional sales department: 800-998-9938 or *corporate@oreilly.com*.

Print History:		**Editor:**	Robert Luhn
January 2005:	First Edition.	**Production Editor:**	Philip Dangler
		Cover Designer:	Ellie Volckhausen
		Interior Designer:	Patti Capaldi
		Art Director:	Michele Wetherbee
		Illustration:	© 2005 Hal Mayforth c/o theispot.com

 This book uses RepKover™, a durable and flexible lay-flat binding.

0-596-00735-3
[C]

Contents

Introduction   xi

1 — EMAIL AND SPAM ANNOYANCES CH. 1

2 General Email Annoyances

Retrieve Web-Based Mail with
   Your Email Program

Can't Send Email from the Road

Clean My Email, Please

Never Forget to Attach a File Again

Give Me an Old-Fashioned Address Book

The Cure for Email Overload

DidTheyReadIt?

Stop Me Before I Flame Again!

Stop URL Sprawl

Stop That Email!

11 Spam

Spam Fighting 101

Stay off Spam Lists

Thirty-Second Guide to Tracing Spammers

Can the Can Spam Act Can Spam?

Beware the National "Do Not E-mail Registry"

Update Outlook's Spam Filter

My Newsletter Gets Blocked as Spam

My ISP Thinks I'm a Spammer

18 Outlook 2003 and Outlook Express 6

Password-Protect Outlook 2003 and
   Outlook Express 6

Fix My Outlook Unread Mail Folder

Outlook 2003 Gives Me Claustrophobia

My Outlook Email Looks Like Sanskrit

Get File Sprawl Under Control

Folder Navigation

More Keyboard Shortcuts

Kill the Express Splash Screen!

Back Up Outlook and Outlook Express

Outlook Email in Two Places at Once

Can't Copy Outlook Express Mail to New Laptop

24 Gmail

Give Me Space, Lots of Space

Why Won't Gmail Receive Newsletters?

Where's My Archived Gmail?

26 Eudora 6

End Auto-Completion Errors

Speed Up Eudora with Keyboard Shortcuts

Help Eudora Take Out the Trash

Speed Up Sluggish Eudora

What Do Those Weird Eudora Icons Mean?

31 MAKING THE CONNECTION ANNOYANCES CH. 2

32 General Connection Annoyances

Instant Fix for Broken Internet Connections

XP Hangs Whenever I Connect to the Internet

What's My True Connection Speed?

Stop My Modem Before It Dials Again

34 Broadband: Cable and DSL Connections

Slow-as-Molasses Cable Modem

Fix This Slow-as-Molasses Cable Modem, Take 2

Revive Your DSL Connection

Internal Wiring Scam

Why Does DSL Hate My Router?

Does Comcast Charge Extra for Home Networking?

Country Boy Has DSL Problems

New Connection Wizard Woes

39 Routers and Home Networks

File-Sharing Traffic Jam

Manage Your Network's Bandwidth

Rock n' Roll and NAT

My Router Won't Connect to the Net

VPN Hates My Home Router

How To Get Real Broadband Help

43 WIRELESS ANNOYANCES CH. 3

44 Home Wireless Networks and Routers

Extend Your Wireless Network's Range

Boost WiFi Speed with a Cantenna

Eliminate WiFi Interference

Jump-Start Your Wireless Router

Test Your True Network Speed

Have I Been Taken for a WiFi Ride?

Why Won't My WiFi Devices Talk to Each Other?

WiFi Printing Woes

Stop Bandwidth Vampires

Speed Up an 802.11g Slowpoke

Wireless Security Cam

A Teen's Dream: Wireless PlayStation

52 Cell Phones and the Net

From Email to Cell Phone

Garbled Web Sites

Become a Wireless Froogle Shopper

Beware Bluetooth Snarfing Attacks

54 WiFi Security

Stop Broadcasting Your Network Name

Protect Your Home WiFi Network

Easy Guide to Setting Up WEP Encryption

Change Your WEP Key Regularly

When Is 40-Bit WEP Really 64-Bit WEP?

Not-So-Easy Guide to Setting Up WPA Encryption

Celtic Runes and Wireless Access?

60 HotSpots

Find HotSpots Before You Hit the Road

Choose the Right HotSpot Provider

HotSpot Gone Cold

Available Versus Preferred Networks

Why Can't I Connect to an "Available" Network?

Easier T-Mobile HotSpot Connections

Protect Your Privacy

Get Technical Support for HotSpot Woes

Cure HotSpot Amnesia

HotSpot, Cold Email

Go War Driving for HotSpots

Go War Driving with Your Pocket PC

Connect to the Right HotSpot

Stop HotSpot "Stuttering"

Tapping into a Private HotSpot—Legal or Not?

Forget HotSpots—Use Your Bluetooth Cell Phone!

Make Your Blog Private

Get Rid of Odd Characters in LiveJournal

Upload a User Picture to LiveJournal

73 WEB HOSTING, DESIGN, AND BLOG ANNOYANCES CH. 4

99 BROWSER ANNOYANCES CH. 5

74 Domain and Hosting Hassles

Become Master of Your Own Domain

Break the Network Solutions Monopoly

Shorten Your Web Site's URL

Choose a New Hosting Service

Stop Sending Site Visitors into Oblivion

82 Design and Maintenance Help

Make Web Pages the Easy Way

Find Out Who's Linking to Your Web Site

Why Won't FrontPage Work with My Host?

FrontPage Extensions Gone Bad

Fix Typos in URLs

Fix Your Spelling Errors

Help Your HTML

Can't View Source in IE

Banish Bad Links

Get Centered

What Happened to My Cool Fonts?

Use Web-Safe Colors

Create Thumbnails on Web Pages

Quick-and-Easy Image Conversion

Get a Free Page Counter

92 Blogging

What Is Blogging?

Why Can't I Use Pictures in My Blog?

Moblog with TypePad

Bust Blog Blockages

Build an Audio Blog

Comment on Web Sites

Syndicate Your Blog

Post to Your Blog via Email

100 Pop-Ups, Ads, and Flash

Pop Away Pop-Ups

I Want My Pop-Ups! (Well, Some of Them)

Make the Internet an Ad-Free Zone

News Flash—I Hate Flash!

Find That Flash File!

104 Favorites and Bookmarks

Where'd My Cool Favorites Icons Go?

Move Favorites and Bookmarks from
Here to There

Search Your Favorites

Alphabetize Your Favorites

Jump Through Your Favorites List

Why Can't I Print My IE Favorites?

The Links Folder: The Most Annoying Favorite

Don't Know Much About History?

109 Working the Interface

Fill Forms Faster

Stop Debugging Me!

End Toolbar Madness

Teach Adobe Acrobat Reader Some Manners

Old News Is Not Good News

Zap Zip

Find the Hidden Button

Save Downloads Where You Want

Print That Web Page—All of It!

Bypass Web Site Logins

Organize Your Web Clippings

Keep Internet Explorer Maximized

Track Down the Google Toolbar

Put Your Brand on Internet Explorer

Keep Tabs in Internet Explorer

Better Tabbed Browsing in Firefox

Pages Don't Display Properly in Firefox

Why Can't I Use Windows Update with Opera or
Netscape?

118 Speedups and Shortcuts

Instant Internet Speedup

Speedup Software Kills Web Site Access

Real Men Don't Use Mice

Stop AutoComplete Reminders

Password Help for the Memory-Impaired

Why Can't I Save Images as GIFS or JPEGs?

Why Won't Internet Explorer Let Me Download?

121 Cookies

Toss Your Cookies

Customize Internet Explorer's Cookie Handling

A Rare Cookie Lover

Can I Trust This Web Site?

127 AOL ANNOYANCES CH. 6

128 General AOL Annoyances

I Don't Care if I've Got Mail!

Who Stole the Back and Forward Buttons?

Stop AOL Window Overload

Cut the Screen Clutter

Speed Up the Long Goodbye

Turn Off Pop-Ups

Stop USPS Junk Mail

Move Favorites from AOL to Internet Explorer

Get Help from a Live Human Being

Save Tech Support Chats

Save Better Web Graphics

Get Caller ID Numbers for Dropped Calls

Uninstall Previous Versions of AOL

Stop AOL from Booting You Off

Check that Local Number!

Keep Your Kids Safe on AOL

Stop AOL from Dialing Unnecessarily

138 Email

Keep Your Sent Email

Fetch AOL Mail with Your Own Email Client

Stop Address-Book Overload

Tell AOL Mail to Send Your File

Send Stalled Emails

No, AOL, I Am Not a Spammer

Get and Send Email in a Flash

Check AOL Email from the Web

"Unsend" an Email

AOL Chews Up My Email!

Sort Mail by Person and Date

Why Can't I Report Spammers?

Fix Flaky Fonts

145 IM ANNOYANCES CH. 7

146 General Instant Messaging Annoyances

Slam IM Spam

Get All-Around IM Protection

Send Text Messages to Cell Phones

Plumb Your IM Program's Memory

IM and Jennifer Aniston's Hairdo

Protect Your Privacy When Using IM

IM Is Killing My Business!

Get a Universal Instant Messenger

Teach Trillian to Talk Again

Help a Mac Friend

Send Files Easily via IM

Stop Viruses Sent via IM

Use IM at Work

157 AOL Instant Messenger (AIM)

Kiss Off AIM Ads

Does AIM Install Spyware?

Be Invisible in Plain Sight with AIM

Use AIM and AOL at the Same Time

My Router Blocks AIM File Transfers!

Make ICQ and AIM Talk

Shrink Your Buddy List

Why Can't I Resize My AIM Screen?

Use AIM Without Installing It

Turn Off AIM Announcements

Shut Up AIM

Stop Obnoxious AIMers

Brave New AIMBots

163 Windows Messenger

Stop Windows Messenger from Autostarting

Kill Windows Messenger Forever

File Transfers Flake Out

Stop Messenger from Launching with Outlook
    and Outlook Express

Send Instant Messages from Outlook

166 Yahoo! Messenger

Clean Out the Yahoo! Messenger Junk

Yahoo! Messenger Crashes Whenever I Send a
File

Can't Log into Yahoo! Messenger

Where Are My Messages?

168 ICQ

Make ICQ a Private Club

Stop the ICQ Typewriter

Get ICQ out of Your Face

169 SEARCHING ANNOYANCES CH. 8

170 General Search Annoyances

Weed Out Sponsored Search Results

Search the Past with the Wayback Machine

Google Toolbar Alternatives

Change IE's Default Search Engine

Super Searches from the Address Bar

Use a Universal Search Engine

Do a Reverse Phonebook Lookup

Why Can't Search Engines Do Science?

Protect Your Kids from Search Engines

175 Government and the Law

Get the Lowdown on Congress

Find Your Congressman's Voting Record

Tell It to the Judge!

Find What Google Can't

178 Google

Search Google Without a Browser

Google Isn't Tech-Smart

Where'd My Original Google Search Go?

Netscape Can Google, Too

Go Local with Google

Show 150 Search Results

Find PDF Files Fast

Find Web Pages by Title

Teach Google to Speak French

Have Google News Delivered

Where's That Picture?

185 Amazon

Search Amazon and the Web Simultaneously

Automatically Seach Amazon for Highlighted
    Words

186 eBay

Better eBay Searching

Fine-Tune eBay Browsing

Quickly Scan eBay Feedback

Search Through a Seller's Items

You've Got Auctions!

189 Yahoo!

Fancy Searching with Yahoo!

Cut Down on Yahoo! Navigation

191 SECURITY ANNOYANCES CH. 9

192 General Security Annoyances
Get Free Security Checkups
Browse in Perfect Anonymity
Beware of Phishing Expeditions
Guaranteed, Foolproof Way to Uncover Spoof Sites
Block Snooping Neighbors
My Kids Keep Downloading Malware
Beware of Spoofed Emails
Kill the Windows Messenger Service
Internet Explorer Blocks My Downloads
Yikes—Someone Stole My Web Site Password!

199 Spyware
My Browser Has Been Hijacked!
Ad-Aware Deleted My Favorite Photos
Ad-Aware Hangs During Scans
Avoid Spyware in the First Place

202 Trojans, Worms, and Viruses
What to Do About Trojans
Hidden File Extensions Feed Viruses and Worms
Home-Grown Email Worm and Trojan Detector
Help! I've Become an AIM Spammer!
Instant Messaging Links Hijacked My PC

205 Firewalls
ZoneAlarm Killed My Home Network
ZoneAlarm Kills Most Web Browsing
Norton Personal Firewall Blocks Forum Discussions
Norton Personal Firewall Blocks Online Banking
Norton Personal Firewall Blocks Web Site Logins
Share Files Safely on Your Network with Windows Firewall
Report Hackers to the Good Guys

211 SHOPPING AND AUCTION ANNOYANCES CH 10

212 General Shopping Annoyances
Beware of Restocking Fees
Swap Your Useless Gift Certificate
Why Can't I Return a Big-Screen TV?
Protect Yourself Against Online Identity Theft
Faster Form Filling
Can I Trust This Lawn-Gnome Site?
Quick Guide to Less Annoying Returns
I Can Get It for You Wholesale!
Tax, Schmax
Why Did I Pay More for a Hotel at Expedia?
Unfreeze Your Frozen PayPal Account
Has My Online Bank Account Been Cracked?

220 eBay Annoyances
Beware of eBay Phishers
When Is Cash Not Cash?
Add a Movie to Your Auction
Get a Great Deal on a Labtop or Camra
Become an eBay Sniper
Beware of eBay Shills
Did I Pay Too Much for Those Opera Glasses?
Don't Get Burned on eBay
Get It Cheaper from the Police

225 Amazon Annoyances
Zap Images for Faster Amazon Shopping
Shop Amazon with Your Cell Phone
Yes, Virginia, There Is an Amazon 800 Number
Stop My $7,600 Amazon One-Click Order
Find Foreign Books on Amazon
Find Books Fast with Amazon Power Search
Search Amazon from IE's Address Bar

Index   231

Introduction

I'm annoyed as hell, and I'm not going to take it any more!

If that's your mantra, this book is for you. I'm here to help you take back the Internet from scamsters, spammers, reality-challenged web developers, sleazy marketers, pop-up ads, spyware, wireless stupidities, sloppy Microsoft programming, and the normal everyday annoyances of dial-up and broadband communications.

I've been using the Internet for longer than I care to remember—since before the days of the Web, when getting onto the Internet meant getting a "shell account" and using an unholy mess of Unix commands to do something as simple as reading your email.

Alas, things are even more annoying today. Don't believe me? Back in those days, there was no such thing as a pop-up ad. Heck, there weren't even *regular* online ads. Spam was a luncheon meat. Annoyance-laden programs like RealPlayer were not even a gleam in their creators' eyes. There were no wireless routers to curse, no sodden browsers like Internet Explorer to kick around, not even a glammed-up AOL to grumble about.

WHY WRITE INTERNET ANNOYANCES?

Over the years, I've made a hobby and a habit (if you combine a hobby and a habit, does that make a Hobbit?) of collecting various Internet-related annoyances and figuring out solutions for them. Word got around, so I'm constantly providing technical support for Internet problems to large swatches of the civilized world (and a substantial section of the uncivilized world, mostly in my hometown of Cambridge, MA). I've gotten email from all over the globe, including from a very sweet 18-year-old boy in Lebanon who, after receiving my help, decided to name his pet rabbit after my daughter's rabbit. (I, of course, was honored, and so there is now at least one rabbit in Lebanon named Polichinelle.)

But you can only help so many people via email and the phone. Why not share my fixes with the world? And so this book was born.

HAVE AN ANNOYANCE?

We feel your pain. If you'd like to share yours—and any solutions, for that matter—feel free to reach out. Send your emails to *annoyances@oreilly.com*. We'll try to sneak them into future editions of *Internet Annoyances*.

HOW TO USE THIS BOOK

This book is organized into 10 chapters, covering email and spam; making the Internet connection; wireless technology; web hosting, design, and blogging; browsers; AOL; instant messaging; searching; security; and online shopping. Each chapter is subdivided into different sections. For example, in the email chapter, you'll find sections devoted to general email annoyances, spam, Outlook and Outlook Express, Gmail, and Eudora. (AOL has more than its share of annoyances, which is why we've set aside an entire chapter for it.)

Don't expect to read this book straight through from cover to cover. It's best to jump around, first solving those annoyances that annoy you the most, then discovering other annoyances you can head off at the pass.

CONVENTIONS USED IN THIS BOOK

The following typographic conventions are used in this book:

Italic is used for filenames, pathnames, URLs, email addresses, and emphasis.

`Constant width` is used for code samples, keywords, and items that should be typed verbatim.

Menu sequences are separated by arrows, such as Data → List → Create List. Tabs, radio buttons, buttons, checkboxes, and the like are identified by name—for example, "click the Options tab and check the 'Always show full menus' box."

O'REILLY WOULD LIKE TO HEAR FROM YOU

Please address comments and questions concerning this book to the publisher:

O'Reilly Media, Inc.
1005 Gravenstein Highway North
Sebastopol, CA 95472
(800) 998-9938 (in the United States or Canada)
(707) 829-0515 (international or local)
(707) 829-0104 (fax)

There is a web page for this book, where you'll find links to the utilities mentioned in this book. You'll also find errata and additional information. You can access this page at:

http://www.oreilly.com/catalog/internetannoy/

To comment or ask technical questions about this book, send email to:

bookquestions@oreilly.com

For more information about books, conferences, Resource Centers, and the O'Reilly Network, go to:

http://www.oreilly.com

ABOUT THE AUTHOR

Preston Gralla first cut his teeth in the online world by dialing into bulletin boards back in the mid-1980s, using an all-powerful 2400-baud modem. He then graduated (or descended, depending on your point of view) to dialing into online services such as Delphi, CompuServe, and America Online, and eventually into the Internet itself (via various annoying means). He now has seven computers at home, which he's networked wirelessly to a broadband Internet connection—which means that he encounters seven times the Internet annoyances of the average user.

Preston is the author of more than 30 books about the Internet and computing, including *Windows XP Hacks* and *Windows XP Power Hound*. He was the founding managing editor of the trade newspaper *PC Week* and a founding editor and then editor and editorial director of *PC/Computing*. He was instrumental in helping establish the ZDNet online service and was on the startup team for a new online service called Interchange that never saw the light of day, thanks to a little thing called the World Wide Web. He was executive editor at both ZDNet and CNET.

Preston has also written about computers and technology for a wide variety of newspapers and magazines, including *USA Today*, the *Los Angeles Times*, *PC Magazine*, *Boston Magazine*, and the *Dallas Morning News* (where he was a technology columnist), among many others. He writes several online columns, including one for *PC Magazine* and one for *PriceGrabber.com*, and is editor in charge of O'Reilly's WindowsDevCenter web site. He's won a number of awards for his writing and editing, including one for Best Feature in a Computer Publication from the Computer Press Association. Under his editorship, *PC/Computing* was a finalist for the National Magazine Award for General Excellence.

As a well-known technology expert, Preston has made numerous TV and radio appearances, including on CNN, the CBS Early Show, MSNBC, ABC's World News Now, and many others. He has also contributed regular commentaries about technology to National Public Radio's *All Things Considered*.

Email and Spam
ANNOYANCES

Let us all praise email. It's the great instant communicator. And, of course, the source of instant annoyances.

No other software is so spectacularly useful and so spectacularly annoying. How annoying? One word: spam.

Of course, there are a lot more email annoyances beyond spam. Like why, when you travel, you sometimes can't send email, no matter how hard you try. Like not being able to access your corporate account. Like getting notices that mail you've sent can't be delivered—even though you never sent it.

There are so many annoying things about email, in fact, that I've had to break up this chapter into several parts. It starts off with general email annoyances. Then it covers that plague of the Internet, spam. After that, it delves into email software that Windows users love to hate, Outlook and Outlook Express. It also shows you how to fix annoyances in that old email standby, Eudora, and dips into the future with a look at Google's Gmail, which has its own set of annoyances. America Online users, don't worry; AOL's email and other annoyances get their very own chapter later on in this book.

GENERAL EMAIL ANNOYANCES

RETRIEVE WEB-BASED MAIL WITH YOUR EMAIL PROGRAM

The Annoyance: It's hard enough to keep track of all the email I handle with my email program, but I also have web-based accounts with Hotmail and Yahoo! This means I have to check three different places for all my email. This is progress?

The Fix: Two free downloads—YahooPOPs! and Hotmail Popper—let you use just about any email program to access your Yahoo! Mail and Hotmail accounts. You'll be able to download and send email with your favorite email app, almost transparently.

YahooPOPs!

A while back, you could fetch your Yahoo! mail for free via a POP3 mail server, using an email program such as Outlook or Eudora. No longer. These days you have to pay $20 a year for the privilege. (Although, to be fair, you get other useful features, such as automatic forwarding of your Yahoo! mail, more storage space, and more.) However, the clever (and free) YahooPOPs! (*http://prdown-loads.sourceforge.net/yahoopops/yahoopops-win-0.6.exe?download*) lets you treat Yahoo! Mail like any other POP3 mail server. YahooPOPs! serves as a go-between, retrieving the mail and then letting your email program grab it.

Install YahooPOPs!, and it idles in the Windows System Tray. You can configure it with a variety of options, directing it to automatically download messages to your email client, leave mail on the server, or download only a certain number of emails per session (see Figure 1-1). Setup is easy—simply create a new mail account in your

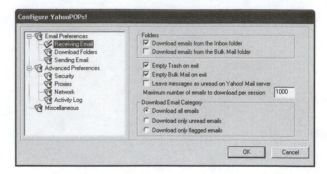

Figure 1-1. Configuring YahooPOPs! to retrieve email from your Yahoo! mail account is a checkbox affair.

email software. Call the incoming and outgoing mail servers "localhost," and use your Yahoo! username and password. Once YahooPOPs! is up and running, you can use your email program to check your Yahoo! Mail account.

OUTLOOK, OUTLOOK EXPRESS, AND HOTMAIL

If you use Outlook 2003 or Outlook Express 6.0, you don't need any special software to send and retrieve email with Hotmail—the capability is built in. In Outlook, go to Tools → Email Accounts and choose "Add a new e-mail account." In the first page that appears, choose HTTP as the server type, and click Next. On the E-mail Accounts settings page, enter your Hotmail username and password and choose Hotmail from the HTTP mail service provider drop-down list. Click Next, then click Finish. In Outlook Express, go to Tools → Accounts, click the Add button, and choose Mail. Type in your name and click Next. On the Internet E-mail Address page, enter your Hotmail email address and click Next. On the E-mail Server Names page (see **Figure 1-2**), choose HTTP for your incoming mail server and Hotmail as your HTTP mail service provider, then click Next. Type in your Hotmail username and password, click Next, then click Finish. That's it!

Figure 1-2. Checking Hotmail from Outlook Express involves only a few menu selections.

Hotmail Popper

Hotmail Popper (*http://www.boolean.ca/hotpop*) works just like YahooPOPs!, except for Hotmail. The setup is similar, too. Configure Hotmail Popper to get your mail, then configure your email client to retrieve it. As with YahooPOPs!, it runs in the Windows System Tray, so if you need to tweak it, right-click its icon and choose Properties. For incoming and outgoing mail servers, use the address 127.0.0.1.

As of this writing, if you're using the free version of Hotmail, you won't be able to use Hotmail Popper to get your email. You must have a "Hotmail Plus" or equivalent MSN account—in other words, a for-pay Hotmail account. Thank you, Microsoft for putting your hands in our pockets again. But Microsoft is well known for changing its mind, so there's a chance that Hotmail Popper will once again work with the free version of Hotmail.

CAN'T SEND EMAIL FROM THE ROAD

The Annoyance: When I'm on the road, I always stay at hotels that offer broadband Internet access. The problem? When I try to send email, my email software tells me it can't deliver the message because my ISP's SMTP server (my ISP is a cable company) chokes on the message. If my cable company can figure out how to charge me extra for movies on demand, surely it can figure out how to send my email!

The Fix: In the earlier, sunnier days of the Internet, this wasn't a problem. But alas, spam is at the root of this annoyance.

When you send email, it wends its way through an SMTP (Simple Mail Transfer Protocol) server. Because SMTP servers can be used to relay spam, many ISPs make sure that any mail sent through them is authorized. The SMTP server checks your IP address, sees you're not on the same network where the SMTP server lives, and rejects your mail, thinking it's spam. There are several fixes. First, find out if your hotel has an SMTP server you can use. If so, create a new mail account in your email software, using that SMTP server for sending mail, but using your ISP's POP3 or IMAP account for receiving.

If the hotel doesn't have an SMTP server, see if your ISP offers web-based access to your email. Many do. You won't be able to use your email software, but at least you'll be able to send and receive mail.

Finally, you can use some clever shareware to create an SMTP server on your own PC, so that your computer can send mail without using someone else's SMTP server. 1st SMTP Server (*http://www.emailarms.com/downloads/1st_smtp.html*), a good tool for this option, is simple to set up and use. If this doesn't appeal to you, you can sign up for an SMTP relay service that provides you with an SMTP server no matter where you are. SMTP.com (*http://www.smtp.com*) offers a variety of plans to choose from, based on how much email you send. For example, for $49.99 a year, or $9.99 for a single month, you can send up to 50 emails a day.

CLEAN MY EMAIL, PLEASE

The Annoyance: When I reply to or forward email, the message includes annoying >> characters in front of every line. Do I really have to spend the rest of my life stripping these things out of my messages by hand?

The Fix: Get a copy of Text Monkey from Boxer Software (*http://www.textmonkey.com*), which will automatically rid your email of these annoying characters (see Figure 1-3).

Figure 1-3. Brackets begone! With a click, Text Monkey strips out those irksome >> characters.

Just copy the text you want to clean to the Windows Clipboard, pop it into Text Monkey, click "Clean it!," and paste the pristine result back into your email app. Text Monkey Lite is free, but the $29.99 PRO version can clean up just about any text you can imagine, stripping out HTML tags, converting tabs to spaces, deleting duplicate lines, and a lot more.

NEVER FORGET TO ATTACH A FILE AGAIN

The Annoyance: My fingers are often faster than my brain, and sometimes I whip off an email and forget to send attachments. I don't want my recipients to think that I suffer from premature senility.

The Fix: If you use Outlook 2000 or 2002, a third-party program can come to the rescue when your brain fails. Attach! from KMGI (*http://kmgi.com/attach*) makes sure that when you intend to send attachments, you actually attach them. It scans all outbound messages for certain words (such as attach, attachment, and so on) and checks whether the messages containing those words actually have attachments. If they don't, Attach! flashes a warning and lets you attach a file. You can add new words to the list of words it checks, as shown in Figure 1-4. The free version of Attach! contains ads; an ad-free

Figure 1-4. Tell Attach! to watch out for specific words in your outgoing email, and it will flag you if it suspects you meant to attach a file but didn't.

version costs $9.95. A similar program, Attachment Forget-Me-Not, sells for $14.95 and is available from *http://www.sperrysoftware.com/Outlook/Attachment-Forget-Me-Not.asp*.

GIVE ME AN OLD-FASHIONED ADDRESS BOOK

The Annoyance: Call me old-fashioned, but I like to have all my contacts printed out neatly in a booklet form, not just in my email program. Why do email apps make this so hard?

The Fix: It's not as hard as you think. In Outlook 2003, in the Contacts view, choose View → Arrange By → Current View → Address Cards. Then choose File → Print. In the dialog box, go to the "Print style" section and select the printout style you want, such as Small Booklet Style or Phone Directory Style (see Figure 1-5). When you've made your choice, click OK, and away it prints.

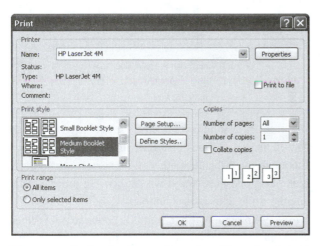

Figure 1-5. Need a printed contacts list in a hurry? Choose from Outlook's prefab formats.

To print your list of contacts in Outlook Express 6, open your Address Book, highlight all the entries you want printed, and choose File → Print. In the "Print style" section, choose Phone List, then click OK to print.

In Eudora 6, open the Address Book and choose Full Name from the View By drop-down list. Then choose File → Print.

You can print out Rolodex-style cards if you select the Card Style option. But if you do that, make sure that you buy special paper that lets you punch out the cards—there's no way you'll be able to cut them out by hand.

THE CURE FOR EMAIL OVERLOAD

The Annoyance: When it comes to email, I'm a pack rat. I use Outlook and have about four or five thousand emails stored in various folders; I rarely delete any of them, just in case I need the information someday. But now I have so much email, I can't find anything!

The Fix: Google Desktop Search to the rescue! You can now use Google technology to search through your email in the same way you use it to search through the Web. It'll dig through more than just email—it'll also search through Word, Excel, and PowerPoint files; text files; AOL Instant Messenger chats; and web pages you've visited. You'll have all the usual Google search operators (from quotes to + signs) at your command. And get this: you don't even have to save your chat logs or the web pages you visit—Google Desktop Search automatically logs and indexes your chats and all the web pages you go to. Even if you clean out your cache, the complete index is still there. One sour note is that Google Desktop Search only indexes sites you visit using Internet Explorer. If you use Firefox, Opera, or some other browser, you're out of luck.

You can download and install the free Google Desktop Search from *http://www.desktop.google.com*. (As with any software, make sure that no other programs are running while you install it.) When you first install it, you won't immediately be able to search—Google Desktop Search must first index everything on your hard disk. Indexing can happen in bits and drabs; if your PC is idle for more than 30 seconds, indexing will kick in. Start using your PC, and indexing will stop. For this initial master index, let Google Desktop Search do its thing. Depending on the speed of your PC and how much data you have on it, the indexing may take less than an hour, or up to a day or more. After the initial indexing, Google Desktop Search will continually index your computer as you use it.

Once it's done indexing, double-click the Google Desktop Search icon in the Windows System Tray. Your web browser will launch into a page that looks just like the Google site. To search your PC, type in search terms just as you would to search the Web with Google. The results will be displayed Google-style in your browser (Figure 1-6). Google Desktop Search will show you relevant results not only from your various in, out, and trash email boxes, but also from files on your PC and web pages you've visited. To see only email search results, click the email link just above the results list.

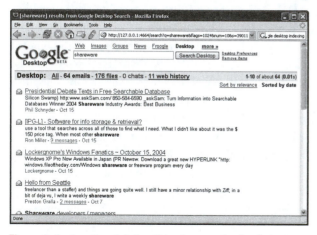

Figure 1-6. Sometimes it feels as if there's no escaping Google, but in this instance, that's a good thing. The free Google Desktop Search does a great job of searching through email and other files on your hard disk, and displays the results Google-style.

To read any of your emails, click the appropriate link. You'll see the text of the email on a web page. To open the email in Outlook, click the View in Outlook link. To see the entire history of an email exchange, click the link that lists the number of messages in the exchange (e.g., "5 messages").

If you're willing to pay for your searching, there's an alternative program that can find information as fast as you can type. X-1 (Figure 1-7) indexes all of your email and lets you search that index instantly. You can get it from http://www.x1.com/download/. X-1 works with Outlook 2000/XP/2003, Outlook Express 5/5.5/6, Netscape 6.2/7, and Eudora 5.2/6.1, and an upcoming version will work with Lotus Notes as well. You can do full-text searches as well as specify senders, recipients, subjects, folders, and attachments, and you can use Boolean searching, so finding exactly what you want is easy.

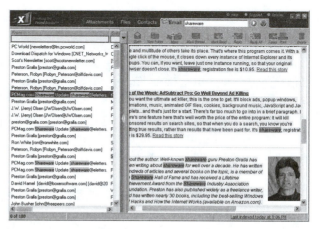

Figure 1-7. When X-1 finds what you're looking for, it highlights your search terms, making it easy to jump to the right spot in your email.

The program also indexes all the files on your hard disk, as well as your Outlook contacts, so you can dig through them quickly. It includes file viewers so you can view attachments and files, and it will launch the program that created a file when you double-click the file. It also has two-way communications with Outlook, so that when you read emails with it, it will mark them as read in Outlook; it will even let you delete emails from Outlook. You can try X-1 for free for 15 days. If you decide to keep it, you'll have to pay $74.95.

So should you use Google Desktop Search or X-1? Free is always good, so Google Desktop Search has that going for it. It also uses the familiar Google interface, and it uses less RAM, so it won't slow down your system, as X-1 can do on occasion.

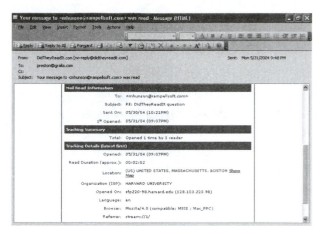

Figure 1-8. *A typical report from DidTheyReadIt notes when the recipient opened your email.*

But for certain purposes, X-1 is superior. It indexes all the files on your hard disk, not just a limited number of them. It searches through your Outlook contacts, which Google Desktop Search doesn't do. And it's easier to narrow your searches using X-1—for example, you can opt to search through only certain Outlook folders, which you can't do with Google Desktop Search.

DIDTHEYREADIT?

The Annoyance: This may sound sneaky, but when I send an email I like to know whether the recipient has read it, and if so, how long he spent reading it. So I signed up for a service called DidTheyReadIt that promises to provide this very information. Sometimes I get a notice that the mail was delivered, but often I don't. What gives?

The Fix: The DidTheyReadIt service (available for $50 a year from *http://www.didtheyreadit.com*) works by tucking a "web bug" (a tiny, invisible .GIF file) in the emails you send. DidTheyReadIt can track when and for how long that .GIF was accessed, and thus tell you when and for how long your email was read (see Figure 1-8). It's

a technique that spammers have used for years, which means that a number of email, antispyware, and firewall programs know how to block it. Also, it only works if the recipient's email program is set up to read HTML email. If the recipient uses a non-HTML mail reader, or if HTML reading is turned off by default (as it is in Outlook 2003, except for messages from senders already in your address book), your little web bug won't work. The web-based email service Gmail also doesn't display HTML by default, so DidTheyReadIt probably won't work there, either.

Additionally, firewall software such as ZoneAlarm blocks web bugs from working, as do some anti-spam programs and ISP filtering software. In fact, some ISPs might consider email containing the web bug spam and never deliver it. In sum, there's no guarantee that the service will work.

There's another way to find out whether an email you've sent has been received, though: use your email program's receipt function. It's not foolproof, because the user can ignore the receipt prompt. However, it'll work most of the time, because most people will probably respond.

If you're using Outlook 2003, here's the procedure to request a receipt that your email has been received and read. When you create a new email, click Options. In the Message Options dialog box, check the "Request a delivery receipt for this message" box if you want to get confirmation that the message was delivered, and the "Request a read receipt for this message" box if you want confirmation that the message was read. In Outlook Express 6, when you create a new message, choose Tools → Request Read Receipt and send your message.

If you use AOL, you can ask for a return receipt—(from AOL recipients only) by checking the "Request Return Receipt from AOL Members" box at the bottom of the screen. But here's a slightly sneaky, if more reliable, trick: in AOL's outbox, if you right-click the message and select Status, you'll learn exactly when the AOLer read the message.

To request a return receipt in Eudora 6, when you create a new email, click the Return Receipt button in the message toolbar, and then send your message. This is only available in paid mode or sponsored mode.

STOP ME BEFORE I FLAME AGAIN!

The Annoyance: I'm a hot-tempered guy, and sometimes I shoot off emails that practically burn up the wires. Later, I regret it. Stop me before I flame again!

The Fix: Switch to Eudora 6.0. Its Mood Watch feature monitors your email messages as you type, underlining offensive phrases in color ("jerk" and "moron," for

A Key to Mood Watch Color Codes

Eudora's Mood Watch underlines offensive words with a squiggly green line and exceedingly offensive words with a squiggly red line. Words such as "stupid," "moron," or "idiot" all get squiggly green lines. As for the words that get squiggly red lines—this is a family book, so I can't print them.

example). If you create a message that Mood Watch figures might be offensive, it pops up a note when you try to send the email, warning you that your message might be considered offensive (Figure 1-9). Mood Watch rates the email on a scale of one to three chili peppers, with three being the most offensive. If you still decide to send the message, or queue it to be sent, you'll get another warning.

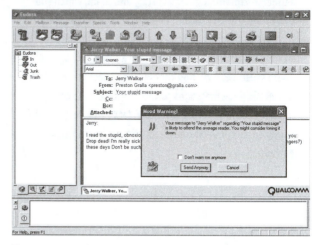

Figure 1-9. Don't send that email! Eudora's Mood Watch checks your email for offensive words or phrases.

If you don't use Eudora, there's a simple technique you can apply to any email program. If you create a new message while you're in a bad mood, don't fill in the sender name, and store it as a draft. Then later, after you've cooled off, read the message. Only send it after you've calmly considered whether it may be offensive.

STOP URL SPRAWL

The Annoyance: Is it me, or have URLs gotten longer and longer over the last few years? These days, when I send a link to someone, it's half the length of the *OED*. Worse, the recipient's email software breaks the link in the middle, which makes it a pain to copy and paste the link into a browser. Is there anything I can do?

The Fix: Cut those URLs down to size. Go to SnipURL (*http://www.snipurl.com*), a free service that shrinks any URL, no matter how long, to a manageable length. Using the service is a snip... er, snap. Head to the site and drag the "SNIP THIS!" link to your Links toolbar in Internet Explorer, or the equivalent in Netscape or Opera. When you're at a site with a long URL that you want to send to someone, click the SNIP THIS! button in the toolbar. A browser box pops up and generates a shortened link, which is automatically copied into the Windows Clipboard. Paste the snipped URL into your email and ship it off; when your friend plugs the snipped URL into her browser, it will take her to the site with the lonnnng address. Note that SnipURL won't work if you use a pop-up blocker, so turn it off before you generate any snips.

STOP THAT EMAIL!

The Annoyance: I guess I should have used Mood Watch—in the heat of an argument with my best friend, I sent him an email telling him off, and now I wish I hadn't. I mailed it only 10 minutes ago. Can I get it back?

The Fix: If you sent the mail from work and your office uses Outlook and Exchange Server, you may be able to recall it—but only if the mail's recipient is logged on, using Outlook, and hasn't yet read the message or moved it from his mailbox.

To recall email:

1. In Outlook's Navigation pane, choose the Sent Items folder.
2. Open the message you want to recall.
3. In the message window, choose Actions → Recall This Message. (Note: If you're not using an Exchange Server, the Recall This Message command won't appear.)

For a more complete solution, you can subscribe to the Bigstring service (*http://www.bigstring.com*). When you send mail, it's first routed to Bigstring's servers, which convert the email to HTML. The recipient of the message then gets an email from Bigstring containing a link. When the link is clicked, the email software goes to the Bigstring server and reads your HTML-based email. Since the HTML message sits on the Bigstring server, you have complete control over it. You can go back and edit the message later, and if you decide that you don't want it to be read at all, you can delete it from the server so it's no longer available. You can also set mail to expire after a certain amount of time. There's a free version of the service that handles 20 emails per month and comes with 1MB of storeage. For $12.95 per year, the service will handle 300 emails per month, offers 25MB of storage, and more. The $29.95 per year service handles an unlimited amount of email, throws in 50MB of storage, and more. Businesses can get five email accounts and many more features covered for $12.95 per month.

WHY AM I GETTING RETURNED MAIL NOTICES?

The Annoyance: I often get emails returned by a Mail Delivery Subsystem, telling me either that the recipient of the email doesn't exist, or that the message I sent has a virus in it. But I don't recognize the recipients—I know I never sent them email. What's the deal?

The Fix: There are several causes for this annoyance. One is that the message is forged and contains a virus. It's a ruse to get you to open any attachments so you'll infect your PC. Spammers also use this technique—you wonder what's getting bounced back, so you open the message, and wham, you're suddenly being sold Vicodin or cheap condos. This could also be a sign that a spammer or virus writer has "spoofed" or forged your email address so that when email is returned, it's sent to you rather than to them. You may get several kinds of returned mail notices for messages you never sent, such as "address unknown" and "email from you blocked because it contained a virus." None of them are your fault, so fear not—you haven't done anything wrong, and you're not being personally targeted by a spammer. Thousands of people are getting the same message.

Your only solution is to ignore the messages and delete them. Don't open them, because they might contain viruses.

In recent years, ISPs and mail services such as AOL, Earthlink, Yahoo!, Hotmail, and Gmail have beefed up their own built-in spam filters, catching a lot of spam before it even reaches you. If you want to stem the flood, your ISP can be your first line of defense.

STOP BUGGED EMAIL AND DANGEROUS SCRIPTS

Email programs that can read HTML are a double-edged sword. They allow you to view colorful, formatted emails that look like web pages, complete with fonts, graphics, animations, and more. But they can also let in web-bugged email and malicious scripts. Spammers often use web bugs to confirm they're sending email to a valid address. According to email-filtering company MX Logic, half of all spam contains web bugs. As for dangerous scripts, they can run inside HTML email and attack your computer in a variety of ways.

The fix? Turn off HTML reading in your email software. In Outlook 2003, HTML email is off by default. To make sure, choose Tools → Options, click the Security tab, and check the Change Automatic Download Settings box. In the dialog box that appears, check the "Don't download pictures or other content automatically in HTML email" box, then click OK. Older versions of Outlook don't let you turn off HTML viewing, but a free add-in called NoHTML (go to *http://ntbugtraq.ntadvice.com/default. asp?sid=1&pid=55&did=38* and click the Download link at the top of the screen) can do the job. There's no way to turn off HTML in any version of Outlook Express, although noHTML for Outlook Express (*http://www. baxbex.com/nohtml.html*) will do the trick. In Eudora, simply choose Tools → Options, click the Display icon, uncheck the "Automatically download HTML graphics" box, and click OK.

SPAM

SPAM FIGHTING 101

The Annoyance: Like everyone else in the world, my mailbox is filled to the brim with more obscene offers, get-rich-quick scams, and other digitrash than I thought existed on the planet. It's so overwhelming that I don't even know where to begin to fight it. I know that there's anti-spam software out there, but which is the best?

The Fix: There's no one "best" piece of spam-fighting software. Truth be told, most of the major anti-spam apps do a good job. The key is to choose a competent anti-spam program and use it to the max. Before buying, look for these features:

Trainable spam filters

Anti-spam software typically lets you mark email as spam. The spam filter should learn as you use it, catching not only email you've identified as spam, but similar emails as well.

Customizable spam filters

You should be able to customize the program's spam filters—for example, by telling it to nab any email that contains certain phrases.

Outlook 2003 includes a reasonably good built-in spam-killer, unlike earlier versions of the program. To turn it on, choose Tools → Options and click the Preferences tab. Then click Junk E-mail. Make sure the "No Automatic Filtering" box is unchecked, or else you'll turn off Outlook's spam-killer. Choose Low if you want to catch only the most obvious spam, and High if you want to be more aggressive—(and can live with it flagging some legitimate mail as spam).

The ability to set filter levels

When anti-spam software is too aggressive, it filters out almost all spam but also treats normal mail like spam. When it is less aggressive, more spam gets through. Look for anti-spam software that lets you choose a range of settings, so you can find the one that's best for you.

The ability to build whitelists and blacklists

The program should let you build a whitelist of senders that you consider safe and not spammers, as well as a blacklist of senders known to be spammers. Look for anti-spam software that lets you build and import these lists.

Integration with your email software

Some anti-spam software works independent of your email software, but many people find it more convenient to use anti-spam tools that work from directly inside the email software.

There are, of course, a lot of spam-killers out there. Here's a very short (and not exhaustive) list of capable anti-spam tools:

Norton AntiSpam

The same company that brings you Norton AntiVirus, Norton Firewall, and other security tools also has a very good spam-killer (*PC Magazine* gave it an Editor's Choice Award). For information, go to *http://www.symantec.com/antispam*.

McAfee SpamKiller

McAfee, like Norton, makes anti-virus software, firewalls, and other security tools, as well as this spam-whacker. It's based on an open source program called SpamAssassin. For information about McAfee Spam-Killer, head to *http://www.mcafee.com*.

Eudora 6.0

Eudora has a built-in spam-killer that's trainable. Choose Tools → Options and click the Junk Mail icon. Look for the Junk Threshold slider. By default, it's set at 50. Move it to the left, to a lower number, if it's catching most or all of your spam, but also some legitimate mail as well. Move it to the right if it isn't catching enough spam.

SafetyBar

This is anti-spam software with a twist. It's an Outlook add-in that uses peer-to-peer technology to fight spam. Everyone who installs it marks messages as spam, and that collective intelligence (at last count, over 1 million users) is then used to determine what's actually spam and what isn't. For information, go to *http://www.cloudmark.com*.

MailWasher

Unlike most spam-fighters, MailWasher sits between your email program and your mail server and blocks spam before it even gets to your mailbox. There's a free version that checks only one account, and a pay version that checks as many accounts as you want. For details, go to *http://www.mailwasher.net*. Some people use MailWasher in addition to other anti-spam tools. That way, spam gets filtered twice.

If you're feeling adventurous, you can also try a free Outlook spam-killing add-in from SpamBayes, an open source project devoted to killing spam. It's perennially in beta or alpha, but people report that it's useful and reliable. Get it from *http://spambayes.sourceforge.net/windows.html*.

STAY OFF SPAM LISTS

The Annoyance: I use spam-fighting email software, but I still get too much mail from friendly Nigerian millionaires and others promising to enlarge my bank account or other, um, assets. How can I stay off these spam lists in the first place?

The Fix: You're right—the best way to avoid spam is to avoid spammer lists. So how do you end up on these lists? The most common technique is "harvesting," according to a 2003 study ("Why Am I Getting All This Spam?") conducted by the Center for Democracy and Technology (*http://www.cdt.org*). Spammers use automated programs, or "bots," to scan web pages, forums, newsgroups, instant messages, and other sources for email addresses. Those addresses are then sold to other spammers, and boom—suddenly you're living in Spamopolis. So if possible, don't post your email address on a personal or public web site. If you post to forums, Usenet newsgroups, and the like, use an email account created specifically for this purpose, such as a free email account from Yahoo!, Hotmail, or Google.

If you must list your email address on, say, a personal web site, you can hide it from the bots in plain view. One easy trick is to spell out your email address—for example, write "preston at gralla dot com" instead of *preston@gralla.com*. Most harvesting programs won't be able to grab a spelled-out address.

Anti-spam mavens also use another classic technique: show your email address in an image file, such as a screen shot of the address in .GIF format. People can read it; spambots can't.

Some clever spammers have figured out ways around these techniques, so another solution is to use an inline JavaScript to generate your email address when the web page loads. Spam-harvester bots only see a `<script>` tag, but users see an address like *preston@gralla.com*.

To get your own bit of personalized code, go to the JavaScript generator at *http://www.u.arizona.edu/~trw/spam/spam.htm*. Feed it your email address and it generates the JavaScript, ready for you to plug into your site.

Yet another solution is to use HTML characters for your address rather than plain-text characters. Anyone visiting your site will see the address, because their browsers will translate the underlying HTML; bots will just see a string of numbers. The trick? Each letter or number in your email address is represented by its ANSI code. Instead of "p", you'd use "112", prefaced by `&#`. Separate each HTML character with a semicolon (`;`), and leave no spaces between characters. For example, in HTML characters, *preston@gralla.com* would be:

```
&#112;&#114;&#101;&#115;&#116;&#111;&#110;&#64;&
#103;&#114;&#97;&#108;&#108;&#97;&#46;&#099;&#11
1;&#109
```

Keep in mind, though, that if you use HTML characters to spell out your email address, you won't be able to use automated HTML "MailTo" links on the page—that requires the email address to be spelled out using regular letters and numbers.

For a comprehensive list of ANSI codes and special HTML characters, go to *http://www.alanwood.net/demos/ansi.html* and click the Symbol link at the top right of the page.

Finally, if you're really drowning in spam, you should carefully choose a new email address, inform your friends, set up an auto-reply on the old one, and never visit the old account again. Sounds too time-consuming? Well, you probably spend at least 30 minutes a day deleting floods of spam—now *that's* too time-consuming!

THIRTY-SECOND GUIDE TO TRACING SPAMMERS

The Annoyance: I'm sick of spam and I'm not taking it anymore. How can I track down these e-scum and turn them in?

The Fix: Two pieces of software, eMailTrackerPro and VisualRoute, can track down the real source of spam and notify the spammer's ISP in as little as 30 seconds.

You can download fully working demos of eMailTracker-Pro and VisualRoute from *http://www.visualware.com*. After 15 days, you can buy the duo for $69.90.

EMailTrackerPro (Figure 1-10) analyzes email headers and traces the messages back to their true senders, when possible, by finding the originating IP address. It even reports on the sender's country of origin. It also reports on the software used to send the message, which isn't especially useful but is something that Net geeks like to know. EmailTrackerPro also tells you if the email address it digs up has been "spoofed," or faked.

Figure 1-10. eMailTracker Pro tracks down the source of spam, including the email program used to send it and the country of origin, and reports if the address has been spoofed.

There are two ways to copy email headers into the program for analysis. If you use Outlook, eMailTrackerPro installs a button on the Outlook toolbar. Just highlight an email and click the button. If you don't use Outlook, copy

WHAT ARE HASH-BUSTING AND SPAMMERWOCKY?

You may have noticed that many spam messages end with gibberish. Some spam filters use a technique known as *hashing*, comparing incoming emails to emails it knows are spam. Spammers hope that by adding the gibberish, the Bayesian filters will let their spam through—a technique known as *hash-busting*. Alas, it often works.

A related technique is called *spammerwocky*. The spam contains a collection of words, such as "inexorable contrive stone brain conclude grandpa trickster." Many spam filters look for spam-like phrases, words, and sentence constructions. These random word collections are an attempt to make the email seem like a legitimate message. However, spam-killers have caught on, and spammerwocky rarely works these days.

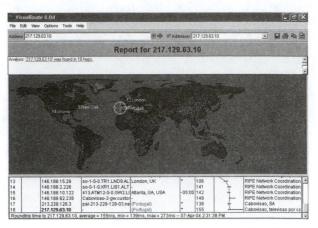

Figure 1-11. Once you know the IP address of the spammer, VisualRoute will find the exact path the spam took to get to you.

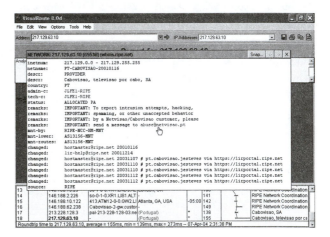

Figure 1-12. VisualRoute finds the spammer's ISP and pops up handy contact info for turning in the slimeball.

the header information from the email, choose Edit → Paste Headers in eMailTrackerPro, and the program will set off to work.

Tracking down the spammer's IP address solves the first part of the problem. To locate the spammer's ISP and send it an email, you must turn to VisualRoute. VisualRoute traces the route back to the IP address of origin, reporting on the path the message took and showing the owner of each server on the Internet over which the message traveled (Figure 1-11).

So while eMailTracker Pro will find the originating IP address, VisualRoute will identify the originating ISP—and that's who you want to complain to. When it finds the originating ISP, click the name, and VisualRoute will summon the WhoIs information for that ISP, including name, address, contact information, and email addresses (Figure 1-12).

If you see an email address for reporting spam, click it, and it will launch your email program. Paste in the header from the spam and send your complaint on its way—you've just reported a spammer.

The Birth of Spam

Most Internet historians generally agree that spam was born on March 8, 1994, when the law firm Canter & Siegel posted a public message on a number of Usenet newsgroups soliciting business. Newsgroups had never been used for commercial solicitations before. Despite the immediate outcry, the firm continued to post, and soon newsgroups were being spammed frequently. Ultimately, the practice spread to email, IM, and everywhere else.

CAN THE CAN SPAM ACT CAN SPAM?

The Annoyance: Congress passed the Can Spam Act. Big deal. I get more spam than ever. Can I really use the law to can spam?

The Fix: In a word, no. Experts hardly expect the act to stop—or even slow—the flow of spam, and evidence indicates that it's not having much impact. For example, Vircom, a maker of security software, examined more than half a million pieces of spam originating in the U.S. (and so covered by the law) and found that only 71 messages complied with the act. Another study, by the anti-spam vendor Commtouch, found that only 10% of all spam originating in the U.S. complies with the act. The law itself has a variety of requirements, including that spammers must use their true return addresses and that they must include opt-out instructions in every email. But the law pertains only to the U.S., and many spammers have simply moved offshore or started sending spam from servers in other countries. In addition, there's no way that any government agency can possibly keep track of, much less prosecute, all the spammers who violate the law.

Still, some of the big ISPs and various law-enforcement agencies are using the law to go after spammers. In March 2004, America Online, EarthLink, Microsoft, and Yahoo! filed civil actions under the law against hundreds of spammers. A month later, the Federal Trade Commission and the U.S. Attorney's Office of the Eastern District of Michigan announced they were prosecuting four spammers.

But let's face it, the law is flawed. It doesn't prosecute those who benefit the most from spam—the companies that sell the products being advertised. After all, if McDonald's paid someone who paid someone to plaster private property with McDonald's posters, the company would be liable. But for some peculiar reason, anti-spam laws haven't taken this tack. Could this be yet one more example of Congress passing a law so it can tell voters it's done something about a problem, even if the problem remains? Look in your email inbox tomorrow morning—then you decide.

BEWARE THE NATIONAL "DO NOT E-MAIL REGISTRY"

The Annoyance: I signed up at the National Do Not E-mail Registry site at *http://www.unsub.us*, to get my name off of spammers' lists. Not only did my spam not stop, but I now get more than ever. Is the federal government trying to reduce the deficit by selling email lists to spammers?

The Fix: You've unfortunately been the victim of a hoax. There is no such federal registry. The site you visited, according to the Federal Trade Commission, "mimics the language, look, and navigation of the web site for the National Do Not Call Registry, a legitimate free service of the federal government." The FTC believes the site might be collecting email addresses to sell to spammers. The site is currently down, but may rise again. Don't get fooled!

UPDATE OUTLOOK'S SPAM FILTER

The Annoyance: I use Outlook 2003's spam filter, but after a few months, it seems like more and more spam is getting through. Is Outlook simply getting as tired as I am sifting through all this junk?

The Fix: New types of spam are created all the time, and on its own, Outlook can't keep up with them. To solve the problem, Microsoft occasionally releases updates to its spam filter. Go to *http://office.microsoft.com/en-us/officeupdate/default.aspx* and click the Check for Updates link to look for the latest.

MY NEWSLETTER GETS BLOCKED AS SPAM

The Annoyance: I send out a weekly newsletter to several thousand people who asked to receive it. But every week, hundreds of them don't get it because their ISP or their anti-spam software considers my email spam. What's the curative?

The Fix: Spam tends to have certain common characteristics, and your newsletter may inadvertently mimic some of those traits. Follow these tips, and you'll go a long way toward making sure your emails don't get bounced:

Don't send an HTML-formatted newsletter

This commonly sets off spam filters.

Watch your language

Don't use the kind of words that got your mouth washed out with soap as a kid. This applies to both the subject line and the body of the message.

WILL MY NEWSLETTER BE CONSIDERED SPAM?

A free service called SpamCheck claims that it can tell you whether your newsletter will be considered spam. Email the newsletter to *spamcheck-thatswise@sitesell. net*. Start the subject line with the word TEST, and make sure that it's capitalized. (After the word TEST, enter the subject line you'd normally include.) You'll get back an analysis of your newsletter, including an overall rating of its spamacious nature, plus specific recommendations for how to fix your newsletter so it won't be considered spam. The recommendations are mildly useful, but not earth-shaking.

How accurate is the service? Not very. I sent it multiple pieces of real spam, and it didn't give any of them a bad enough rating to be considered spam. One spam I sent even contained the subject line "Cure for Erectile Dysfunction." If that's not spam, nothing is.

Don't overuse capitalization

THIS MIGHT LOOK LIKE SPAM to a spam filter. Follow proper grammatical rules for capitalization. This applies to both the subject line and the body of the message.

Don't overuse punctuation

Use too many exclamation points and question marks, especially in a row, like this !!?!, and the newsletter may be flagged as spam.

Avoid spam-like phrases

Phrases commonly used by spammers, such as "free investment," "cable converter," or even "stop snoring" could put your newsletter in the spam bin. For a list of phrases to avoid, head to *http://www.wilsonweb. com/wmt8/spamfilter_phrases.htm*.

Pick your mass email software carefully

Some anti-spam software looks for fingerprints left behind by mass-emailing programs commonly used by spammers. Use that software, and your newsletter could be targeted as spam. The web site run by Dr. Ralph F. Wilson, an e-commerce consultant, notes that some mass-emailer programs that might be penalized include jpfree, VC_IPA, StormPost, JiXing, MMailer, EVAMAIL, and IMktg.

Link to domain names instead of IP numbers

If you have links in your newsletter, always use the domain name, such as *http://www.oreilly.com*, rather than the IP address, such as *http://208.201.239.36*.

Check if you're on blacklists

Many spam filters use blacklists to help determine what's spam. If you end up on a blacklist, your newsletter won't get through to people using some anti-spam programs—and many ISPs use the blacklists to block spam as well.

Some of the most common blacklists:

http://www.spews.org
http://www.spamhaus.org/sbl/index.lasso
http://www.abuse.net/lookup.phtml
http://www.njabl.org/lookup.html
http://razor.sf.net
http://www.rhyolite.com/anti-spam/dcc
http://pyzor.sf.net

If you find your newsletter or your IP address on any of the lists, contact the site, and ask how to be taken off the list. Keep in mind, though, that actually getting off one of these lists can be very difficult. For advice, go to *http://www.spamcop.net/reported.shtml*.

For more tips, head to *http://www.wilsonweb.com/wmt8/spamfilter_avoidance.htm* and *http://www.thatswise.com/free/lessons/0503.html*.

MY ISP THINKS I'M A SPAMMER

The Annoyance: I've got a much worse problem than some spam filters thinking I'm sending spam. My ISP thinks I'm a spammer, and it won't let me send out a newsletter at all. In fact, it's about to kick me off the service entirely. How can I change my ISP's mind?

The Fix: Don't bother trying. If you're sending out a newsletter to more than 25 people, you should be using a service that does it for you. Don't do it from your own computer and your own email account unless you're absolutely sure it's kosher with your ISP. Check your ISP's rules before sending. On AOL, for example, head to *http://postmaster.info.aol.com/tools/whitelist_guides.html*. From this page, you can request to be put on AOL's whitelist, which means that you'll be able to send a newsletter and AOL won't block it as spam. However, you'll have to agree to a set of rules: your mailings will have to comply with the Can Spam Act, valid contact information must be included, all of your subscribers must have requested the newsletter, and so on.

Some ISPs and web-hosting services offer free newsletter-mailing services, so check with yours. If they do, it'll most likely be limited to newsletters with a few hundred

---

---

subscribers. You can also go with a free newsletter service such as Coollist (*http://www.coollist.com*) or Yahoo! Groups (*http://groups.yahoo.com*). To use the Yahoo! Groups service, first create a new group by clicking the "Start a new Group" link. After you've created the group, go to the Members section and click Invite Members. That will allow you to add subscribers to your newsletter, which you can then send out whenever you want. Pay sites, such as *http://www.dundee.net*, *http://www.sparklist.com*, and *http://www.topica.com*, are good if you're distributing to several thousand readers.

For a more complete list, head to *http://directory.google.com/Top/Computers/Internet/E-mail/Mailing_Lists/Hosted_Services/*.) The actual amount you'll pay varies according to the number of subscribers and the size of your newsletter.

OUTLOOK 2003 AND OUTLOOK EXPRESS 6

PASSWORD-PROTECT OUTLOOK 2003 AND OUTLOOK EXPRESS 6

The Annoyance: I'll admit that I'm paranoid. I worry that anyone can read the Outlook 2003 and Outlook Express 6 email that I've received or am about to send, so I log off my computer every time I leave my desk. Isn't there an easier way to protect my email privacy?

The Fix: Outlook and Outlook Express both let you password-protect your inbox, out-box, and all mail folders. In Outlook, choose File → Data File Management. Select the folder you want to protect, then choose Settings → Change Password. Choose a password, verify it, and click OK, and then click OK again. From now on, only someone who knows the password can read your mail. By the way, the folder you're password-protecting isn't a single folder—it's an entire collection of folders, such as all your archived mail, or all your personal mail folders (inbox, sent mail, outbox, and so on).

In Outlook Express, choose File → Identities → Manage Identities and select the Identity that you want to protect. Then click the Properties button, check the "Require a password" box, and enter and confirm your password. Click OK, and then click Close. A password will now be required to access all folders.

FIX MY OUTLOOK UNREAD MAIL FOLDER

The Annoyance: One of Outlook 2003's best features is its Unread Mail folder, which shows me all the unread mail in all of my mail folders. Unfortunately, two weeks ago Outlook went on the fritz. Now when I delete unread mail in other folders, it still shows up in my Unread Mail folder. And when I try to delete mail in the Unread Mail folder, it doesn't get deleted; it just sits there. What can I do about this?

The Fix: The Unread Mail folder will at times mysteriously exhibit this behavior. There's an easy fix: delete the folder. Right-click the Unread Mail folder and choose Delete "Unread Mail" (Figure 1-13). Then right-click Search Folders, select New Search Folder → Unread Mail, and click OK. You'll have your Unread Mail folder back, and this time it'll actually work.

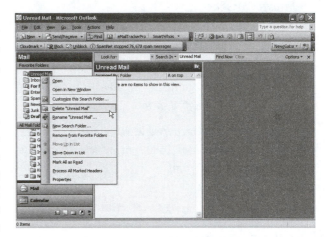

Figure 1-13. If your Unread Mail folder is giving you conniptions, simply delete it, then recreate it.

OUTLOOK 2003 GIVES ME CLAUSTROPHOBIA

The Annoyance: The whole point of an email program is to make it easy to read email. So why does Outlook 2003 make the message window so tiny? There's a window on the left that displays folders and a middle window listing emails in the current folder, with the remaining puny space devoted to displaying message contents. Is there any way to expand this window?

The Fix: There are several ways to fix the problem. You can change the width of any pane by dragging its edge. You can shrink the left window and the middle window, giving the message window more room. Or you can get rid of the left window altogether by simply pressing Alt-F1; press it again and the window reappears. Keep the left window open when navigating to the folder you want; once you're there, press Alt-F1 to hide it. Whatever you do sticks, so once you're done arranging windows, Outlook should stay that way until you change it.

MY OUTLOOK EMAIL LOOKS LIKE SANSKRIT

The Annoyance: A lot of the email I get via Outlook 2003, especially newsletters, looks like it's written in Sanskrit. My uncle was a Sanskrit scholar, but I didn't follow him into the field. What can I do?

The Fix: As they say, that's a feature, not a bug. To help protect you from potential dangers that can arrive via HTML email, Outlook 2003 turns off HTML reading by default. When HTML email arrives, you won't see any images or fancy fonts; instead, you'll see the coding and other digital gibberish underneath. To view the full HTML email, right-click where you see "Right-click here to download," and then choose "Download pictures." You'll now see the email in all its glory. If, after you right-click, you choose "Add sender to safe sender list," you'll always download the pictures and HTML from that sender, and you won't have to go through this process again. If you want to always receive HTML email from everyone, choose Tools → Options, go to the Security tab, and click the Change Automatic Download Settings button. In the screen that appears (Figure 1-14), uncheck the "Don't download pictures or other content automatically in HTML e-mail" box, then click OK. Just remember that you are now vulnerable to HTML-borne dangers!

GET FILE SPRAWL UNDER CONTROL

The Annoyance: The Outlook *.pst* file that stores all my mail and contacts is growing faster than mushrooms after a spring rain. I frequently delete email messages, but sometimes I think that only encourages the file to grow larger. Help!

The Fix: There are two problems here. First, when you delete a message in Outlook, it isn't actually deleted. Instead, it's moved to the Deleted Items folder. To truly remove it, you must empty that folder. To do this manually, choose Tools → Empty "Deleted Items" Folder. A better bet is to have Outlook automatically delete all items in the folder when you exit the program. Simply choose Tools → Options, click the Other tab, check the "Empty the Deleted Items folder upon exiting" box, then click OK.

This alone won't solve the problem, though. Even after you delete the messages, your *.pst* file won't shrink, because Outlook doesn't automatically delete the space in its database that was used by the deleted messages. You must compress the *.pst* file. To do this, choose File → Data File Management. Select the *.pst* file you want to compress, then choose Settings and click the Compact Now button (Figure 1-15), and the file will be compressed. Depending on its size and the number of deleted files, compression can take from several seconds to several minutes.

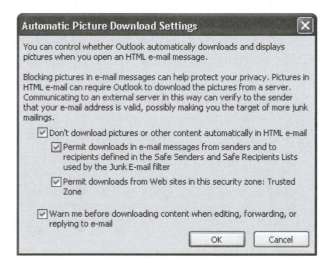

Figure 1-14. Outlook 2003 blocks HTML by default. If you want to see pretty pictures and text, change the defaults at this screen.

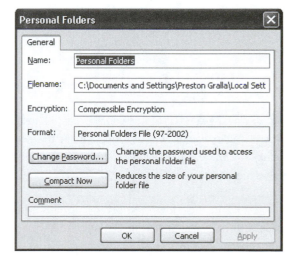

Figure 1-15. Got Outlook bloat? Compact your mail regularly and you'll get it under control.

FOLDER NAVIGATION

The Annoyance: I get a lot of email from a lot of different people, so I keep everything organized neatly in Outlook's folders. But I've created so many levels of folders that navigating through them is like wending my way through the Department of Motor Vehicles. Isn't there a faster way for me to get to folders like *Personal*\ *Family**Reunion**2004**How To Avoid*?

The Fix: Keyboard shortcuts to the rescue! Ctrl-Y opens the Go to Folder dialog box, which lets you quickly navigate to a folder. Type the plus sign (+) to expand a folder or the minus sign (–) to collapse folders. There are more keyboard navigation shortcuts as well, as you can see in Table 1-1.

Table 1-1. Keyboard shortcuts for Outlook navigation

Keyboard shortcut	What it does
Ctrl-Comma	Goes to the next item (when you have an item open)
Ctrl-Period	Goes to the previous item (when you have an item open)
F6 or Ctrl-Shift-Tab	Switches between the Folder List and the main Outlook window
Ctrl_y	Goes to a different folder
Plus or Minus on the numeric keypad	Expands/collapses a group (when you have a group selected)

MORE KEYBOARD SHORTCUTS

The Annoyance: I like your keyboard shortcuts for faster folder navigation. But what about the rest of Outlook? Are there other keyboard shortcuts that will let me give the mouse a rest?

The Fix: In fact, there are several dozen keyboard shortcuts to help you speed up Outlook. Table 1-2 lists the most useful ones for email.

Table 1-2. Keyboard shortcuts for email in Outlook

Keyboard shortcut	What it does
Ctrl-Shift-M	Creates a new email message
Ctrl-Shift-E	Creates a new folder
Ctrl-Shift-I	Switches to the inbox
Ctrl-Shift-O	Switches to the outbox
Ctrl-R	Replies to a message
Ctrl-Shift-R	Replies to all (sender and other recipients).
Ctrl-Shift-S	Posts to a folder
Ctrl-M or F5	Checks for new mail
Ctrl-N	Opens a received message
Ctrl-Shift-B	Displays the Address Book
Ctrl-Shift-O	Converts an open HTML or RTF message to plain text
Ctrl-Q	Marks a message as read

For a more complete list, go to *http://www.microsoft.com/ enable/products/keyboard/keyboardresults.asp?Product=24* (click the "Search for Additional Keyboard Shortcuts" link at the bottom of this page to get shortcuts for other Office apps and other versions of Outlook).

KILL THE EXPRESS SPLASH SCREEN!

The Annoyance: I hate Outlook Express's splash screen. How can I turn it off?

The Fix: The secret solution lies in the Windows Registry. Select Start → Run, type regedit, and press Enter. Then follow these steps:

1. In the Registry Editor, go to HKEY_CURRENT_USER\ Identities\{Unique Identity}\Software\Microsoft\ Outlook Express\5.0. (Note: {Unique Identity} will be a string such as {E46F102B-802C-4FF4-B1D3-B574483B2F75}.)

2. Right-click the 5.0 key, select New → DWORD value, and type NoSplash.

3. Double-click NoSplash, type 1 in the "Value data" field, then click OK and exit the Registry. When you start Outlook Express, it will no longer have a splash screen. (To turn it on, enter a NoSplash value of 0 or delete the NoSplash item.)

BACK UP OUTLOOK AND OUTLOOK EXPRESS

The Annoyance: Where in the world does Outlook hide my messages? I want to back up all my email. How do I do this?

The Fix: This is a problem Outlook and its smaller brother share. Depending on what you want to back up, the process is relatively easy (which means you can do it manually) or a nightmare (which means you'll have to turn to third-party software).

Back up Outlook manually

If you just want to back up your Outlook mail messages and contacts, it's a breeze. Outlook keeps all messages, contacts, and your calendar in a single file that ends with a *.pst* extension (typically *Outlook.pst* in the *C:\Documents and Settings\<Your Name>\Local Settings\Application Data\Microsoft\Outlook* folder). If it's not there, you can find it by right-clicking the Outlook Today icon in Outlook, choosing Properties → Advanced, and looking in the Filename box. If you archive old email, look for a file named *Archive.pst* in the same folder. Just copy these files to a disk or another computer. To restore them, copy them back to their original locations. That's it—you're done.

t i p

If you use Outlook on a network with Exchange Server, there won't be any *.pst* files on your system. You won't be able to back up your messages, contacts, or the calendar—your Exchange administrator should be doing it for you.

Things get a little more complicated if you don't use Outlook to store your contacts, and instead use the Windows Address Book. (I think Outlook's tools are far superior for this task, but yes, some folks prefer the Windows Address Book.) In this case, your contact information will be in a file with the extension *.pab*, which you'll need to back up along with your *.pst* mail file. To restore the Windows Address Book, copy it back to its original location.

Backing up is simple enough, if you only want to back up your email and messages. But there's a whole host of other Outlook information you might want to store, such as Outlook bar shortcuts, mail rules, custom toolbar settings, stationery, signatures and templates, and other customizations. The relevant files may be in the same folder as *Outlook.pst*, or they may be in *C:\Documents and Settings\<Your Name>\Application Data\Microsoft\Outlook*, or even in another folder. Various versions of Outlook are notorious for keeping these files in different locations. Back up these files up as you would *Outlook.pst*—to a disk or another computer—and restore them by copying them back into their original folders.

Table 1-3 lists Outlook's files and what each does. Depending on how you use Outlook, some files won't be on your system. To locate the files, use Windows Explorer's Search tool.

SynchPst

If all this sounds like too much work, turn to SynchPst for Outlook, available at *http://www.synchpst.com/download.htm*. It allows more than just basic synchronization—you can choose individual folders to copy from PC to PC. You can try it for free for 30 days; after that, you can buy it for $39.95 for the basic version or $69.95 for the professional version, which includes extras such as scheduled automatic synchronizations.

Table 1-3. Outlook files and their extensions

Type of file	Filename/extension
Personal folders	.pst (*Outlook.pst* is typically the file with all of Outlook's folders; *Archive.pst* is typically the file with archived folders)
Personal Address Book	.pab.
Outlook bar shortcuts	.fav
Rules Wizard rules (Outlook 2000 and earlier versions)	.rwz
Nicknames for AutoResolution	.nick
Nicknames for AutoComplete (Outlook 2002)	.nk2
Customized print settings	OutlPrnt
Customized toolbar settings	Outcmd.dat
Customized system folder views	Views.dat
Macros and VBA programs	VbaProject.otm
Send/receive group settings (Outlook 2002)	.srs
Stationery	.htm
Templates	.oft
Dictionary	.dic
Junk and Adult Senders lists	Junk Senders.txt and Adult Senders.txt

Back up Outlook Express manually

Outlook Express is a different beast than Outlook. It stores your email in multiple files, and you must back up Windows Registry keys to save your personal settings.

Messages in Outlook Express are kept in files with *.dbx* extensions. To locate them, open Outlook Express and chose Tools → Options. Click the Maintenance tab, and click the Store Folder button. A dialog box notes the location of the *.dbx* files. Go to that folder and back up all the *.dbx* files. To restore them, just copy them back to their original folders.

But that's only part of the job—you must also back up the Registry keys. The information about your mail settings, accounts, and preferences is stored in a single Registry key, `HKEY_CURRENT_USER\Software\Microsoft\Internet Account Manager`. Back up the key (namely, `\Internet Account Manager`) and its subkeys to a single *.reg* file by choosing File → Export. Restore the key as you would using any other *.reg* file, by double-clicking it in Windows Explorer to get its information into the Registry.

Outlook Express uses the Windows Address Book to store contact information, so you need to back up the relevant *.pab* file or files. Typically they're stored in *C:\Documents and Settings\<Your Name>\Application Data\Microsoft\ Address Book*, but you might have to look elsewhere. Back up the files, and restore them by copying them back to their original locations.

Mail rules are stored in the `HKEY_CURRENT_USER\ Identities` Registry key and its subkeys. Back up this key and its subkeys to a *.reg* file, and restore it using the steps noted above.

Back up with third-party software

Shudder at the thought of doing all these manual backups and restores? Try Outlook Express Backup and Genie Outlook Backup, from Genie-Soft (*http://www.genie-soft. com/products.html*). You get a wide variety of backup options with these tools, including backing up multiple identities and information, viewing emails from inside the backup and copying text from them, using an automated backup scheduler, encrypting your backups, spanning multiple disks when you back up, and more. You can download fully working demos and use them free for 15 days; after that, expect to pay $29.95 for each. If you regularly back up either Outlook or Outlook Express, they're worth the money.

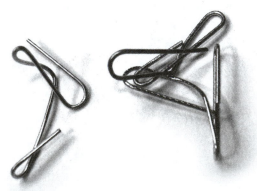

OUTLOOK EMAIL IN TWO PLACES AT ONCE

The Annoyance: I have a desktop PC that I use at my office and a laptop I use when I travel, and I use Outlook on both. But that means I have two separate email stores, and no way to combine them. Do I really have to live this schizophrenic email life?

The Fix: As you saw in "Back Up Outlook and Outlook Express," Outlook keeps email in *.pst* files. There's no automatic way to synchronize the *.pst* files on separate computers, but you can keep them in sync manually by simply copying the *Outlook.pst* file from one to the other. For example, when you're working normally at home or the office, your desktop PC should have the complete, current version of the *Outlook.pst* file. Before you travel with your laptop, copy the file over to it, and your laptop will now have the current version of your files. When you're traveling, get and send mail as you would normally on your laptop. When you return from your trip, copy the file from your laptop back to your desktop PC, and it will have the most current version.

CAN'T COPY OUTLOOK EXPRESS MAIL TO NEW LAPTOP

The Annoyance: I have Outlook Express 6 on my old laptop, and I want to move all my mail and folders over to Outlook Express on my new laptop. I moved the *.dbx* files on my old machine to the proper folder on the new machine, but this didn't maintain the elaborate arrangement of mail folders within mail folders I had. What's the trick?

The Fix: The trick is using Outlook Express's import feature. Once you locate your *.dbx* files, copy them to your new laptop, then import them into the new laptop's Outlook Express. Here's how:

1. On the old laptop, choose Tools → Options in Outlook Express, click the Maintenance tab, and then click the Store Folder button.

2. Highlight the location of the folder and press Ctrl-C to copy it to the clipboard. Make sure that you highlight the entire location, from start to finish.

3. In Windows, select Start → Run, paste the location into the Open box, and press Enter. Windows Explorer will open to the folder location that holds your Outlook Express mail.

4. If your new and old laptops are both connected to a network, or to one another via a cable, copy the folder to a temporary location on your new laptop. Don't copy it to any folders holding Outlook Express information.

5. If the laptops are not connected, copy the folder to a floppy, Zip disk, CD-R, or some other removable disc and put the disc in your new laptop.

6. On your new laptop, open Outlook Express and select File → Import → Messages. Choose Microsoft Outlook Express 6 from the dialog and click Next.

7. In the next screen, choose "Import mail from an OE6 Identity," highlight "Main identity," and click OK (Figure 1-16).

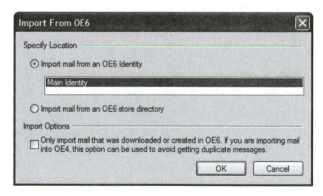

Figure 1-16. Make sure you import mail into Outlook Express from an identity.

8. In the next screen, click the Browse button, and browse to the folder or CD where you copied the old laptop's Outlook Express message store. Choose it and click Next.

9. Choose "All folders" (Figure 1-17), then click Next. (If you want to import an individual folder, click "Selected folders" and then choose the folder.)

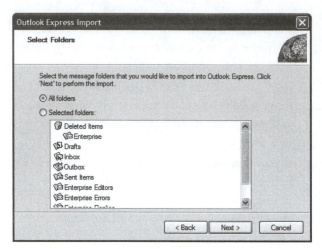

Figure 1-17. You can import your entire folder structure from your old copy of Outlook Express, or only the folders you select.

10. Outlook Express will import your mail and your custom folder structure. When the importing is done, click Finish. All your email—and your convoluted folder structure—should now be in your new version of Outlook Express.

GMAIL

GIVE ME SPACE, LOTS OF SPACE

The Annoyance: I use Yahoo! Mail, and I'm constantly running out of storage space—the free 250 MB isn't enough. I get the feeling they're "encouraging" me to upgrade to the Plus service, for $20 per year. (Granted, that does buy you 2 GB of space.) Is there a better (and cheaper) alternative?

The Fix: Get 4 times the space with Google's free email service, called Gmail (Figure 1-18). You get an astounding 1 GB of free storage, so it'll be a long, long time before you have to delete a piece of email. Sign up at *http://gmail.google.com*.

The service offers a lot of extras besides a ton of storage space. For example, you can search through your mail using Google's search technology, so even though you might have a lot of mail, finding what you want is easy. Also, there's a nice set of tools for creating folders (which

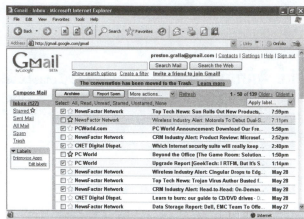

Figure 1-18. You can import your entire folder structure from your old copy of Outlook Express, or only the folders you select.

Google calls "labels") and for creating rules for automatically handling mail (for example, routing messages to the appropriate folders based on the sender or on words in the text).

WHY WON'T GMAIL RECEIVE NEWSLETTERS?

The Annoyance: I've signed up for half a dozen email newsletters using my Gmail account, but I haven't received a single one yet. What's with Gmail—is it losing more mail than the U.S. Postal Service?

The Fix: The culprit is Gmail's spam filter, which can be a bit aggressive when it comes to newsletters (especially any initial messages that require you click internal links to confirm your free subscription). Click the Spam link in your Gmail account; you'll probably see that Gmail has filtered out all your newsletters as spam. To let future newsletters through, scroll to the bottom of each newsletter, and click the Not Spam button. Each one you marked will be moved to your inbox, and future newsletters should now get through to you.

DOES GMAIL INVADE YOUR PRIVACY?

Almost as soon as Gmail was launched, it caused an outcry among some privacy advocates. That's because Gmail delivers ads along with the mail, based on the contents of your incoming messages. So, in theory, a friend could send you a message about a new car he just bought, and Gmail could serve up ads for that car, for other cars, for car-repair services, and so on.

No human at Google actually examines the email; computers examine the incoming messages on the fly and deliver ads based on their content. The technology is similar to the one used by Google to serve up ads based on your searches.

However, privacy advocates contend that Google's practice still violates your privacy. In April 2004, 31 privacy and civil liberty groups, including the Consumer Federation of America, the Electronic Privacy Information Center, and the National Consumers League, sent a public letter to Google, asking that the Gmail service be suspended until privacy issues are addressed. The groups claim that "The scanning of confidential email violates the implicit trust of an email

service provider. Further, the unlimited period for data retention poses unnecessary risks of misuse...the Gmail system sets potentially dangerous precedents and establishes reduced expectations of privacy in email communications." Their biggest fear is that Google might keep copies of your mail, and those copies could be misused in some way.

Google and its defenders say that all ISPs examine mail to determine whether it's spam. According to Google's page about Gmail privacy at *http://gmail.google.com/gmail/help/more.html*, "All email services scan your email. They do this routinely to provide such popular features as spam filtering, virus detection, search, spell checking, forwarding, auto-responding, flagging urgent messages, converting incoming email into cell phone text messages, automatic saving and sorting into folders, converting text URLs to clickable links, and reading messages to the blind." The page also notes that all ISPs back up mail, so Google's policy on retaining mail messages is similar to that of other ISPs. In this instance, an invasion of privacy is in the eye of the beholder.

WHERE'S MY ARCHIVED GMAIL?

The Annoyance: I regularly go through my Gmail account and archive mail that I may want to re-read at some later point, but that I don't want cluttering up my inbox. But archiving the mail makes it vanish! Where's it gone?

The Fix: Google could use some help with the English language, because unlike in other email programs, "archiving" mail in Gmail just makes it invisible. Click the All Mail link—you'll find the archived mail there, mixed in with all your other mail.

EUDORA 6

END AUTO-COMPLETION ERRORS

The Annoyance: Eudora 6 has a useful, but sometimes annoying, auto-completion feature. It captures the email address of just about everyone you send and who sends you email including the errors. I've sent email repeatedly to a nonexistent address because the $#@#$ feature captured a typo I entered three weeks ago.

The Fix: Tell Eudora to stop using its History file to fill in addresses. In Eudora, select Tools → Options, click the Auto-completion icon, uncheck the "History File" box and the "Don't auto-complete, just list matches" box, and click OK (see Figure 1-19). To do away with individual auto-completion entries that are incorrect, open a new message form and type the first letter of a recipient's address. A list of potential matches will pop up. Scroll to the incorrect item, select it, hit the Delete key, and it's gone for good.

Outlook has a similar auto-completion feature. To turn it off, you'll have to dig deep through the menus. Choose Tools → Options, click the Preferences tab, then click the E-mail Options button. Click the Advanced E-mail Options button, and uncheck the "Suggest names while completing To, cc, and bcc fields" box. Click OK, and keep clicking OK until the dialog boxes disappear. You can delete individual auto-complete entries using the same procedure as in Eudora.

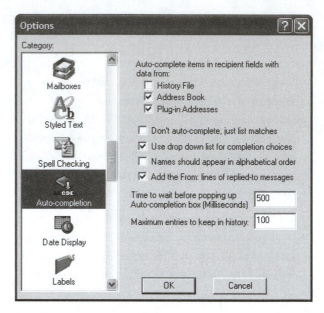

Figure 1-19. If Eudora's auto-completion feature is sending you around the bend, turn it off from this screen.

SPEED UP EUDORA WITH KEYBOARD SHORTCUTS

The Annoyance: I read your advice on how to use keyboard shortcuts to speed up Outlook. But I'm a Eudora user. What keyboard shortcuts will let me give the rodent a rest?

The Fix: Ask and you shall receive. Table 1-4 lists some helpful keyboard shortcuts for Eudora. (You can also look for "shortcuts" in Eudora's help system.)

Table 1-4. Helpful Eudora keyboard shortcuts

Keyboard shortcut	What it does
Ctrl-0 (zero)	Opens the Out box
Ctrl-1	Opens the In box
Ctrl-6	Checks your spelling
Ctrl-'	Pastes the contents of the clipboard at the insertion point, with > characters at the beginning of each line to indicate quoted text
Ctrl-A	Selects all
Ctrl-B	Makes text bold
Ctrl-C	Copies selection to clipboard
Ctrl-D	Deletes a message
Ctrl-E	Sends immediately
Ctrl-F	Opens the Find Messages window
Ctrl-Shift-F	Opens the Find Text dialog box
Ctrl-H	Attaches a file
Ctrl-I	Makes text italic
Ctrl-J	Filters messages
Ctrl-K	Makes a nickname Address Book entry
Ctrl-L	Opens the Address Book
Ctrl-M	Checks your mail
Ctrl-N	Opens a new message
Ctrl-O (letter O)	Opens a file
Ctrl-P	Prints a message
Ctrl-Q	Quits Eudora
Ctrl-R	Replies to the message
Ctrl-Shift-R	Replies to all (sender and other recipients)
Ctrl-S	Saves the current window
Ctrl-T	Sends queued messages
Ctrl-U	Underlines text
Ctrl-V	Pastes from the Clipboard
Ctrl-X	Cuts and places the selection onto the Clipboard
Ctrl-Y	Opens Directory Services
Ctrl-Z	Undoes the last operation
Ctrl-Shift-Z	Redoes the last undone operation
F3	Finds again
Home	Scrolls to the beginning of the mailbox window or to the beginning of the line in a message
End	Scrolls to the end of the mailbox window or to the end of the line in a message

HELP EUDORA TAKE OUT THE TRASH

The Annoyance: I get a ton of spam in Eudora. I delete it from my In box; then, later, to truly get rid of it, I have to delete it from my Trash box. Is there any way to delete something *completely* from the In box, so I can avoid this extra step?

The Fix: When you delete mail, it always first goes to your Trash. But you can have Eudora automatically delete all messages in your Trash folder when you exit. Choose Tools → Options, click the Miscellaneous icon, check the "Empty Trash when exiting" box (Figure 1-20), and click OK.

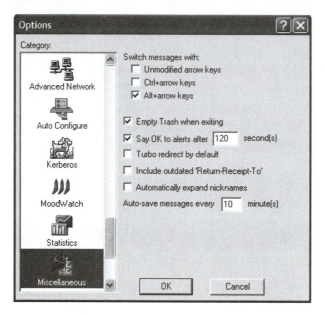

Figure 1-20. Don't take out the trash yourself—have Eudora automatically delete it whenever you exit the program.

SPEED UP SLUGGISH EUDORA

The Annoyance: When I first started using Eudora, it was speedy and stable. Now, three months later, it's like trying to get a teenager out of bed before noon on a weekend. What's the problem?

The Fix: You've probably created and opened too many mailboxes. Each open mailbox eats up RAM, and if you have a bunch open, Eudora slows to a crawl.

The answer? Consolidate your mailboxes, and only keep important mailboxes open. You open a mailbox by double-clicking it, or choosing it from the Mailbox menu. You often don't even realize that you've opened mailboxes, because they each recede into the background when you open another one. To see all the mailboxes you have open, choose Window → Cascade. That will arrange all of your open Eudora windows, including mailboxes, in a stack. Close any you don't need.

> **t i p**
>
> Confused about what's a folder and what's a mailbox in Eudora? Join the club. Mail lives in a mailbox (such as In); mailboxes live in folders that you name. Thus, a folder might contain an In, Out, Family, Sent, and other mailboxes, and each of those mailboxes could have mail in them.

WHAT DO THOSE WEIRD EUDORA ICONS MEAN?

The Annoyance: I know that the weird icons in the status column to the left of the mailbox are supposed to tell me something, but I can't figure out what the heck they mean. Do you have the secret decoder ring?

The Fix: The Eudora status icons certainly have caused more than a few people to scratch their heads. But once you know what they mean, they're very useful. Table 1-5 reveals all.

Table 1-5. Eudora status icons

Icon	What it means
Blue ball	Message hasn't been read
Blank	Message has been read
Left green arrow	Message has been replied to
Right green arrow	Message has been forwarded
Diagonal green arrow	Message has been redirected
Green check mark	Message has been sent
Blue button	Message is queued to be sent
Green ball with circle	Message has been saved but not sent
Blue alarm clock	Message is queued to be sent at a specific time
Black dash	Message was transferred to the Out box before it was sent
Dotted grey line	Message is being sent
Red button with X	Message can't be sent because of an error

2

Making the Connection
ANNOYANCES

What's more basic—or more annoying—than making a connection to the Internet? This should be the most mundane of tasks, but it can all too often turn into a three-hour soap opera, and even then the annoyance may not be solved.

Connecting to the Internet was annoying enough when you only had to worry about dial-up connections. But now, with cable and DSL broadband access, home routers and networks, and using the Internet to make phone calls via Voice over IP (VoIP), the mere act of making an Internet connection has become the Mother of All Annoyances.

GENERAL CONNECTION ANNOYANCES

INSTANT FIX FOR BROKEN INTERNET CONNECTIONS

The Annoyance: I sometimes lose my Internet connection. When I call my ISP's tech support line, they ask me for details such as DNS entries, gateway information, IP addresses, and the like, but they still don't fix the problem. I have better things to do with my time—like watching the Yankees lose to the Red Sox. Again. Isn't there a simpler way to fix a broken connection, without resorting to pointless (and often, useless) tech support?

The Fix: This quick fix can automatically repair a surprising number of broken connections. First, right-click My Network Places and choose Properties. Then right-click the connection that's broken and choose Repair, as shown in Figure 2-1. This is a great starting point and often solves the problem without further troubleshooting.

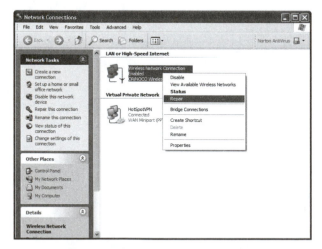

Figure 2-1. This instant solution will fix a surprising number of Internet connection snafus.

XP HANGS WHENEVER I CONNECT TO THE INTERNET

The Annoyance: This has to be one of the worst Internet annoyances! Whenever I try to connect to the Internet, XP hangs so badly that I have to reboot. It's like living in 1995—which is the last time I used a PC without an Internet connection.

The Fix: Chances are you've installed the Advanced Networking Pack, which uses the IPv6 protocol, at the behest of your network's system administrator. This new-ish networking protocol is supposed to lead to more reliable networking, but instead it usually leads to disaster because it doesn't always play nice with other protocols and the Internet. The protocol and related services start by default, and that's what's crashing XP. You'll have to uninstall IPv6 to solve the problem. Here's how:

1. Log onto XP using the administrator's account (if this isn't possible, ask your network administrator to do it for you).

2. Right-click My Network Places, and choose Properties.

3. Right-click your Internet connection, choose Properties, and click the General tab.

4. Select IPv6 Protocol and click the Uninstall button. Follow the directions and restart your PC.

5. After your computer restarts, log onto XP as the administrator.

6. Type `services.msc` in the Windows Start → Run box or at the command prompt to run the Microsoft Management Console.

7. In the Services area to the right, right-click IPv6 and choose Properties. Then choose Disabled from the "Startup type" drop-down box. If IPV6 doesn't show up in the Microsoft Management Console, don't worry—that means your problem has been solved.

WHAT'S MY TRUE CONNECTION SPEED?

The Annoyance: My cable connection frequently slows to a crawl, particularly in the evening. When I complain to my broadband ISP, it has only two words for me: "Prove it!" How can I show just how slow my connection really is?

The Fix: There are a lot of free programs and web sites that will report on your connection speed. Keep in mind that these tools may report different connection speeds, so it's a good idea to use more than one. A good free application is NetStat Live, available from *http://www.analogx.com/contents/download/network/nsl.htm*. It reports your current incoming and outgoing connection speeds, as well as your average connection speed, how much data you've transferred this month and last month, plus other details, such as your current and average CPU use (see Figure 2-2).

It doesn't generate a printed report, so if you want to send the onscreen report to your ISP, take a screen shot of it with the Windows PrintScreen feature, or use a screen-capture program such as SnagIt (available from *http://www.techsmith.com/download/snagitfreetrial. asp*).

If you use NetStat Live, note that the program has its eccentricities. There's no way to keep it on top of your other programs, so every time you visit a web site or open a new application, you'll have to Alt-Tab to get back to it. Also, be wary of the average connection speed rating, because it includes the time when you're not uploading or downloading data, which is most of the time you're on the Internet. (When you browse the Web, the actual downloading of web pages is only a small fraction of your online time.) To get an accurate picture of your current connection speed, visit a site, start downloading a large file, and Alt-Tab to NetStat Live to get the news.

For a web-only alternative, check out the PC Pitstop site (Figure 2-3), which has a series of free diagnostic and tune-up tools for your PC, plus a set of very good upload and download tests. Go to *http://www.pcpitstop.com/internet* and click the Measure Download Speed or Measure Upload Speed links. If you're testing download speed, the site will send a file to your hard disk and calculate the average download speed; for the upload test, it creates random text data on your PC, uploads it, and measures the average upload speed.

Figure 2-2. NetStat Live reports on your current connection speed.

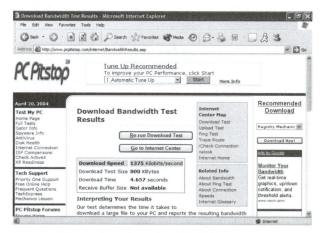

Figure 2-3. Prefer a web-only speed test? The PC Pitstop site tests your connection speed for free.

To take a screen shot, press Shift-Print Scr, which pastes the current screen to the Windows clipboard. Then open Paint or another graphics program and press Shift-Insert to paste in the screen. You can then save the screen and send it to your ISP.

It's a good idea to run the test several times and then average the speeds for the most accurate results. In fact, I recommend that you run both NetStat and PC Pitstop several times and average the results before sharing them with your ISP.

STOP MY MODEM BEFORE IT DIALS AGAIN

The Annoyance: I recently got cable Internet access, so I have an always-on connection. But my computer seems to think I have an always-off connection, because every time I launch Internet Explorer it tries to connect using my dial-up modem. How can I stop this annoying annoyance?

The Fix: Somehow, your dial-up settings were never changed, so your computer still thinks it's using a dial-up modem. To fix it:

1. Launch Internet Explorer.
2. Select Tools → Internet Options and click the Connections tab (see Figure 2-4).
3. Select "Never dial a connection."
4. Click the LAN Settings button and then click OK.

BROADBAND: CABLE AND DSL CONNECTIONS

SLOW-AS-MOLASSES CABLE MODEM

The Annoyance: When I installed my cable modem, it was faster than greased lightning. Now it's slow as molasses. It's *really* slow when it rains. Am I crazy, or can there be some cause and effect here?

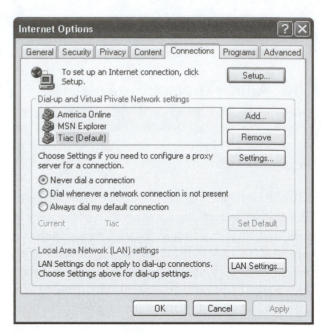

Figure 2-4. If you have an always-on broadband service, tell Windows to nix the dial-up option.

The Fix: It sounds like your outside cable connection is loose or in some way exposed to the elements. That's why, when it rains, your Internet speed heads south. Get your cable company to check the cable connection to your house, as well as the connection from the pole. If no problems are found, have them check for a cable splitter installed in your house. Splitters are sometimes used to separate data and video connections, and if there's a problem with your splitter, you may have problems with your Internet connection.

FIX THIS SLOW-AS-MOLASSES CABLE MODEM, TAKE 2

The Annoyance: I followed your advice and had the cable company check my connections. The connections were fine, but the connection's still slow as a dog. I forgot to mention that I use a router at home, which my cable company set up for me when they installed my cable modem. Is the router the problem?

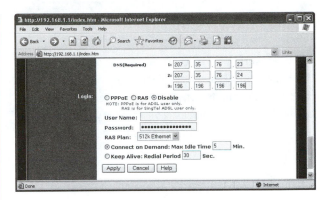

Figure 2-5. Enter the DNS addresses for a Linksys router.

The Fix:

Ah, I see the solution. When your cable company installed your router, they set it to use specific DNS (Domain Name Service) addresses—and chances are they've since changed them without telling you. While you can still make an Internet connection, it's painfully slow because you're going to DNS servers that are outside your cable network, which slows things down. How you change DNS settings varies from router to router, but here's how you'd do it on a Linksys home router:

1. Call the tech support line of your ISP (or cable company) and ask for the current DNS settings. Some ISPs also publish this information on their web sites, so check the tech support area as well.

2. Open the Linksys setup screen by loading your browser and going to the address *http://192.168.1.1*. In the screen that appears, leave the username blank, type admin as your password, and press Enter. (That's the router's default password; if you've changed it, use the new password.)

3. The Setup screen will appear. Scroll down to the DNS area and type in the DNS settings you got from tech support (see Figure 2-5). Click the Apply button.

4. Turn off your router and cable modem for five minutes, then turn them back on. The problem should be fixed.

If your ISP didn't set up your router and enter DNS addresses (or have you enter them), don't go through this process, because it won't help. Your problem isn't related to DNS. Try plugging your cable modem directly into your PC's Ethernet port, bypassing the router. If that solves the problem, you have trouble with your router, and you may need a new one.

REVIVE YOUR DSL CONNECTION

The Annoyance: For reasons I can't fathom, my DSL connection is suddenly dead. No matter what I do, I can't get onto the Internet. I've used every troubleshooting tool known to bipeds; I've reset my TCP/IP setting, turned off my firewall and pop-up blocker, and more, but still, no Internet.

The Fix: Often the fix is a simple finger flick away. (No, not that finger!) Simply turn off your DSL modem for five minutes, and then turn it back on again. It's amazing how frequently that will solve your problem. The solution works with cable modems as well.

Of course, this doesn't always work. Sometimes you can revive the connection by reloading your DSL dialer application, or by rebooting your PC and then reloading the dialer app. Look, too, for sources of electromagnetic radiation that might be annoying your modem (such as 900-MHz to 2.4-GHz portable phones, security alarms, or digital phone systems), or even a kink in the cable.

INTERNAL WIRING SCAM

The Annoyance: My DSL connection drops intermittently and slows down without warning. The phone company claims that the problem is my house's "internal wiring" and wants to charge me big bucks to check it out. Are they scamming me?

The Fix: In the Byzantine economics of DSL service, if a tech guy or gal steps into your house to troubleshoot a problem, the high-priced meter starts ticking. But if the techie finds the problem outside the house, you get the problem fixed for free. So tell your ISP to send out a techie to run a line test from the telephone pole to your house. Next, have him check the configuration of that gray phone box on the outside of your house. Many problems may lurk here. If neither is the source of your problem, and the tech has to check your house's internal wiring, hold onto your wallet. It can easily cost $80 per hour, which sometimes is charged in 15-minute increments of $20. But the costs can go way beyond that—some ISPs

will also charge you a "dispatch fee," which can run to over $200. Note: If you need your home's internal wiring checked, you don't have to turn to your ISP or Baby Bell. Third-party companies can do the job as well, and often for less money.

WHAT IS PPPOE?

PPPoE stands for Point-to-Point Protocol over Ethernet, and it lets users, such as those on a DSL "network," make broadband connections to the Internet. With PPPoE, you typically use a little dialer application that does the dialing for you. PPPoE connections can be more problematic than Ethernet connections because they may require extra router configuration. Also, with PPPoE, if you're idle for a long amount of time, your connection may be terminated. In short, PPPoE isn't exactly "always on." However, ISPs like PPPoE because it easily integrates with existing dial-up phone networks (which is one reason why PPPoE is commonly used with DSL connections, and not with cable lines).

WHY DOES DSL HATE MY ROUTER?

The Annoyance: I can't get my DSL connection to work with my home router. The router maker blames my ISP, and my ISP, of course, blames the router vendor. Which of these turkeys should I baste?

The Fix: The most common cause of DSL/router woes is simple to fix: you haven't properly enabled PPPoE on your router, or maybe you haven't enabled it at all. Most DSL connections require this protocol. How you configure it varies by router, but here's how to do it with a Linksys router:

1. Log into the Linksys administrator's setup screen by opening your browser and surfing to *http://192.168.1.1*. Leave the username blank and enter the password admin (assuming you haven't changed the router's default password).

2. Scroll down to the PPPoE section, and select the radio button next to PPPoE.

3. Type in your DSL username and password (which you can get from your DSL ISP) and click OK. Your router should now work properly with PPPoE.

DOES COMCAST CHARGE EXTRA FOR HOME NETWORKING?

The Annoyance: I have a Comcast Internet cable connection, and I want to install a home network so that, among other things, several PCs can share the line. But I just checked its web site (*http://homenetworking. comcast.net)*, and bless Comcast's greedy little heart, it tries to sell me a home networking package that'll cost me a whopping $149 for installation, plus $180 or $5 a month rental for a home router that I can buy for less than $50. Worse, it says I can only have five PCs on the network, but I have six and plan to buy two more. What is this, the Soviet Union? Can Comcast force me to pay for this service? Network free or die!

The Fix: Comcast's home networking site implies that you must buy a special package if you want to set up a home network to share your cable connection. But if you look elsewhere on the general Comcast site, the company implies that you can set up a home network and share the line without charge. In general, the Comcast site is fairly unclear and unhelpful when it comes to home networking. For example, one page notes that if you want to, you "may order additional network addresses in order to connect several computers to the service through one cable modem." Of course, when you set up a home network, you don't *need* additional network addresses, because your home router handles the necessary network addresses.

I tried clearing up the matter with Comcast, but the company said via email that "we will need to decline" to provide the information I requested. Ah, cable company customer service. Can't beat it.

The upshot? I know many people, including myself, who use Comcast's high-speed Internet service with a home network, and none of us has paid Comcast a dime for sharing the line with two or more computers. Based on our tests, it appears that Comcast doesn't really care—we all easily set up home networks, sharing the lines with several PCs, and no one at Comcast griped.

If you're still worried about your broadband ISP charging you extra for a home network, you can "hide" the router from your ISP. When you connect a router to a cable modem, your ISP may require you to supply the router's MAC address in order to give it Internet access. The MAC address is a number that uniquely identifies routers, network cards, and similar communications hardware. When you call in with your router's MAC address, the ISP will naturally know you're sharing the line with other computers. If you're paranoid about your broadband ISP finding out, Linksys and other routers let you clone your PC's MAC address and use that for the router. You won't have

Sharing your high-speed Internet connection with other PCs in your home is fine, but sharing it with a neighbor (say, via a wireless WiFi connection) is generally considered verboten. The issue surfaced as far back as 2001, when a spokesperson for AT&T Broadband told the *San Francisco Chronicle*, "We view it the same way as cable theft… and that's against a variety of state and federal laws." The spokesman went on to say that AT&T Broadband conducted "flyovers" in selected areas, looking for unauthorized "leakage" of cable and broadband signals, and then disconnected any customers responsible for the leakages.

Comcast's service agreement notes that "The Service and the Comcast Equipment shall be used only by you and by members of your immediate household living with you at the same address," which certainly seems to rule out sharing Internet access with neighbors.

to call your ISP with the new MAC address, and to the ISP, it'll look like your original PC—not a router—is connected to the cable modem.

To clone a MAC address on a Linksys router, go to *http://192.168.1.1* and log into the Linksys administrator's setup screen, leaving the username blank and entering admin (or whatever you've changed the default to) as the password. Select Advanced → MAC Addr. Clone, then enter your PC's MAC address in the User Defined WAN MAC Address box. Click the Apply button, and you're done. If you don't know your PC's MAC address, open a command prompt, enter ipconfig /all, and press Enter. In the information that appears, look for your network adapter's physical address (e.g., 00-06-5B-1C-49-08)—that's its MAC address.

COUNTRY BOY HAS DSL PROBLEMS

The Annoyance: I live on the edge of a suburb and recently subscribed to DSL. The DSL company said I'd get a 1.5-Mbps connection, but my real-life connection speed isn't a whole lot faster than it was with my old dial-up modem. I've spent four lifetimes on the phone with tech support, and they know even less about DSL than I do—which is approximately zero. Is there a way to fix the problem?

The Fix: What DSL providers don't always tell you is that you must be within a certain distance of the "central office" (the phone company's local switching station) to get top speeds. As a general rule, you should be within 14,000 feet (closer is better), or you won't get a solid, speedy connection. Also, remember that the distance is not as the crow flies, but rather as the phone line twists and turns its way from the central office to you. In this case, it sounds like you're past the point of reasonable performance. There's not much you can do except complain until they put a switch nearer to your home (don't hold your breath) or cancel your service. If you can get cable service, make the switch now—cable doesn't suffer from the distance limitations.

HOW DSL WORKS

DSL (Digital Subscriber Line) doesn't require a special phone line—the signals travel over the same telephone wires and telephone system you use for voice calls. How do DSL and voice coexist on the same line? DSL and voice use different frequencies; you simply plug a special filter into the phone jack to keep the two signals from interfering with each other. As with cable Internet access, DSL download speeds are higher than upload speeds. For example, you may be able to download at 1.5 Mbps, but upload speeds may top out at 128 Kbps.

NEW CONNECTION WIZARD WOES

The Annoyance: I want to create a new DSL connection using XP's New Connection Wizard (via the Network Connections control panel), but the "Connect using a broadband connection that requires a user name and password" option is grayed out. Why in the world won't XP let me make a DSL connection?

The Fix: You've most likely upgraded from Windows 98 to Windows XP, since others who have made this move report the same problem. Luckily, there's a quick fix you can apply to the Registry:

1. Run the Registry Editor. Select Start → Run, type Regedit in the Run box, and press Enter.
2. Go to the key HKEY_CURRENT_USER\Software\ Microsoft\Windows\CurrentVersion\Telephony\ Cards.
3. In the righthand pane, click NextID.
4. Choose Edit → Delete.
5. When asked to confirm your deletion, click Yes.
6. Exit the Registry.

From now on, the "Connect using a broadband connection that requires a user name and password" option won't be grayed out, so choose that option and continue with the wizard.

ROUTERS AND HOME NETWORKS

FILE-SHARING TRAFFIC JAM

The Annoyance: I just installed a home network so my wife, my music-loving 14-year-old son, and I can use the Internet at the same time. But for no apparent reason, my cable connection is getting slower and slower. For this I pay $45 a month? Strangely enough, if I turn off my router and then turn it back on again, things speed up for a while, then gradually slow down again.

The Fix: The key here is your music-loving 14-year-old son. He's probably using file-sharing software such as BitTorrent or Kazaa to download music or movies and share them with others. Not only is he sucking up your network's bandwidth, but file-sharing software can fill up the router's routing tables and slow the entire network to a crawl. When you restart your router, the routing tables are cleared out—hence the temporary speed boost. To solve the problem, first tell your son that he can't use file-sharing software when other people are using the network. Have him queue up all his files for nighttime download, when everyone is asleep.

Want to, um, confirm compliance? Depending on your router, you can probably see all the inbound and outbound traffic between your network and the Internet, on a PC-by-PC basis, by peeking into the router's logs. If you see a single PC with a constant stream of inbound and outbound URLs, it's a sign that file sharing is going on. Here's how to check the logs on a Linksys router:

1. Log into the Linksys administrator's setup screen, at *http://192.168.1.1*. Leave the username blank and enter the password admin (assuming you haven't changed it).

2. First, check the IP addresses of all your networked computers, so that you can match the traffic log to each PC. Click the DHCP tab, which appears when you log into the router, then the DHCP Client table. A small browser window will pop up, showing you the IP address and hostname of each PC (see Figure 2-6).

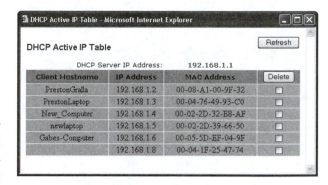

Figure 2-6. Here's how to find the IP address of every PC and device on your network. The 192.168.1.8 refers to a PS/2 game system, which doesn't have a hostname.

3. Now that you know the IP address of each computer on your network, it's time to check the router logs. Click the Log tab, choose the Enable radio button, and click the Apply button. (If the log is already enabled, you can skip this step.)

4. Now you can check the incoming and outgoing logs. Click on Incoming Access Log to see incoming traffic by IP address, and click on Outgoing Access Log to see outgoing traffic. Click the Refresh button every few seconds. If you notice more new outgoing URLs each time you click the button, someone may be using a file-sharing program. It's a better bet to check the Outgoing Access Log (Figure 2-7) rather than the Incoming Access Log, because multiple people connecting to your network and downloading files is typically what causes the slowdown. A single outgoing connection won't cause this problem.

Even if the culprit isn't actively using his computer, file-sharing software can cause slowdowns. Teens often leave file-sharing software going all the time, even when they're at school. In that case, the outgoing connections will again be the source of your slowdowns—another good reason to check the Outgoing Access Log.

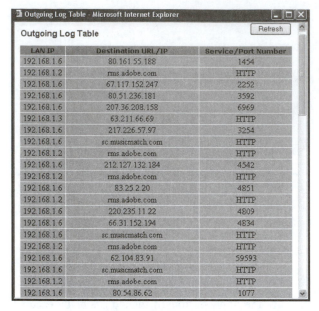

Figure 2-7. Here's the outgoing traffic log—someone is playing music online, as you can see by the connection to sc.musicmatch.com.

MANAGE YOUR NETWORK'S BANDWIDTH

The Annoyance: Thanks for the tip on nipping my son's file sharing in the bud. Now he's gone on a hunger strike. Is there another solution for this annoyance?

The Fix: You can use software that limits the bandwidth that any PC on your network can use. So, if you have a 3-Mbps connection, you could limit his bandwidth to, say, 500 Kbps.

With these limits he can share music at reasonable speeds, and everyone else will be able to use the Internet for browsing the Web without any serious slowdown.

A great program for doing this is NetLimiter (*http://www.download.com/NetLimiter/3000-2071_4-10227459.html*). Not only can you set bandwidth limits per PC, but you can also limit upload and download transfer rates for individual programs on a PC (Figure 2-8). For example, you can give more of an individual PC's bandwidth to file sharing and less to email. NetLimiter is shareware; you can try it out for free, but after 28 days, you're expected to pay $29.95 to the developer.

If NetLimiter isn't available, you can turn to SoftPerfect Bandwidth Manager, which does much of what NetLimiter does, but is $99 (ouch) shareware. It's available from *http://www.softperfect.com/products/bandwidth/*.

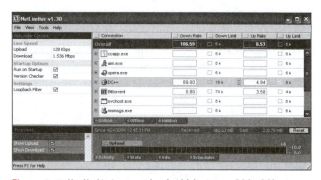

Figure 2-8. Use NetLimiter to set bandwidth limits on a PC-by-PC basis on your network, and keep both file sharers and web surfers happy.

UNDERSTANDING DHCP AND NAT

Your router allows all the computers on your network to access the Internet using two related technologies: DHCP (Dynamic Host Configuration Protocol) and NAT (Network Address Translation). Using DHCP, it assigns different IP addresses to each computer so that each computer can be uniquely identified on the network. Every time a computer is turned off or disconnects from the network, it loses its

IP address; the next time the computer logs back onto the network, it's given a new IP address by the router.

Those IP addresses, however, are internal to the network; they're not visible out on the Internet. NAT presents only one IP address to the Internet—the router's. NAT provides a dollop of security, because it masks specific IP addresses, shielding your PCs from attack.

ROCK N' ROLL AND NAT

The Annoyance: Now my 14-year-old son is making my life hellacious because the router's NAT protections stop him from playing certain online games. To get back at me, he plays his favorite Green Day power riffs on his Fender Stratocaster at full volume late into the night. Help!

The Fix: Some routers, such as those from Linksys, include a special DMZ zone that lets you expose one computer directly to the Internet. Certain games require this kind of access, but the computer in the DMZ zone doesn't get the normal protections offered by NAT.

To put a PC into the DMZ zone with a Linksys router, log into the Linksys administrator's setup screen (go to *http://192.168.1.1*; leave the username blank and enter admin or the new password you've selected). Click the Advanced tab and choose DMZ Host. Enter the IP address of the PC that you want to put into the DMZ zone, and click the Apply button. If you don't know the IP address of the PC, see "File-Sharing Traffic Jam."

MY ROUTER WON'T CONNECT TO THE NET

The Annoyance: I just brought my new Linksys router home, and it connects all my PCs to one another like a charm. I called up my cable provider and told them the router's MAC address so that all my connected PCs could hop onto the Internet, but the router simply refuses to connect them to the Net. Why?

The Fix: The problem lies in the MAC address that you gave to your cable provider. Routers have two different MAC addresses: a LAN address used for your internal network, and a WAN address used when the router accesses the Internet. You probably gave the LAN MAC address to the cable company. Call back and give them the WAN MAC address. You'll find the address on your router's setup screen.

VPN HATES MY HOME ROUTER

The Annoyance: My company lets me telecommute and connect to its network, but only if I use a Virtual Private Network (VPN). I installed the VPN software, but it won't work with my home router, and my company's tech support team has washed its hands of me.

The Fix: A few minor changes to your router's setup should do the trick. But first, upgrade your router's firmware by visiting the manufacturer's web site. Download the firmware and carefully follow the instructions for installing it.

Once you've done that, go into your router's setup screen and change three settings:

- Disable the Block WAN Requests setting.
- Enable IPSec Pass Through.
- Enable PPTP Pass Through.

Apply the settings, and your VPN should work with no problems.

HOW TO GET REAL BROADBAND HELP

The Annoyance: I think broadband ISPs and router manufacturers have outsourced their tech support to the same place—somewhere four light years past Pluto. How can I get good tech support for my broadband/router woes?

The Fix: Amazingly enough, there are two great free sites that offer superb technical support. The Navas Cable Modem/DSL Tuning Guide (*http://cable-dsl.home.att.net*) has questions and answers, message boards, how-to articles, and links to countless web sites with more information. Cable Modem Resources on the Web (*http://rpcp.mit.edu/~gingold/cable*) is great when you're looking for a web site that can help—it has comprehensive listings of cable modem manufacturers, broadband ISP web sites, and other useful places. Some of the links on this site are out of date, so keep that in mind when you visit.

Wireless
ANNOYANCES

3

Ah, wireless technology. It's the closest thing we have to magic—extremely annoying magic, that is. No other technology frees us so completely from having to be in a fixed place: with wireless devices you can get high-speed Internet access while you roam through your house, through your office, or even across the country. But no other technology is so thoroughly annoying, either. When you turn on your wirelessly connected PC or laptop, you have to worry about filing cabinets, walls, pesky RF-absorbing coworkers, or someone in the kitchen microwaving a burrito disrupting your signal. And as you'll see in this chapter, there are countless other annoyances you'll face as well.

Although there are other wireless networking standards (notably, Bluetooth and HomeRF), this chapter largely focuses on *WiFi networks*—that is, wireless networks built around the 802.11x standard.

HOME WIRELESS NETWORKS AND ROUTERS

EXTEND YOUR WIRELESS NETWORK'S RANGE

The Annoyance: I just installed a WiFi network, but the connection to my upstairs PC is so slow and flaky, I might as well use the Pony Express to send mail. How can I speed things up?

The Fix: Flaky is the right word for WiFi connections—they can be affected by a mind-boggling array of objects and phenomena, from cordless phones to filing cabinets. You should also keep in mind that wireless networks rarely deliver data at their rated bandwidth speeds. You're lucky to get half the rated speed, even in the best of conditions.

One of the biggest factors affecting connection speed is the distance between the access point and the wirelessly equipped PC. Compaq, for example, notes that at a distance of 150 feet, the throughput of its wireless access point drops by half, and at 300 feet, it drops even more. And that's understating the case: in real-world conditions, you'll find a much more severe drop-off in speed.

Reducing the distance between your upstairs computer and your access point will go a long way toward boosting network performance, but interference from other devices and the layout of your house or office can dramatically affect network speed as well. Here's what you can do to get more throughput throughout your home:

- **Put your wireless access point in a central location.** That way, all of your wirelessly equipped PCs will get reasonable throughput. If you tuck your access point away in a corner of the house, nearby PCs may get high throughput, but for others it may drop significantly.
- **Make sure the access point's antennas are not obstructed.** Make sure there are no obstructions within two to three inches of the antennas. Transmission may also improve if the antennas are vertically oriented, but every house is different, so experiment.
- **Point the antennas of your wireless PCs in the direction of the access point.** Many of the WiFi adapter cards you stick in a PC's slot have external, adjustable antennas. So, too, do external USB wireless adapters and some of the wireless network cards you snap into a laptop's PCMCIA slot. If you can, point the adapter's antenna toward your access point. If the antenna is built into the adapter, change the orientation of your PC or laptop until you get the best signal strength—hopefully, in a position that still lets you get work done! Note: these tips only pay off if your devices are using directional antennas.
- **Don't place access points or wireless PCs near filing cabinets and other large metal objects.** Any metal within 100 feet can cause multiple reflections of the signal, which can cut throughput dramatically.
- **Consider using external and booster antennas.** Some access points can accept booster antennas that can increase the range of the signal and boost the throughput for those who are further away from the router. So can some wireless PC cards, such as Proxim's Orinoco cards, which have a small connector that allows you to attach a "pigtail" cable and, on the other end, a store-bought or home-built antenna (for more on building your own antenna, see the next annoyance: "Boost WiFi Speed with a Cantenna").

BOOST WIFI SPEED WITH A CANTENNA

The Annoyance: In spite of all your advice, the access speed of one of my laptops is still pretty pokey. I'd like to get an antenna to boost its throughput, but I'm short on cash. Is there any help for the cheapskates of the world?

The Fix: You can build your own wireless antenna for a few dollars using a tin can and other stray parts, as long as you're willing to do a little bit of soldering. Because they're built out of tin cans, these homemade

GIVE YOUR ACCESS POINT A BOOST

There are two key ways to extend the range of your access point, and thus your wireless network: *booster antennas* and *relay stations* (also known as *repeaters*). Not all access points accept them, but some will. For example, with some Linksys wireless routers, you can turn to the company's $99 repeater, the Wireless-G Range Expander (WRE54G), or pick up a Wireless High-Gain Antenna for as little as $59. Both approaches promise to extend your router's range and strengthen its signal—a claim I can confirm with my own, admittedly informal, tests. With a repeater, you don't have to connect anything. Just place it in range of your router, and it will boost and relay the signal throughout your house. With a booster antenna, you take the antennas off your router, attach them to the booster, then attach the booster to the router via cables.

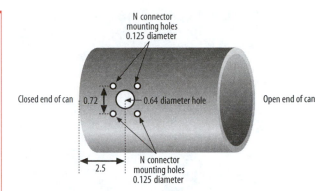

Figure 3-1. The cantenna connector location.

affairs are called *cantennas*. (For more details, see Chapter 3, "How to Hack 802.11b Antennas," in Scott Fullam's *Hardware Hacking Projects for Geeks*, also published by O'Reilly.)

You often see cantennas built out of Pringle's cans, but you'll get much better results with one of those giant 34.5-ounce coffee cans. (And a caffeine buzz is better for you than carb-heavy potato chips, anyway.)

If you haven't bought a WiFi card, look for a Proxim Orinoco card or a similar product that accepts "pigtails." These slim RF cables let you connect WiFi cards, routers, and other devices to external antennas, typically via an N–Male connector. (The connection on the card or router end can vary wildly. There are RPTNC, MC-Card, MMCX, and other connectors. Get the scoop on what connects to what at *http://www.cantenna.com/pigtailfinder.html*.) You can even connect to a homemade antenna built out of copper wire and a tin can (Figure 3-1). A good place to get all the parts (minus the tin can, of course) is Hyperlink Technologies, at *http://www.hyperlinktech.com*.

There are many sites where you can find directions for making cantennas. Three good places to start are *http://www.oreillynet.com/cs/weblog/view/wlg/448*, *http://www.netscum.com/~clapp/wireless.html*, and *http://www.turnpoint.net/wireless/cantennahowto.html*. Here's a brief preview of the steps involved:

1. Empty the can of coffee or chips, then give it a good washing.

2. Solder a short piece of thick copper wire to a small piece of hardware called an N connector (available at *http://www.hyperlinktech.com* and other fine outlets). This wire is the antenna.

3. Drill a hole in the can and insert the small antenna that you just soldered.

4. Attach the antenna to the can by securing it with small screws and bolts.

5. Attach one end of the pigtail cable to your wireless card and the other end to the N connector.

Once you're done, sit back and enjoy improved throughput (Figure 3-2). Make sure to experiment with the direction you point the cantenna; it can make a big difference in throughput.

Note: some PC pros don't recommend the cantenna approach. A home-built cantenna is neither weatherproof nor stable, and using accessories that are not approved by your card or access point vendor could void your warranty.

Figure 3-2. Using a cantenna can help extend yout wireless range—even in the great outdoors.

Buy a Prebuilt Cantenna

Like the idea of using a cantenna, but don't like the idea of using a soldering iron? No problem—you can buy one already made from *http://www.cantenna.com*. They don't come cheap, though: $19.95 for the cantenna itself, and $19.95 for a pigtail. You can also buy related hardware, such a mini-tripod, to keep your cantenna in place.

> **t i p**
>
> You should never look into the open end of your cantenna when it is operating. Although the signal levels from the antennas built into your wireless card are considered safe by the FCC, your new antenna focuses the signal to levels that could be harmful.

ELIMINATE WIFI INTERFERENCE

The Annoyance: Communications devices are at war in my house, and I'm the victim. Every time I talk on my phone, my WiFi connection cuts out. How can I get my phone and WiFi network to declare a truce?

The Fix: The problem is caused by your cordless phone, not your landline phone. WiFi and many cordless phones operate in the same part of the radio spectrum, at 2.4 gigahertz (GHz). When you use a cordless phone near your network, it generates enough interference to knock out your WiFi connection. The high-tech solution: get a 900-MHz or 5.8-GHz phone. The low-tech solution: don't use cordless phones near your network. You might also try relocating your access point and your wireless PCs to see if that helps.

JUMP-START YOUR WIRELESS ROUTER

The Annoyance: I installed a new Linksys wireless router a week ago, and every morning when I wake up, every PC's Internet connection is dead. If I restart the router, they work fine again, but then the next morning the same thing happens. Does this router need a double dose of espresso every morning, or what?

The Fix: A double dose of espresso isn't a bad idea, but save it for yourself. There's a better way to fix your router problem. The problem is related to how the router assigns IP addresses to all of the PCs on your network. The router uses the Dynamic Host Configuration Protocol (DHCP) to assign each PC a unique IP address. Without an IP address, a PC can't connect to the Internet.

The problem is that newer Linksys routers have one of the most annoying "features" of all time—by default, the IP addresses they assign last for only one day. Theoretically, they should automatically get new IP addresses each day without your intervention. But some people find that this doesn't always happen, and that they must restart their routers every day to make sure that all their PCs get new IP addresses.

Upgrading your router's firmware often fixes the problem. Go to the Linksys site at *http://www.linksys.com*, click the Products tab, and then click through the categories until you find the product page for your router model. Once you find it, click the Firmware link, and follow the instructions for downloading and installing the firmware upgrade.

If that doesn't fix the problem, there's a workaround: you can drastically lengthen the amount of time each assigned IP address will last (known as the "lease" on the IP address). That way, your PCs will lose their IP addresses much less frequently, so you'll have to restart your router only once every, say, 45 days. Here's how:

1. In your browser, go to *http://192.168.1.1.* Log into the Linksys administrator's setup screen by leaving the username blank and entering the password admin. (That's the default password. If you've changed your username and password, use those.)

2. Click the Setup tab, then click Basic Setup.

3. In the Client Lease Time box, type in 65535. That's how long in minutes (approximately 45 days) the IP address on each PC will last before it expires. Note: routers may limit you to a smaller number.

4. Click the Save Settings button, then exit.

TEST YOUR TRUE NETWORK SPEED

The Annoyance: When it comes to WiFi connections, XP seems to have an issue with telling the truth. No matter how slow my 802.11b connection is at home or at a HotSpot, it always reports that I'm getting the maximum 11 Mbps. Why can't I get the *true* throughput?

The Fix: XP won't help you here. When you double-click the network icon in XP's System Tray, it pops up the Wireless Network Connection Status window, which reports only your theoretical connection maximum, not your real connection speed. But the free Qcheck software from Ixia (see Figure 3-3), which you can download from *http://www.ixiacom.com/products/qcheck/*, does an admirable job of reporting your true network speed. Install it on each PC on your network, and you can then test the connection speed of any PC—handy if you're trying to optimize network performance.

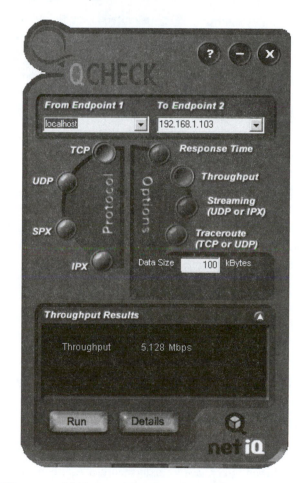

Figure 3-3. Qcheck measures the true speed of a PC connected to a WiFi network (here, 5.128 Mbps, rather than the 11 Mbps reported by Windows XP).

HAVE I BEEN TAKEN FOR A WIFI RIDE?

The Annoyance: I just bought an 802.11g WiFi router that promised me a 125-Mbps network speed. But I measured it using Qcheck, and I'm only getting 25 to 30 Mbps. What am I doing wrong—or have I been taken for a WiFi ride?

The Fix: You've been victimized by marketing hype. Some manufacturers promise that you can get 125-Mbps throughput from their 802.11g routers, even though the 802.11g standard only calls for 54 Mbps. The trick? They use proprietary methods to get speeds higher than 54 Mbps, so it only works with hardware from the same manufacturer using the same proprietary methods. If you mix and match hardware from other manufacturers, you won't get the same speed boost.

Besides, 125 Mbps is a purely theoretical speed—it's not achievable in real-world conditions, even if you use the same proprietary hardware for your entire network. It assumes that there's no interference; that all devices on the network use the same, compatible hardware; and that you're transferring a file made up of all 000000s that is incredibly compressible.

WHY WON'T MY WIFI DEVICES TALK TO EACH OTHER?

The Annoyance: I bought WiFi cards and a router from different manufacturers and discovered that they don't work together. Doesn't anyone understand the meaning of "standard"?

The Fix: That's the nice thing about standards—there are so many to choose from. In theory, a WiFi-compliant device should work with any other WiFi-compliant device. But what does "WiFi-compliant" really mean? Make sure the hardware has passed the WiFi Alliance certification test. If it hasn't, there's no guarantee it will work with other vendors' equipment. Even if two devices are certified, they may not work with each other, thanks to

---

THE TRUTH BEHIND SPEEDBOOST

Linksys is one of the WiFi vendors that claims that some of its wireless routers and cards (with "SpeedBooster" technology) increase "real-world" wireless network performance by 35%. But is that really true? The answer is both yes and no, according to tests conducted by Tom's Networking (*http://www.tomsnetworking.com/Reviews-142-ProdID-WRT54GS.php*). SpeedBooster gets its kick from an "Afterburner" chip made by Broadcom. To get the speed boost, both the access point and the network adapter must incorporate Afterburner technology. If they do, says Tom's Networking, you'll get a speed boost—maybe. If the access point and computers with the network adapter are in the same room and have no walls between them, and the PCs are running 1-GHz or faster CPUs, you could see a speed boost of up to 45%. But when the access point is located further away from the computer, with walls in between, there appears to be no speed gain. Given that these SpeedBooster devices often cost about 20% more than non-SpeedBooster devices, they'll only make sense if your computers are located near your access point and all use SpeedBoost technology. For more details, see *http://www.tomsnetworking.com/Reviews-142-ProdID-WRT54GS-1.php*.

---

the vagaries of a new standard. The Alliance says that an estimated 25% to 30% of equipment fails certification. To find out before buying, go to *http://www.weca.net/OpenSection/certified_products.asp?TID=2* and search its list of certified products.

WIFI PRINTING WOES

The Annoyance: In my WiFi network, my printer is attached to my computer downstairs. So if I want to print out something from my laptop upstairs, I have to jog downstairs, turn on my downstairs computer, then jog back up and print. I know this is good for my cardiovascular system, but I'd rather get my workouts at the gym.

The Fix: There's no need to connect your printer to a PC—you can connect it directly to your wireless network using a USB wireless print server, made by Linksys, D-Link, and other companies. Plug one of these paperback-sized units into your printer's USB port, configure it using a web browser, and you'll be able to print to it even when your PCs are turned off. At press time prices were at just over $100, but expect them to drop.

If your printer lacks a USB port, you're not out of luck. Some models, such as the Linksys Wireless-G PrintServer for USB (WPS54GU2) and D-Link DP-G321 Multi-Port Print Server (shown in Figure 3-4), include a parallel port connection so that any printer, not just those with USB ports, can connect to a wireless network.

Figure 3-4. Cast off your USB and parallel printer cables and go completely wireless with the D-Link wireless print server—just plug it into a printer, and everyone on your network can start printing wirelessly.

STOP BANDWIDTH VAMPIRES

The Annoyance: I have a sneaking suspicion that one of my close neighbors is leeching off of my WiFi network and getting access to the Internet on my dime. I notice that the evenings when he's home, my network slows down; I suspect he's using it to download gigabytes of MP3s and movies. How can I confirm he's a digital freeloader?

The Fix: Download the free AirSnare for the PC, which will monitor your network for wireless intruders, report on who they are, show you their activity, and even send them alerts telling them that you know they're using your bandwidth. (To stop these intrusions, however, check out the "WiFi Security" section later in this chapter.) Here's how to use it:

1. Before you can use AirSnare, you must download and install the required WinPcap library of tools (available from *http://winpcap.polito.it/install/default.htm*).

2. Download and install AirSnare from *http://home.comcast.net/~jay.deboer/airsnare*.

3. After you install the program, go to *C:\Program Files\ AirSnare*, open *trustedMAC.txt* with WordPad, and add the MAC addresses of any network cards that will be using your wireless network. (The MAC address is a number that uniquely identifies a network card or other piece of communications hardware.) Enter the MAC address, such as 00-08-A1-00-9F-32, on a new line by itself in the file, follow it by a space, and then type in a description of the computer. For example: 00-08-A1-00-9F-32 Preston's Upstairs Laptop.

4. Go to *C:\Program Files\AirSnare* and run the file *AirSnare.exe*.

5. You must run the file from this location, because the program doesn't install an icon on the desktop or show up as an entry in Windows's All Programs menu.

6. Choose your network adapter from the list that appears, and you're all set.

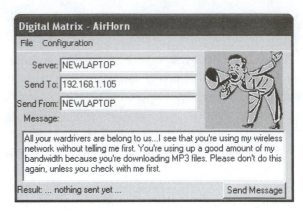

Figure 3-5. AirSnare not only detects intruders, but lets you send them messages telling them you know what they're up to.

Whenever an unrecognized device slips onto your wireless network, you'll be alerted. You can also monitor the intruders' Internet activity, including sites they're visiting. You can even log their activity to a file and send them personalized alerts letting them know you're watching what they're doing (Figure 3-5). That should solve the leeching problem fast.

By the way, AirSnare won't work with every WiFi card. If the program crashes when you launch it, it's not compatible with yours. (Click the Supported Equipment button on the AirSnare site to view known problems.) One plus: you can use AirSnare to monitor a Mac network, too—just connect a PC to the network and run AirSnare from there.

UNDERSTANDING 802.11 STANDARDS

There are several versions of the 802.11*x* WiFi standard. So when you're buying WiFi equipment, make sure that you know exactly what you're buying—and that the products are certified. The 802.11b standard was the first one to be ratified, and it's the one commonly used by public wireless "HotSpots" in coffee shops, airports, hotels, and other locations. It operates in the 2.4 GHz part of the spectrum, and its maximum throughput is 11 Mbps.

The increasingly popular 802.11g standard also operates at 2.4 Ghz, but it has a much higher maximum throughput of 54 Mbps. 802.11b cards will connect to a 802.11g access point, but only at a maximum of 11 Mbps. 802.11g cards will also connect to an 802.11b network, but again, only at a maximum speed of 11 Mbps.

The WiFi alphabet doesn't end with "b" and "g." 802.11a hardware, which is relatively rare, operates at 5 GHz and has a maximum data rate of 54 Mbps. Other standards are in the works as well, including 802.11i, which features enhanced security.

SPEED UP AN 802.11G SLOWPOKE

The Annoyance: I just bought a new high-speed 802.11g router to replace my 802.11b slowpoke. I don't know why I bothered to fork out the cash—the network speed remains the same. How can I kick-start this network?

The Fix: Just buying a router won't bump up your performance; you must buy 802.11g network cards for *every* computer on your network. If there's a single 802.11b network card connected to your 802.11g network, the throughput slows down to 802.11b speeds for everyone on the network, not just those with 802.11b cards.

WIRELESS SECURITY CAM

The Annoyance: I've just spent tons of money on a wireless network, and now I'm about to spend even more on a separate security camera for my house. Isn't there some way to have my wireless network tied to a security camera?

The Fix: Yes there is, and you won't have to break the bank to get one. The D-Link Wireless 2.4GHz Internet Camera (DCS-900W) connects to your network and displays streaming video at 320 X 240–pixel resolution at up to 20 frames a second, which is more than adequate for a security camera. It includes a built-in web server and free Dynamic Domain Name Service (DDNS) utility, so you can easily create a personal web site for viewing the video feeds. You can also automatically save the feeds to disk so that you can have a permanent record. It costs about $150 online or at retail stores. For more details, head to *http://www.dlink.com/products/?pid=297*.

A TEEN'S DREAM: WIRELESS PLAYSTATION

The Annoyance: My Fender-wielding son is at it again, this time because I replaced our Ethernet network with a WiFi network. Now he can't hook up his PlayStation and kill his virtual Internet friends in late-night shootouts.

The Fix: Buy a wireless game adapter designed to hook up PlayStation and other game boxes to the Internet. They're amazingly easy to set up. Plug the adapter into the Ethernet connection on the game box and turn on the adapter; it will automatically recognize your wireless network and become part of it.

As of this writing, several models are available from different manufacturers (two from Linksys have gotten good reviews). The **Linksys WGA11B Wireless–B Game Adapter for** 802.11b networks sells for as little as $60. The **Linksys WGA54G Wireless–G Game Adapter** for 802.11b and 802.11g networks (Figure 3-6) costs about $100. Microsoft sells the Wireless-G Xbox Adapter for the Xbox for about $80.

Figure 3-6. Instant fun: the Linksys WGA54G Wireless-G Game Adapter connects a gaming system to a WiFi network.

Make sure the adapter you buy is designed specifically for gaming platforms; avoid wireless bridges and other products that promise to hook up any kind of device to a wireless network. Configuring one of these to work with a game box can be a nightmare.

WIRELESS GAME ADAPTERS DO DOUBLE DUTY

The Linksys Wireless Game Adapter can do more than connect a gaming system to a WiFi network—it can connect PCs to it as well. Simply plug the adapter into the Ethernet port on your PC, and you'll be able to connect to a WiFi network. The Linksys adapter even has an advantage over normal WiFi adapters—it needs no drivers, so it can often work when other WiFi adapters won't. My son, for example, installed Linux on his PC, and Linux refused to connect to our WiFi network with his normal wireless adapter. So he plugged his game adapter into the PC's Ethernet port, and he connected to the network without a hitch. The drawbacks: you can't pick which wireless network to connect to if you're near more than one (it automatically connects to the one with the strongest signal), nor can you connect to networks that require encryption.

CELL PHONES AND THE NET

FROM EMAIL TO CELL PHONE

The Annoyance: I want to send a text message to my daughter using my email program. I know that the email address is her phone number, followed by a certain domain, but I can't remember the domain name. We're living in the age of communications—there's got to be some way to do this!

The Fix: Traditionally (namely, until a few months ago), to send someone a text message, you had to know her cell phone carrier's domain—and they're seldom obvious. To send email to a Cingular user, for example, the domain is *mobile.mycingular.net*. But technology soldiers on. Thanks to Teleflip, now all you need to send a message to someone's cell phone is that person's cell phone number. Just send an email to *cellphonenumber@teleflip.com*, where *cellphonenumber* is the person's cell phone number. The service is free, although the recipient will probably have to pay to receive the message. For more details, go to *http://www.teleflip.com*.

It soon could become easier to find web sites to browse with your cell phone. Microsoft, Nokia, Hewlett-Packard, Samsung, and five other companies have banded together to promote a top-level Internet domain (such as *.com* or *.net*) devoted to web sites designed to be accessed by cell phones. The Internet's oversight body has given initial approval to the use of *.mobi*, and it might be in use by the time you read this. For more information, go to *http://www.mtldinfo.com*, the home page of the mobile Top Level Domain initiative, the group that's pushing for the new domain.

GARBLED WEB SITES

The Annoyance: What's so great about browsing the Web with a cell phone? Almost every site I visit is completely garbled!

The Fix: Your phone's included browser can only display sites that are built using WML (Wireless Markup Language) and that conform to the WAP (Wireless Access Protocol) standard. If you browse non-WML sites (which, alas, is most of them) with your cell phone browser, you can't view them properly.

To find WML sites, check out these directories: Yahoo! (*http://mobile.yahoo.com*), Google (*http://www.google.com/intl/en_extra/wap.html* on your PC or *http://wap.google.com* on your cell phone browser), *and Waptiger* (*http://www.waptiger.com*). For still more, check out the SearchEngineWatch article on WAP and WML search engines at *http://searchenginewatch.com/links/article.php/2156391*.

BECOME A WIRELESS FROOGLE SHOPPER

The Annoyance: I'm shopping at the local mall and I see a new gadget that I absolutely must have, but the voices of my ancestors whisper in my ear, "I can get it for you wholesale!" But if I can't get it cheaper, I'd like to buy it now. Why can't I do some quick comparison-shopping using my cell phone?

The Fix: You can, if you have a WML-capable cell phone. (Virtually any phone that has a web browser is WML-capable.) Go to http://wml.froogle.com on your phone and search the Internet for the lowest prices on the product. You'll be able to use your cell phone's keypad to browse through the results, as shown in Figure 3-7.

For more information about how to use Froogle, see Chapter 10.

BEWARE BLUETOOTH SNARFING ATTACKS

The Annoyance: Nokia has revealed that some of its Bluetooth cell phones may be vulnerable to hackers, who can get at your address book and calendar information, as well as photos, videos, and audio files stored on the phone. Which phones are vulnerable, and how can I prevent an attack?

The Fix: You're referring to *snarfing*, or *bluesnarfing*. (The term comes from the '60s slang word "snarf," which means "to eat like a pig." Unix users later redefined the word as "to take a large file or document from someone

Figure 3-7. Compare prices online versus at a retail store using your cell phone and wireless Froogle.

without their permission.") The only Nokia phones vulnerable to the attack, says the company, are older phones—models 6310, 6310i, 8910, and 8910i. Of those, the only one sold in the U.S. was the 6310i.

There are several ways Bluetooth phones can be attacked. In one, the victim must accept "pairing" from another Bluetooth phone, which allows for two-way communications between the two phones. So practice safe phone sex and never accept pairing from a stranger. (Or candy, for that matter.) In another kind of attack, you don't even know you've been victimized—you can be attacked even if your phone is in nonvisible mode, and you assume no one has made a connection to you. Be alert to your digital surroundings. If you're in an area where there is likely to be a large gathering of people with Bluetooth-enabled cell phones—at a trade show, for example—turn off your phone's Bluetooth features and you'll be safe.

t i p

Nokia isn't the only company whose older phones can be attacked, according to A.L. Digital Ltd. Several models from Ericsson and Sony Ericsson are also vulnerable. (For a full list, go to *http://www.bluestumbler.org*.)

What's in a Name?

Bluetooth is a wireless technology that lets devices instantly recognize and communicate with one another in a kind of ad hoc network that requires no central server. The idea is that many different kinds of devices—cell phones, PDAs, even kitchen appliances—can talk to one another. Bluetooth gets its name from the Danish Viking King Harald Blåtand, whose name means Bluetooth in English. He united Denmark and Norway, and so is the inspiration for a technology designed to unite devices.

WIFI SECURITY

STOP BROADCASTING YOUR NETWORK NAME

The Annoyance: I have a Linksys wireless router, and the other day, using AirSnare (see "Stop Bandwidth Vampires"), I found someone on my network, stealing bandwidth. When I sent an angry note to the leech, he had the gall to write back, "Then stop broadcasting your SSID, stupid!" What's an SSID, and how do I stop it from being broadcast?

The Fix: Your SSID is your network's name, and if people know what it is, it's easier for them to find your network and connect to it.

That's only one part of the problem, though. Even if you stop broadcasting your network's name, people may still be able to connect to it. That's because manufacturers generally ship their wireless routers with the same generic SSID—for example, Linksys routers are called "Linksys" by default. So even if you stop broadcasting your SSID, these bandwidth vampires may be able to easily guess your router's name and log on to your network. So you need to first change your SSID's name, then hide it.

Change your SSID name

The steps you'll follow with most vendors' wireless routers should be similar. This is how you'd change the SSID name on a Linksys router:

1. Log into the setup screen by opening your browser and going to *http://192.168.1.1*. When the login screen appears, leave the username blank, type admin as the password, and press Enter. (If you've changed the username and password, obviously, use those.)

2. On the Setup tab (Figure 3-8), go to the ESSID box and type in a new name for your network, then click the Apply button. (With some Linksys routers, you'll instead need to go to the Wireless tab, locate the "Wireless Network Name (SSID)" box, enter a new name, and then click the Save Settings button.)

3. After you change your network name, reconnect each WiFi computer to the network, using the new network name. To reconnect a PC running Windows XP with Service Pack 2 (SP2), right-click the small wireless icon in the Windows System Tray, choose Available Wireless Networks, click Change Advanced Settings, then click the Wireless Networks tab. Click the Add button in the Preferred Network section, type in the network name, click OK, then click OK again. To reconnect a PC running Windows XP pre-SP2, click the small wireless network icon in the Windows System Tray and select the Wireless Networks tab. Click the Add button, type in the network name, click OK, and then click OK again.

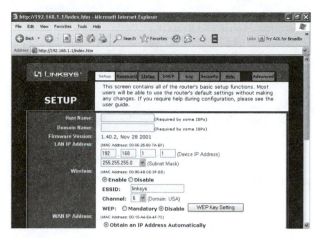

Figure 3-8. Changing your router's ESSID and the channel number will make it harder to find.

Stop broadcasting your SSID

To stop broadcasting your SSID, on the same router setup screen, scroll down to SSID Broadcast and choose Disable. Make sure that you don't disable your wireless network—just disable SSID broadcasting. If you choose Disable under the Wireless setting, you'll disable your wireless network. (On some Linksys routers, you'll find these options on the Wireless tab.)

Not all Linksys routers let you disable SSID broadcasting.

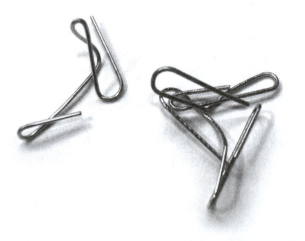

PROTECT YOUR HOME WIFI NETWORK

The Annoyance: I've stopped SSID broadcasting, but occasional leeches still hop onto my WiFi network. Isn't there anything I can do to block these bandwidth bandits once and for all?

The Fix: There's no single fix that will keep you protected, but if you follow these steps, you'll go a long way toward keeping out intruders. Before doing any of this, go to your wireless router vendor's web site and download and install any firmware updates for the router. The firmware may have newer security features built in. After you've installed the firmware, take these steps:

1. Regularly change the channel your router transmits over. That way, people who have tapped into it before won't know which channel it's broadcasting over. This only works if you change your SSID (or stop broadcasting it, as described in "Stop Broadcasting Your Network Name"), though, because XP automatically connects to a WiFi network, no matter what channel it's on, if it knows the network's SSID.

   Log into your router's setup screen. With a Linksys router, for example, go to *http://192.168.1.1* and log in by leaving the username blank and, assuming you haven't changed it from the default, entering admin as the password. Go to the Setup tab, choose a new channel from the Channels drop-down list, and click the Apply button. Then restart each of your computers. Since they all know your network name, they'll automatically connect on the new channel.

2. Limit the number of IP addresses on your network to the number of computers on your network. That way, no one else will be able to get an IP address from your network's DHCP server, and so they won't be able to hop onto your network.

   Your router's built-in DHCP server hands out IP addresses whenever a computer needs to use the network. The router lets you set the maximum number of IP addresses it hands out. With a Linksys router, for example, go to the setup screen and click the DHCP tab. Enter the number of computers that will use your network in the "Number of DHCP Users" field (Figure 3-9), and click the Apply button. If you add another computer to your network, make sure you go back to the screen and increase the number of DHCP users by one.

Figure 3-9. If you limit the number of IP addresses your DHCP server hands out, only PCs in your home will be able to connect to your network.

3. Filter out MAC addresses. You can tell your network to only allow access to network cards with specific MAC addresses. That way, only hardware that you specify can use your network. (Note that not all routers have this capability, although Linksys routers do.)

To find the MAC address of a network adapter, see the sidebar "Find Your WiFi Adapter's MAC Address" earlier in this chapter. Write down the MAC addresses of all the network adapters to which you're granting network access. How you filter MAC addresses varies by router. With the Linksys WRT54G, go to the setup page and choose Advanced → Filters → Advanced. In the Advanced Wireless section, set the Wireless MAC Filter option to "Enable." Set the option under Wireless MAC Filter to "Permit only," and then click the Edit MAC Filter List button. Then click the Wireless MAC List button and, in the list that appears, check the box under Enable MAC Filter for each of your PCs that are listed under Active PC. When you've done that, click the Update Filter List button. You'll be sent back to the MAC Address Filter List window. Click the Apply button.

4. Use encryption. The WEP encryption standard is relatively weak, but it will keep out anyone except a determined expert. So turn on WEP. The WPA standard is stronger, but you can only use that if your hardware supports it. If it does, use WPA instead. For details, see "Easy Guide to Setting Up WEP Encryption" and "Not-So-Easy Guide to Setting Up WPA Encryption."

EASY GUIDE TO SETTING UP WEP ENCRYPTION

The Annoyance: Help! It feels like I've spent years of my life trying to set up WEP encryption on my home wireless network, but no matter what I do, I can't get it to work. I'm wondering if it's worth it—WEP encryption isn't the end-all of security measures, after all.

The Fix: It's true that a dedicated cracker can break through WEP encryption, but it will keep casual snoopers from getting into your network.

WEP can be confusing to set up, and the process varies by make and model of wireless router. Following are the basic steps for setting up WEP on a typical Linksys wireless router. Check your documentation for details, but it should be similar to this:

1. Go to the setup screen of your router. For a Linksys router, you typically fire up your browser, go to *http://192.168.1.1*, and type in your password (leaving the username blank). The default for a Linksys router is typically admin.

2. In the WEP section, click Mandatory.

3. Click WEP Key Setting. A screen will appear that will let you set your WEP preferences, as well as generate a required WEP key that will be used by the router and any PC that wants to use the network.

4. Choose 128-bit encryption from the top drop-down menu, as shown in Figure 3-10—it's the strongest encryption you can use with WEP.

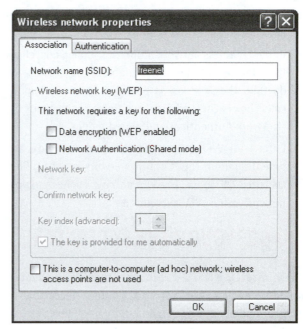

Figure 3-11. You're almost there: enable WEP encryption, type in your WEP key, and you should be set to go.

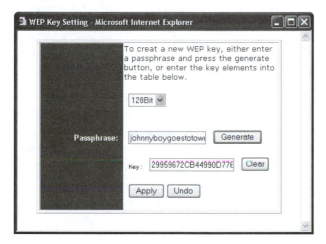

Figure 3-10. When setting up WEP, use the strongest encryption, 128-bit, and let the router generate the key for you.

5. Generate your WEP key by typing words or a phrase in the Passphrase box and clicking the Generate button. A key will be created in the Key box (see Figure 3-11).

You don't have to generate your key this way—you can create one yourself and type it in manually. But chances are it will be far easier to crack than one randomly generated by the software.

6. Write down the entire key that was just generated. Get yourself a lot of paper—it's going to be a long one, filled with strange characters. You'll need to use the key for each PC that is going to access the network.

7. Click the Apply button. That will apply the key to your network. Now only PCs that use WEP encryption and the key you just generated will be able to get onto your network. When you're sent back to the Setup screen, click Apply.

8. Now you have to configure each wirelessly connected computer on your network to use WEP and the key you just generated. On each PC, double-click the wireless connection icon in the Windows System Tray and choose Properties → Wireless Networks. (In Windows XP with Service Pack 2, click the wireless connection icon in the Windows System Tray, click View Wireless Networks, click Change Advanced Settings, then click the Wireless Networks tab.)

9. In the "Available networks" section, highlight your network and click the Configure button.

10. In the "Wireless network properties" dialog box, check the "Data encryption (WEP enabled)" box. When you do that, the "The key is provided for me automatically" box is checked. Uncheck this box and check the "Network Authentication (Shared mode)" box.

11. Enter your WEP key in the "Network key" box, and type it again in the "Confirm network key" box. Click OK, then OK again. The PC can now connect to your network using WEP encryption.

CHANGE YOUR WEP KEY REGULARLY

The Annoyance: I thought that WEP encryption would be enough, but last week I found traces that an intruder had been sniffing around my hard drive. Clearly, WEP is the 98-pound weakling of the encryption world. What else can I do?

The Fix: The problem is that you've used the same WEP key for too long. If a snooper monitors your network packets (each with the same WEP key) for long enough, he'll be able to crack the encryption. However, if you regularly change your key, it will be much harder to crack the encryption. You should change your encryption key regularly—i.e., every week. To set up a new key, see "Easy Guide to Setting Up WEP Encryption."

WHEN IS 40-BIT WEP REALLY 64-BIT WEP?

The Annoyance: My access point lets me generate a key for 64-bit WEP encryption, and I've done that. Now I want to connect my Palm Tungsten C handheld to my network, but there's no option for typing in a 64-bit key—it only accepts a 40-bit key. How can I connect my Palm to my network with maximum WEP protection?

The Fix: Believe it or not, 40-bit WEP encryption and 64-bit WEP encryption are actually two terms for the same thing, so just go ahead and type in your 64-bit-encryption WEP key. WEP uses a 24-bit *initialization vector*,

> Changing your key regularly can be a pain, but there's a nifty little utility that can make life a bit easier for you. The WEP Key Generator utility will automatically generate WEP keys and print them out for you. You can then take that printout from PC to PC and type in the WEP key. The program is free from *http://www.clariondeveloper.com/wepgen.*

and you don't control that part of the key. That's why some manufacturers refer to the standard as 40-bit, and others call it 64-bit. In the same way, 128-bit WEP encryption is sometimes called 104-bit WEP encryption. And you thought programmers were good with numbers!

NOT-SO-EASY GUIDE TO SETTING UP WPA ENCRYPTION

The Annoyance: Everything I've read says WEP security is a joke. I don't want a 98-pound weakling protecting my network—I want the Charles Atlas of encryption. I don't want every 15-year-old in the neighborhood breaking into my network and getting his virtual fingerprints on my files. I've heard WPA is far superior—how can I use it?

The Fix: If your network hardware is more than a year or two old, it may not support WPA. Check with your manufacturer and find out. If your manufacturer doesn't have details, you can also turn to the Wi-Fi Alliance's web site at *http://www.wi-fi.org* for information about what hardware can handle WPA. Just remember that *all* your network hardware has to support WPA—your router and your wireless network cards. So do the operating systems running on every networked PC.

If you can use WPA, set some serious time aside for installing it—it's not for the weak of heart. There's no room here to give you a comprehensive blow-by-blow description of how to use WPA, but here are the steps you'll take (for more detailed instructions, see the *PC Magazine* article "*Wireless Security: WPA Step by Step*" at *www.pc-mag.com/print_article/0,3048,a=107756,00.asp*):

1. Install the WPA software. WPA isn't built directly into many versions of Windows XP (although it is built into SP2), so you'll have to download it. Go to *http://support.microsoft.com/default.aspx?kbid=826942* to download an update that will let XP use WPA. Then head on over to *http://support.microsoft.com/default.aspx?scid=kb;en-us;815485* for information about how to install and configure WPA.

2. Update your router's and network cards' firmware. Your hardware may not take advantage of WPA. Check with the relevant manufacturers and see if a firmware update will do the job. If so, download and install the firmware. Remember that you'll have to upgrade all your wireless networking hardware, not just a few components.

3. Configure WPA on your router. This can be a fairly complex process, depending on your router, so check the manufacturer's documentation. It's similar to setting up WEP, but requires several extra steps.

4. Configure WPA on your network cards. Using the key you generated on your router (see "Easy Guide to Setting Up WEP Encryption"), configure WPA on your network cards. You'll use the "Wireless network properties" dialog box, much as you did when you configured WEP.

CELTIC RUNES AND WIRELESS ACCESS?

The Annoyance: I think I've been targeted by some kind of anti-WiFi cult. Ever since I installed my wireless network, odd, cryptic symbols that look like Celtic runes, or perhaps symbols of devil worshippers, have been appearing on the sidewalk outside my house. Should I contact an exorcist?

The Fix: No need to call Father Damien, but you should strengthen the security of your WiFi network (see the annoyance "Protect Your Home WiFi Network"). What you've noticed are "war-chalking" symbols (see Figure 3-12) that tell passersby that there is a WiFi network nearby, and that it might unwittingly provide free Internet access. Anyone who recognizes the symbols will know you have a WiFi network and may try to connect. Look closely at the symbols—there's information on how to connect to your network, such as your SSID. The symbols were inspired by the practice of hoboes, who during the Great Depression would make chalk marks near hobo-friendly homes that would hand out free food. For more information about war chalking, go to *http://www.blackbeltjones.com/warchalking/index2.html*.

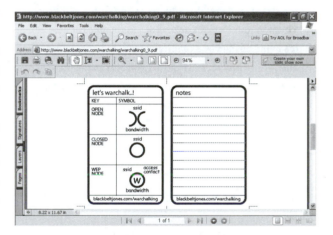

Figure 3-12. Some typical war-chalking symbols: the top one means the network is open and unencrypted, so anyone can connect to it (an SSID may be included as well), the middle one means that the network is private and closed, and the bottom one indicates a network using WEP encryption.

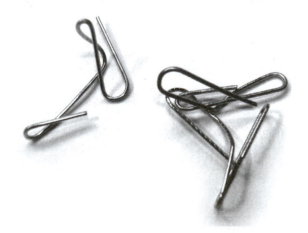

HOTSPOTS

FIND HOTSPOTS BEFORE YOU HIT THE ROAD

The Annoyance: I spend more time in airports and hotel rooms than I do at home. I'd like to access HotSpots wherever I travel, but finding a HotSpot on the road is about as easy as finding a good sushi bar in Saskatchewan.

The Fix: Before you hit the road, check these online HotSpot finders: *http://www.wi-fihotspotlist.com*, *http://www.wifinder.com*, *http://www.wifimaps.com*, and *http://www.jiwire.com*. They'll help you find free as well as for-pay HotSpots. If you're looking for only free HotSpots, head to *http://www.wififreespot.com*.

You can also combine the power of Google's location search with the JiWire search to locate HotSpots near any zip code, street, or any other location, complete with a map. Go to *http://labs.google.com/location*, and type jiwire in the "Search terms" box. In the "Street address, city, or zip" box, type in the location and press Enter (or click the Google Search button). You'll get a list of HotSpots near the location, with addresses, directions, related web links, and more (Figure 3-13). With a click, you can summon a map with the locations neatly pinpointed.

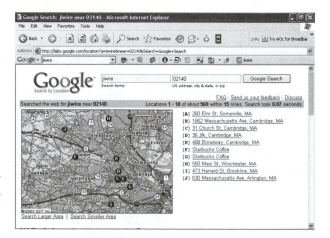

Figure 3-13. Combine the power of a Google location search with the JiWire HotSpot finder to find HotSpot locations where you'll be traveling.

CHOOSE THE RIGHT HOTSPOT PROVIDER

The Annoyance: I'm tired of always scrounging around for free-access HotSpots. I'm ready to take the plunge and pay for HotSpots. How can I find one that'll give me access whenever I want it, wherever I go (within reason), without putting a serious dent in my bank account?

The Fix: There's no one-size-fits-all solution when choosing a Wireless Internet service provider (WISP). You'll have to balance price, connection speed, the number of HotSpots the WISP has, and whether you need to access HotSpots close to home or when you're out of town.

For close-to-home use, look for local or regional WISPs—they tend to be less expensive than national WISPs, and they may offer extra benefits as well. For example, Ottawa Wireless (*http://www.ottawawireless.net*) covers the city of Grand Haven, Michigan, and costs $24.99 per month. You can use it not just when you're roaming around town, but *inside* your home as well. Not a bad deal for 256-kbps access.

If you travel widely and need HotSpots in many different locations, you'll need a national service, or a WISP aggregator—the latter bundles access to HotSpots from different companies. Boingo (*http://www.boingo.com*), for example, gives you access to 8,500 HotSpots nationwide from many providers, including Wayport and Surf and Sip. Pricing is pretty reasonable: $21.95 a month for unlimited access for the first year, and $39.95 per month thereafter.

T-Mobile (*http://www.t-mobile.com/hotspot*) has over 4,200 locations offering T1-type speeds, at places such as Starbucks, Kinkos, and Borders Books. They offer a variety of pricing plans, including $19.99 per month for T-Mobile cell phone subscribers, $29.99 per month for unlimited access for non–cell phone subscribers, and per day, per month, and metered plans. Wayport (*http://www.wayport.com*) has more than 3,000 HotSpots, primarily at hotels

and airports, and even at some McDonald's restaurants. Wayport charges $29.95 per month for unlimited access and offers a variety of prepaid, per-connection, and month-to-month plans. Surf and Sip, which is big in Internet cafes, hotels, and restaurants, offers a $20 per month annual membership plan, plus a variety of daily, weekly, and monthly plans. As this book went to press, it was available at 400 locations, with 300 more on the way.

As in real estate, the key to choosing a HotSpot provider is location, location, location. If a WISP has a lot of HotSpots, but they're not in places you visit, there's no point in signing up. Here's where to go to find out where each major HotSpot provider has locations:

- T-Mobile: *http://locations.hotspot.t-mobile.com*
- Boingo: *http://www.boingo.com/search.html*
- Wayport: *http://www.wayport.net/locations*
- Surf and Sip: *http://www.surfandsip.com/location.htm*

PUBLIC VERSUS PRIVATE HOTSPOTS

Increasingly, you'll find HotSpots just about everywhere you go—in cafes, airports, apartment buildings, and outside people's homes. Some of these are "public" HotSpots, to which anyone can connect, and others are "private," to which only certain people are allowed to connect.

Bear in mind that a public HotSpot isn't necessarily free. For example, the T-Mobile HotSpots you find in Starbucks coffee shops across the country are all public HotSpots, but you have to pay to use them. You may find free public HotSpots too, in some cafes or in downtown areas.

Private HotSpots, on the other hand, are not meant to be used by anyone except the people who own them. For example, if you have a WiFi network at home, the signal may reach beyond your house. In essence, you've created a HotSpot, but it certainly isn't a public one!

Finally, find out if your cell phone company or existing dial-up or broadband ISP offers a wireless package. Verizon DSL users, for example, can get free access to Verizon's HotSpots. T-Mobile gives HotSpot discounts to its cell phone subscribers, and if Comcast Internet cable customers sign up for a $9.99 T-Mobile HotSpot Day Pass, they get a free day pass to T-Mobile's network once a month for a year.

HOTSPOT GONE COLD

The Annoyance: I did everything right—I checked ahead of time to find a HotSpot, I made sure my WiFi card was working and configured properly, and I ordered a piping hot latte, which is essentially the price of admission for this HotSpot. But when I turned on my laptop and tried to connect to the HotSpot, nothing happened. How can I turn this cold spot into a HotSpot?

The Fix: Several things may prevent you from connecting to a HotSpot. Try these steps:

- **Make sure the HotSpot is actually working.** Free HotSpots frequently go on the fritz. Double-click the wireless connection icon in the System Tray and choose Properties → Wireless Networks. Look in the "Available networks" section. If you don't see a network listed, the HotSpot isn't available. If you do see a network listed, but there's a red X across it or the tower icon next to it doesn't have the small circle around its top indicating that it's transmitting, either the network signal is too weak or the network is offline. If you use XP Service Pack 2 (SP2), click the wireless connection icon in the Windows System Tray and click View Wireless Networks. If you don't see a wireless network on the screen that appears, one isn't available.

- **Manually connect again.** Highlight the HotSpot in the "Available networks" section of the Wireless Network Connection Properties dialog box, and click the Configure button. In the "Wireless network properties" dialog box (shown in Figure 3-14), make sure the "Data encryption (WEP enabled)" box is unchecked, unless the HotSpot requires encryption. Click OK, then click OK again. If you use XP Service Pack 2

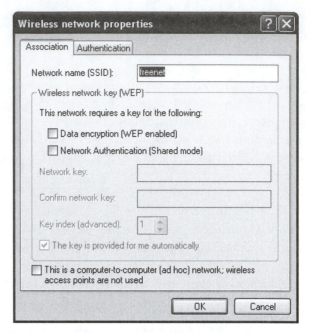

Figure 3-14. If you're connecting to a public HotSpot, you probably won't need encryption. But if you're connecting to a private HotSpot, encryption might be required, so check with the owner and then fill in the necessary information.

(SP2), click the wireless connection icon in the Windows System tray and click View Wireless Networks. From the screen that appears, highlight the network to which you want to connect, and click Connect.

- **Use encryption if the HotSpot requires it.** Public HotSpots don't use encryption, but private HotSpots do. If you're trying to use a private HotSpot, first get all the information about it, including the WEP key. Then, in the "Wireless network properties" dialog box, check the "Data encryption (WEP enabled)" box, fill in and confirm the network key, and pick a key index from the drop-down list (if the HotSpot requires it). To finish, click OK, then click OK again.

- **Make sure you're using infrastructure mode.** WiFi lets you connect directly to another PC, in ad hoc mode, or to a HotSpot or network, in infrastructure mode. If you're accidentally using ad hoc mode, you won't be able to connect to a WiFi network. In the "Wireless network properties" dialog box, make sure the "This is a computer-to-computer (ad hoc) network; wireless access points are not used" box is *not* checked.

- **Move closer to the HotSpot.** Wireless transmissions are notoriously erratic and eccentric. You may be seated in an area with very poor transmission, so try moving to another table or seat—reception there might be better.

AVAILABLE VERSUS PREFERRED NETWORKS

The Annoyance: What's the difference between an "available" wireless network and a "preferred" wireless network? And how do "preferred" networks get to be "preferred"? I sure never told Windows I preferred them—how can it know which are my favorite ones?

The Fix: Someone needs to sic the language police on Microsoft, because "preferred" networks are not necessarily "preferred." In the Wireless Networks tab of the Wireless Network Connection Properties dialog box (Figure 3-15), you'll find two sections. The top one shows you available networks, and the bottom one shows "preferred"

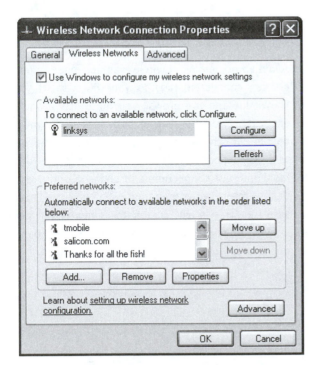

Figure 3-15. Networks that are currently broadcasting within your PC's range are listed under "Available networks." Networks you've connected to in the past are listed under "Preferred networks."

networks. An available network is simply one that's within the range of your wireless network card. Networks show up here without you doing anything; your network card finds them. (If you're running Windows XP SP2, available networks aren't listed in the top section. Instead, click the View Wireless Networks button to go to the Wireless Network Connection page, which shows you all the available networks.)

A "preferred" network is one that you've connected to in the past. If you often connect to many different HotSpots, this listing can get pretty big. You can also manually add a network to your preferred list, even if it's currently out of your range. Here's how:

1. Click the small network icon in the Windows System Tray and select the Wireless Networks tab.

2. Click the Add button, and fill in the required information for the network, including its SSID; whether it uses WEP and, if it does, its WEP key information; whether it's an ad hoc network; and so on. When you're done, click OK, then click OK again.

That network will now always show up in your "Preferred networks" section. Whenever you turn on your PC with its wireless card installed, XP will look at the "Preferred networks" section and try to connect to the networks in the order they're listed.

WHY CAN'T I CONNECT TO AN "AVAILABLE" NETWORK?

The Annoyance: A HotSpot shows up as an available network, yet no matter what I do, I can't connect to it. Doesn't "available" mean that it's ready for you to use?

The Fix: Chances are its signal is too weak for you to make the connection. A network can show up as available even if the signal isn't strong enough for a sustained connection. Look at the small icon next to the network's name. A tower that doesn't have a small circle on top means that the signal is too weak for a connection. A tower with a small circle on top means that the signal is strong enough for a connection.

EASIER T-MOBILE HOTSPOT CONNECTIONS

The Annoyance: I have a monthly subscription plan to T-Mobile HotSpots, and it drives me crazy having to check T-Mobile's web site for HotSpot locations before I travel. I'd also like to be able to connect to its HotSpots more quickly, without fiddling around with dialog boxes and signing onto web pages.

The Fix: Download the free T-Mobile Connection Manager from *http://client.hotspot.t-mobile.com*. It maintains a constantly updated list of T-Mobile HotSpots and automatically recognizes nearby networks. When you're in a HotSpot, just run the software and it'll automatically log you in, without any extra setup.

PROTECT YOUR PRIVACY

The Annoyance: Public WiFi HotSpots at places like coffee shops and airports are notoriously insecure—they don't use encryption, so whatever you do is open to snoopers. How can I protect myself?

The Fix: Because public HotSpots don't use wireless security technology, you'll have to take matters into your own hands. For the most security, sign up for a wireless virtual private network (VPN). Wireless VPNs encrypt any information that's sent or received by your PC when you're on a HotSpot, so you can't be snooped on. HotSpotVPN (*http://www.hotspotvpn.com*) is one excellent choice. It's simple to set up and use, and it costs $8.88 a month. To use it, go to the site, sign up, and follow the instructions for installing a VPN. (For instructions on how to set up a VPN, turn to "Protect Yourself with a Virtual Private Network" in Chapter 9.) You won't need to download any software to use the service; XP's built-in VPN software is all you need.

Of course, if you don't use public HotSpots frequently, $8.88 a month is clearly overkill. But you can still take the following security measures, and they won't cost you a penny:

- **Only send your name and password over a secure logon connection.** When you use for-pay HotSpots such as T-Mobile's, you have to enter your username and password to log on. You launch your browser, and a login page pops up. Most HotSpots encrypt this information, but nothing else. But some HotSpots may not even encrypt the logon, which means nearby snoopers can easily capture your username and password and run up a sizable bill on your account. Only log on if the site tells you on the opening web page that it's secure and if the URL starts with *https://*, which means it's using SSL encryption technology.

- **Use a personal firewall.** This will prevent anyone from connecting to your PC unless you want them to. The best one, ZoneAlarm, is available for free from *http://www.zonealarm.com*. You can also use Windows XP's built-in Windows Firewall. For more details, see Chapter 9.

- **Turn off file sharing.** You don't need to share files with fellow latte lovers, so disable this feature. To turn it off in Windows XP, open Windows Explorer, right-click on the drive or folders you normally share, chose Sharing and Security, and uncheck the "Share this folder on the network" box.

- **Avoid ad hoc mode.** In wireless ad hoc mode, snoopers can connect directly to your PC without your knowledge and can browse your hard disk if you've enabled network file sharing. To disable ad hoc mode, double-click the wireless connection icon in the System Tray, choose Properties → Wireless Networks, highlight your connection, and choose Configure. In the "Wireless network properties" dialog box, make sure the "This is a computer-to-computer (ad hoc) network; wireless access points are not used" box is unchecked.

GET TECHNICAL SUPPORT FOR HOTSPOT WOES

The Annoyance: I love wireless computing and lattes, but let's face it—the tech support you get at cafes is limited to "Do you want a tall or grande?" When the cafe's HotSpot tanks (or my laptop has a problem), where can I turn?

The Fix: Take along the tech support numbers for your HotSpot provider. True, you might be kept on hold while waiting for a technician, but you can at least have a few cuppas while you wait. Here are the tech support phone numbers for the top HotSpot providers who may well be providing wireless services for your local cafe. Email addresses are included as well, although if you can't connect, they won't help you much:

- Boingo: (800) 880-4117, *support@boingo.com*
- Surf and Sip: (415) 974-6321, *support@surfandsip. com*
- T-Mobile: (800) 981-8563, *hotspotcustomerservice@t-mobile.com* (Note: T-Mobile hides its tech support option when you call its 800 number. When you dial in, you're told to press 1, 2, or 3 on your phone to get to various T-Mobile services. None of them offers HotSpot technical support. To get to the hidden technical support, you must press 5 on your phone, even though you're not given that option when you dial in. Strange but true.)
- Verizon: (800) 567-6789 (Note: When you call, ask to be sent to the general tech support line for all Verizon products; otherwise, you may be transferred several times until you end up at the right place.)
- Wayport: (877) 929-7678, *callcenter@wayport.net*

CURE HOTSPOT AMNESIA

The Annoyance: Whenever I come back home after using a HotSpot network, I can't reconnect to my own WiFi home network. Instead, my PC keeps trying to hook up to the last HotSpot I used while I was traveling.

The Fix: The HotSpot you connected to outside your home has essentially jumped the queue in your "Preferred networks" list. To fix the problem, you must tell your PC to look for your home network first, before it searches for any other HotSpot:

1. In the Windows System Tray, double-click on the small wireless network icon.

2. Go to the Wireless Networks tab of the Wireless Network Connection Properties dialog box. (Note: To get to the Wireless Network Connection Properties dialog box in SP2, click the small wireless network icon in the Windows System Tray, click View Wireless Networks, click Change advanced settings, then click the Wireless Networks tab.)

3. In the "Preferred networks" section of the dialog box, highlight your home wireless network. Click the "Move up" button until it's at the top of the list (Figure 3-16). Then click OK.

Your PC should now automatically connect to your home network whenever you return home.

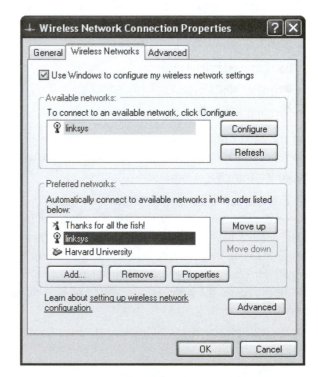

Figure 3-16. If your PC keeps trying to connect to a HotSpot instead of your home network, move your network to the top of the "Preferred networks" list.

HOTSPOT, COLD EMAIL

The Annoyance: Whenever I try to send email from my favorite HotSpot, I get an error message from my ISP telling me that it won't send it. Why am I paying the HotSpot for Internet access and my ISP for mail service if I can't send email?

The Fix: Because of widespread spam problems, some ISPs won't let you send email using their SMTP servers unless you're on their network. When you're using a HotSpot, you're not on their network, so they refuse to let you send mail. (For a similar conundrum facing those on the road, see "Can't Send Email from the Road" in Chapter 1.)

To get around the problem, some HotSpot providers have their own SMTP servers that you can use to send mail. When you use those HotSpots, you'll have to change your email account settings to reflect their SMTP server settings.

SMTP server settings for the major HotSpot providers are:

- T-Mobile: *myemail.t-mobile.com*
- Boingo: *mail.boingo.com*
- Wayport: *mail.wayport.net*
- Surf and Sip: *mail.surfandsip.net*

You shouldn't run across this problem with Verizon Hot-Spots, because they are only available to Verizon customers, who already use a Verizon SMTP server.

You can also pay to use an SMTP relay service so that you can send mail from any HotSpot, even if the HotSpot provider doesn't have an SMTP server. SMTP.com (*http://www.smtp.com*) will let you use its SMTP servers for $49.99 per year, unless you send more than 50 emails a day. In that case, the price goes up, based on how many messages you send.

Here's how to set up Outlook and Outlook Express to use the SMTP servers.

Outlook 2003

1. Choose Tools → E-mail Account → View or change existing e-mail accounts, and select the email account you plan to use at the HotSpot.

2. Click the Change button.

3. Write down the name of the existing outgoing SMTP mail server. You'll need this information later, when you change back to your original settings after you leave the HotSpot.

4. In the "Outgoing mail server (SMTP)" box, enter the name of the HotSpot's SMTP server (see Figure 3-17).

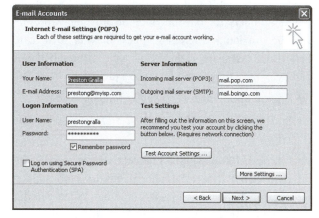

Figure 3-17. If you can't send email from your HotSpot, configure Outlook to use your HotSpot's SMTP server, using this screen.

5. Click the More Settings button, then click Outgoing Server.

6. On the screen that appears, click "My outgoing server (SMTP) requires authentication." Select "Log on using," and enter your HotSpot username and password where indicated. (If you have trouble sending mail with these settings, try it without using a username and password.)

7. Click OK, Next, and then Finish.

You should now be able to send email while connected to the HotSpot.

Outlook Express

1. Choose Tools → Accounts, select the Mail tab, click the Properties button, then click the Servers tab.

2. Write down the name of the existing outgoing SMTP mail server. You'll need this information later, when you change back to your original settings after you leave the HotSpot.

3. In the "Outgoing mail (SMTP)" box, enter the name of the HotSpot's SMTP server.

4. Check the "My server requires authentication" box and click the Settings button.

5. On the screen that appears, select "Log on using," and enter your HotSpot account name and password where indicated. (If you have trouble sending mail with these settings, try it without using a username and password.)

6. Click OK, then OK again, and then Close.

You should now be able to send email when you're connected to the HotSpot.

GO WAR DRIVING FOR HOTSPOTS

The Annoyance: I just know there are wireless networks and HotSpots practically everywhere I go, but I have no idea how to find them. Isn't there a simple way to use my laptop as a HotSpot detector?

The Fix: Ah, you're ready to do a little "war driving," as it's called. There is a way, with a free program called Network Stumbler (Figure 3-18), available from *http://www.netstumbler.com/downloads/*. *Network Stumbler* checks for any WiFi network in range of your network card and gives you all the details for connecting to it, including its SSID, the manufacturer of the access point, the channel on which it's broadcasting, the signal strength, the signal-to-noise ratio, and whether the network's encryption is enabled, among other details. (If a network uses encryption, a small lock appears next to it.)

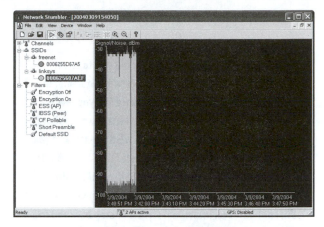

Figure 3-18. Network Stumbler can help you find WiFi networks within range of your wireless card.

Look for any networks that aren't encrypted, and once you've found one, copy down its SSID. Then exit Network Stumbler, double-click the small wireless network icon in the Windows System Tray, and choose Properties → Wireless Networks. If the network Network Stumbler found isn't listed here, click the Refresh button. The network should show up (if it doesn't, its signal is probably too weak for you to connect). To connect to it, click the Configure button and fill out the required information. You'll then be able to connect to the network.

Network Stumbler won't work with some WiFi cards. It does work with Lucent Technologies's WaveLAN/IEEE (Proxim Orinoco); Dell's TrueMobile 1150 Series (PCMCIA and mini-PCI); Avaya's Wireless PC Card; Toshiba's Wireless LAN Card (PCMCIA and built-in); Compaq's WL110; Cabletron/Enterasys's Roamabout; Elsa's Airlancer MC-11; Artem's ComCard 11Mbps; IBM's High Rate Wireless LAN PC Card; and 1stWave's 1ST-PC-DSS11IS, DSS11IG, DSS11ES, and DSS11EG. For more details, download the release notes from the Network Stumbler web page.

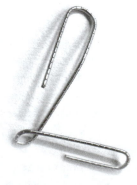

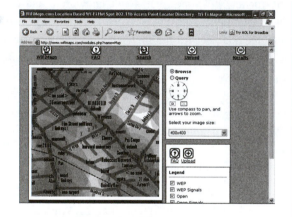
GO WAR DRIVING WITH YOUR POCKET PC

The Annoyance: I don't use a laptop. I have a Pocket PC with a WiFi card. How can I war drive with this setup?

The Fix: Pocket PC owners aren't left behind. There's a version of Network Stumbler (discussed in "Go War Driving for HotSpots"), called MiniStumbler, that works the same way. And there's a similar caveat—it won't work with all WiFi cards or all versions of the Pocket PC.

CONNECT TO THE RIGHT HOTSPOT

The Annoyance: On the Cambridge/Somerville line where I live, there's a HotSpot war of sorts going on among the cafes. Two are directly across the street from each other. There's also a free HotSpot down the block. My problem is that when I sit down at a cafe, I want to connect to the HotSpot with the strongest connection. But my laptop, with a twisted mind of its own, often automatically connects to the weakest one. What can I do?

The Fix: When there is more than one available network nearby, your laptop doesn't opt for the network with the strongest connection. Instead, it connects to whichever nearby network is listed closest to the top of your "Preferred networks" list. (For more information about preferred networks, see "Available Versus Preferred Networks".)

There's no automated way to tell XP to look for the strongest available network. Your best bet is to install Network Stumbler (discussed in "Go War Driving for HotSpots"), look at each network's signal strength, and then manually connect to the strongest. In NetStumbler, any network with a green circle next to it is a strong connection; yellow means sporadic and weaker, and red or grey means extremely weak.

STOP HOTSPOT "STUTTERING"

The Annoyance: When I'm near several Hot-Spots, and most are weak, my connection "stutters" and jumps—when one connection fades out, XP automatically connects me to another one, then that one stutters, and XP jumps to another connection, and so on. With all this disconnecting and reconnecting going on, I can't get any work done. Can't I just connect to one HotSpot, and leave it at that?

The Fix: Your problem is caused by the very thing that allows you to easily connect to HotSpots—XP's Windows Zero Configuration (WZC) applet, which runs automatically on startup. WZC looks for a new network connection every three minutes, and if at that point your current connection fades out, it will search for a new one and automatically connect to it. That's why you get the stuttering and jumping.

The fix is to disable WZC after you've made a connection—that way, you can stay with your one connection, even as it fades in and out. But you'll want to enable WZC again after you're done, so that the next time you want to connect to a HotSpot or your home WiFi network, it will do its job.

To temporarily disable WZC, select Start → Run, type `services.msc` in the Open box, and press Enter. This runs the Services console. Scroll down until you see the Wireless Zero Configuration entry. Right-click it, and choose Stop. That turns off the service; you'll stop the stuttering and jumping. When you're done with a HotSpot, repeat the steps, except choose Start (Figure 3-20).

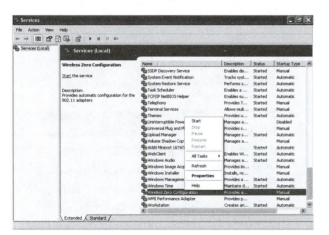

Figure 3-20. To stop Windows from hopping from one HotSpot to another in search of a stronger connection, temporarily turn off the service that automatically detects and connects to wireless networks.

If you expect to do this a lot, create a desktop shortcut for stopping WZC and another for starting it up again. Here's how:

1. In Windows Explorer, go to *C:\Windows\System32*.

2. Drag the file *Net.exe* to the desktop. Right-click it and select Create Shortcut.

3. Give the shortcut a name—right-click it, select Rename, and call it "Halt WZC."

4. Right-click the shortcut again, choose Properties, and click the Shortcut tab. The target field will read something like `C:\Documents and Settings\Administrator\Desktop\net.exe`.

5. Replace this with `C:\WINDOWS\system32\net.exe`, enter a space, and then type `stop wzcsvc` and click OK. The contents of the target field should now be "C:\WINDOWS\system32\net.exe stop wzcsvc."

Repeat these steps to create a shortcut for starting WZC. Name it "Start WZC," and type `C:\WINDOWS\system32\net.exe start wzcsvc` in the target field.

Whenever you want to stop WZC, double-click the Halt WZC shortcut. To start WZC again, double-click the Start WZC shortcut (Figure 3-21).

Figure 3-21. Create a shortcut to halt WZC so that you can easily turn it off; create another one to start WZC so that you can easily turn it back on.

TAPPING INTO A PRIVATE HOTSPOT—LEGAL OR NOT?

The Annoyance: I've found several convenient HotSpots in my area. There's only one problem: none of them are public; they're people's private networks. I'd like to use their bandwidth when I need it, but I don't know the legalities or etiquette involved. Where's Miss Manners—or Matlock—when you need them?

The Fix: The legalities involved with using someone else's bandwidth without his knowledge are murky, but it's most likely illegal. State laws generally prohibit accessing other people's networks without authorization, but is it a crime to merely hop on to use their Internet access, if you're not actually snooping through the networks, gathering information and using network servers? That's why God created lawyers—and the legalities will vary from state to state.

However, most law seems to consider it illegal. Bob Hillery, senior security consultant and partner in the security firm IntelGuardians.com, has done a great deal of research on the issue, and he notes that both state and federal legislation may apply. For example, it is probably considered a theft of services, in the same way that it's illegal to tap into cable TV or satellite TV without paying for it. His conclusion: "It is inappropriate, if not explicitly illegal, to snitch bandwidth from a network for which you do not know you have authorized access." However, he also notes that at least one state, New Hampshire, has passed a law saying that the owners of the WiFi networks have some responsibilities. The owners must issue a warning of some kind that their networks are private, and they must take steps to stop intruders if they want to prosecute people for breaking into their networks. But the law mostly applies to businesses, not people at home.

As a practical matter, while it may possibly be illegal, you're not likely to be prosecuted for using someone else's bandwidth. As for the etiquette, that's something completely different. Just as you wouldn't walk unannounced into the home of a stranger who left the front door open, you shouldn't use someone else's bandwidth without asking. So check with the person first, ask if it's OK, and, if you do use his bandwidth, don't use it for downloading large files (such as MP3s) unless you ask first.

FORGET HOTSPOTS—USE YOUR BLUETOOTH CELL PHONE!

The Annoyance: WiFi, schmi-fi—why should I pay someone to use a HotSpot if I have a Bluetooth-enabled cell phone that can access the Internet?

The Fix: You don't have to—if you have a laptop with Bluetooth capabilities. And as you can see in the sidebar "Bluetooth-Enable Your Laptop," it's easy to enable any laptop with Bluetooth. You'll use the laptop/cell phone duo to connect to your ISP.

> ## Bluetooth-Enable Your Laptop
>
> If your laptop doesn't have Bluetooth capabilities, you're not out of luck—they're exceptionally easy to add. All you need is a USB Bluetooth adapter. Companies such as D-Link, Keyspan, Belkin, and many others sell them, often for around $30. Just plug the little device into your USB port, follow the installation instructions, and you'll be set.

Here's how to connect to the Internet with a Sony Ericsson T68i Bluetooth-enabled phone. The steps with other Bluetooth-enabled cell phones should be very similar:

1. Turn on your cell phone and make sure it's within range of your laptop.

2. Turn on the phone's Bluetooth. On the Sony Ericsson T68i, press the joystick button and select Connect → Bluetooth → Options → Operation Mode → On.

3. Make the phone "discoverable." On the Sony Ericsson T68i, press the joystick button and select Connect → Bluetooth → Discoverable.

4. Discover the phone in Windows XP. Go to My Bluetooth Places and select View Devices in Range. You should see the Sony Ericsson T68i icon. Right-click it and select Discover Available Services. You'll get to a group of icons that show the list of available services.

5. Right-click the Dial-up Networking service, and select Connect Dial-up Networking (Figure 3-22). You'll be asked whether you want to accept or decline the connection, or "add to paired." Pairing the phone and the computer will let you make the connection in the future without going through the discovery process outlined above, so it's a good idea to select the "add to paired" option.

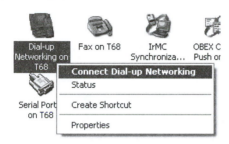

Figure 3-22. After you discover your cell phone's Bluetooth services, right-click the Dial-up Networking icon and choose Connect Dial-up Networking to connect to the Internet.

6. In the screen that appears (Figure 3-23), make up a PIN and enter it to pair your phone with your computer. You'll have to enter the same PIN code on your phone.

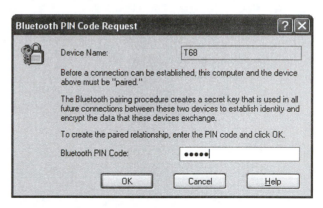

Figure 3-23. Pair your phone and laptop to make connecting the two via Bluetooth easier the next time.

7. Click OK, and in the dialog box that appears, enter the information you normally use to connect to your ISP, including your username, password, and phone number. Click the Dial button, and you'll be connected to your ISP. Those who have used this method of connecting report reliable connections. The exact speed you'll get varies according to the precise technology your cell phone uses. You'll get 20 to 40 kbps with a GSM/GPRS cell phone, 20 to 150 kbps with EDGE, about 50 to 120 kbps with CDMA 1xRTT, and from 300 to 500 kbps with CDMA 1xEV-DO. If you don't know which technology your cell phone uses, check with your cell phone carrier.

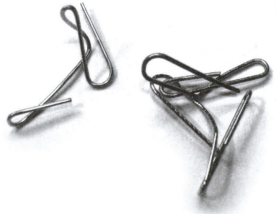

Web Hosting, Design, and Blog
ANNOYANCES

4

If you've ever tried to create your own web page or blog, you know the true meaning of the word "annoyance." Hosting services whose tech support departments treat you like a dolt. Wrestling with the incomprehensible vagaries of HTML. Creating your first blog and trying to figure out why no one can read it.

Yes, getting a web site up and running is a journey to Angst City. But you don't need to be an accidental tourist when you get there, because this chapter is here to help. It covers hosting hassles, domain woes, design and HTML help, and advice on how to get your blog up and running. Whether you're building a web site or already have one, help is on the way.

Looking to buy your own domain, or want to find a good hosting service, but annoyances get in the way? I've got solutions for you. Can't get FrontPage to work with your hosting service? Problem solved. Tired of bad links and poorly written HTML bedeviling your site? Help in many forms is just around the corner. Want to post to your blog, but not via the Web? No problem—we'll look at how to do it via email, or even from your cell phone. Can't figure out how to get past an annoying login screen in Movable Type? You'll find out how. Dig in; there are plenty of web hosting and design annoyances to solve.

DOMAIN AND HOSTING HASSLES

BECOME MASTER OF YOUR OWN DOMAIN

The Annoyance: My ISP gives me free web hosting, but the URL I'm stuck with is as long as the Manhattan phone book. How can I get a domain name that people won't get carpal tunnel from typing?

The Fix: Getting your own domain is a good idea, and not just because of the shorter URL. When you own your own domain, no one can take it from you—it's your own little piece of the Internet, and it's yours for as long as you pay for it.

The first step is to find out what domain names are available. During the height of the Internet boom, there was a domain land grab, with people registering domains they didn't need in the hopes that some large company would buy them for big money. (Some did.) So if you're looking for a domain using a common word (e.g., *food.com*) or you have a common last name, you're probably out of luck. But you might find an available domain name based on a combination of your first, middle, and last names, such as *alexawilliams.com* or *peterlsmith.com*.

How do you find out what's available? Turn to an Internet facility called Whois, which searches through a database of all registered domain names and lets you know if the one you want is available. You can run a search with a free Whois utility such as Whois Web Professional 4.2 (*http://www.rietta.com/whoisweb/*), but it's easier to search via a dedicated Whois web site (such as *http://www.whois.net*) or a domain-registration site. It doesn't really matter which approach you use—they all access the same servers and report the same results. The advantage of searching via a registrar is that if the domain name you want isn't available, some will suggest dozens of variations that are available. Some registrars can even "backorder" the domain you want and notify you when the domain is back on the market.

Once you find a domain that's available, register it at any registrar. For a guide to registrars, go to *http://www.reg-select.com*. Some popular registrars to check out are *http://www.networksolutions.com*, *http://www.domain-direct.com*, *http://www.register.com*, and *http://www.godaddy.com* (Figure 4-1).

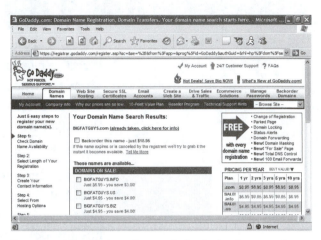

Figure 4-1. Do a Whois search to see whether the domain you want is available—if it's not, registrars will show you similar ones that you can buy.

Once you've registered a domain name, you need to find a company that can host your web site—specifically, one that supports *domain name hosting*, so you can use your custom URL. While some sites, such as Yahoo! GeoCities, offer free basic web hosting, if you want to use your own

---

MAKE SURE YOU'RE LISTED AS THE DOMAIN CONTACT

When you register a domain, you're asked a series of questions, including who should be listed on the domain record as the administrative and technical contacts. (This domain record can be viewed by anyone running a Whois search.) Make sure that you're listed as the contact, and not someone at the ISP or hosting service that you're using. If someone at the ISP or hosting service is listed, that could make it harder to transfer the domain if you decide to host it at a different ISP or hosting service.

domain, you'll have to pay a bit for the service. The fee for domain name hosting at Yahoo! GeoCities is $8.95 per month, but for that modest fee you also get email accounts, more server space for your files, more data transfers per month, and so on. For more details about finding a hosting service, see "Choose a New Hosting Service" later in this section.

BREAK THE NETWORK SOLUTIONS MONOPOLY

The Annoyance: I used Network Solutions (*http://www.networksolutions.com*) to register my domain, but dealing with the company is about as pleasant as dealing with the IRS—and almost as expensive. Isn't there an easier and cheaper way to register my domain?

The Fix: Network Solutions was the original Internet domain registrar, and because it's so well known, it still acts at times as if it's a monopoly. But many competing registrars provide the same services for a lot less. As of this writing, Network Solutions charges $34.99 per year to register a site; GoDaddy (*http://www.godaddy.com*) asks only $7.95 a year. Check *http://www.regselect.com* for more information about bargain hosts.

SHORTEN YOUR WEB SITE'S URL

The Annoyance: I don't want to go through the whole domain name hassle. I'd like to keep using my current web site address, but I want a shorter URL. There's gotta be way.

The Fix: There is. The answer is to use a free domain forwarding service. These services offer some of the benefits of owning your own domain, but without the cost.

Here's how it works. Let's say your web site has a long, hard-to-remember address, such as *www.anotherisp.com/homepages/personal/longname/pgralla*. If you use a domain forwarding service, a visitor can type something like *www.gralla.cjb.net* and be automatically routed to your web site. Another benefit is that if you move your site to another hosting service, the domain forwarding

Snip Your URLs

Don't want to fuss with a domain forwarding service? Consider using *http://www.snipurl.com* or *http://www.tinyurl.com*. They shrink any URL, no matter how long, to a manageable length, so that you can easily send your web site address to others via email. For details, see "Stop URL Sprawl" in Chapter 1.

service can simply send people to your new location; your shortened URL remains the same.

Using these services is a no-brainer. Sign up, tell the service what the front of the domain should be (such as "gralla"), and it generates the last part (such as "cjb.net"). Send your brand new (and shorter) URL to the people you want to visit your site. There are a number of domain forwarding services, including *http://www.webalias.com*, *http://www.cjb.net*, and *http://www.internetjump.com* (all of which are free), and *http://www.redirection.net* (which costs $5 per year). Before signing up, check the terms of service. Will visitors to your site be barraged by ads? Will you have to put an ad banner or pop-up ads on your site pointing to the forwarding service? The terms vary according to the service.

CHOOSE A NEW HOSTING SERVICE

The Annoyance: My current web hosting service makes the cable company look like a model of customer service. I want to switch. But where do I look? And how do I evaluate a hosting company?

The Fix: Which hosting service you should choose depends primarily on how much traffic you expect, what you're using your site for, and what you're willing to pay. The three main kinds of hosting services available are:

Internet service providers (ISPs)

Almost every ISP, including America Online, includes web hosting as part of its basic service. Often, this hosting is bare-bones and offers little beyond the most basic features. But many ISPs, for a modest monthly fee, offer a lot more. For example, for $19.95 per month, Earthlink provides 200 MB of disk space, 10 GB of data transfers, 30 email addresses, and 24/7 service.

Free web hosting services

Free hosting services such as Yahoo! GeoCities (*http://geocities.yahoo.com*), Angelfire (*http://www.angelfire.lycos.com*), or the hosting you get with your ISP won't offer as much server space or data transfers as paid services, but you'll often find web-based site-building and blog-building tools. In return, you may have to agree to put advertising on your web site.

Paid hosting services

Paid services such as Verio *(http://www.verio.com)* or for-pay Yahoo! services (GeoCities Plus or Pro, or Yahoo! Web Hosting) provide lots of storage space for your web site, have multiple and redundant connections to the Internet's "backbone" (which means visitors will get speedy access to your site), provide solid technical support, and may offer a variety of extras, such as extra email accounts or prebuilt "shopping carts" for people who want to build simple e-commerce sites.

So how do you decide? The biggest choice to make is whether to go with a free or pay service. If you don't care about having your own domain, and the site is only for personal use, free hosting services are a pretty good deal. If you're using the web site for business purposes, especially for e-commerce, opt for a paid hosting service. You'll be able to use your own domain name, and you'll get the speed, extra storage space, and better technical support that a business site requires. If you're creating a personal site using your own domain name, you'll also have to go with a for-pay service.

How do you pick a paid hosting service? Here are some tips on what to look for:

- **How much server space will you get?** Expect at least 200 MB. Although individual web pages may not take up a lot of space, you may want to host files for download (pictures, PDFs, music, and the like).

- **Can you use your own domain name?** If a service doesn't support domain name hosting, look elsewhere.

- **How many email addresses do you get?** This is particularly important if you're running a business. You'll want email addresses that end in your domain name, and enough addresses for all of your employees, plus general addresses for customer support, sales, and so on. If nothing else, make sure you can buy extra addresses later if you need them. Also, make sure that your for-pay hosting service doesn't limit the size or number of emails you send and receive each month. Bear in mind that some services combine your email storage with your hosting storage when calculating the total amount of storage available to you—so a service offering you 200 MB of combined space may not be such a great deal.

- **How much total bandwidth are you allowed?** Some sites limit the amount of bandwidth you're given each month (that is, how much data can be transferred from your site to visitors, be it pages they're viewing or files they're downloading). If you have a lot of visitors each month who view lots of pages or download files you've posted, you'll have to pay extra. Find out what the monthly limit is, and how much extra you'll pay if you exceed it. There may also be a limit on how much you can upload to your site.

- **How long has the hosting service been in business?** You want a company with a long track record, that's been at the same location for three to five years and has a good rating with the Better Business Bureau.

- **What kind of technical support does the hosting service offer?** If you're running a business site, you'll want 24/7 technical support via phone, email, and maybe instant messaging. Look for a solid knowledge base or FAQ list so that you can troubleshoot some problems yourself. Test technical support: call the support line and note how long you're kept on hold, the professionalism of the techs, and the quality of their advice.

- **What types of e-commerce features does it have?** If you're going to sell anything from your site, make sure the service offers built-in shopping cart software, will let you easily build online product catalogs, and offers secure credit card authorization. Check the prices for these services as well.

- **What kinds of web-building tools does it offer and support?** If you don't plan to create web pages on your own, look for tools that do more than just let you build very basic web sites. And if you use specialized tools, such as FrontPage extensions, make sure the hosting service supports them.

- **Does it support features you plan to add to your site, such as blogs, RSS feeds, or streaming audio and video?** If so, does the company provide the appropriate tools and technical support?

- **Do you have CGI-bin access?** CGI scripts are used for a variety of interactive features for web sites. Even if you don't think you need CGI-bin access, you might eventually, so make sure that your hosting service offers it.

- **Is the hosting service connected to the Internet's backbone via multiple high-speed connections?** Multiple connections via T3 and optical lines not only guarantee speedy access to your visitors; they also guarantee that your site will stay live if one connection goes down, because your hosting service has backup access to the Internet.

There are far too many for-pay hosting services out there to include them all in this book, but Table 4-1 provides a comparison of some of the more popular services that you can use as a starting point for making your decision.

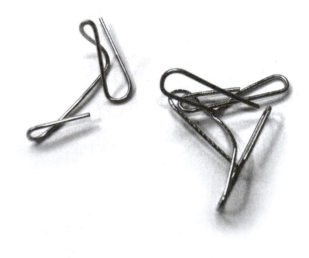

Table 4-1. Popular hosting services compared

	Price (Base cost)	Storage (MB)	Bandwidth/ month	CGI–bin access?	# of email accounts	Domain name hosting?
AppSite Hosting http://www.appsitehosting.com	Starter: $17.95/mo.	50 MB	3 GB/mo.	Yes	5	No
	Basic: $19.95/mo.	250 MB	10 GB/mo.	Yes	25	Yes
	Enhanced $37.95/mo.	500 MB	20 GB/mo	Yes	50	Yes
	Premium: $149.95/mo.	1.5 GB	30 GB/mo.	Yes	150	Yes
Bigstep http://www.bigstep.com	$29.95/mo.	200 MB	10 GB/mo.	No	10	$20/yr.
	Pro: $49.95/mo.	1 GB	50 GB/mo.	No	10	$20/yr.
EarthLink Web Hosting http://www.earthlink.net/biz	Starter: $19.95/mo.	200 MB	10 GB/mo.	Yes	30	Yes
	Pro: $34.95/mo.	300 MB	20 GB/mo.	Yes	100	Yes
	Premium: $84.95/mo.	500 MB	30 GB/mo.	Yes	200	Yes
Interland http://www.interland.com	Value: $9.95/mo.	200 MB	5 GB/mo.	Yes	5	Free for 1 year with signed 1-year contract
	Business: $19.95/mo.	500 MB	20 GB/mo.	Yes	30	
	Advanced: $29.95/mo.	1 GB	100 GB/mo.	Yes	70	
Microsoft Small Business Web Hosting http://www.microsoft.com/ smallbusiness/products/online/ wh/detail.mspx	Standard: $24.95/mo.	200 MB	10 GB/mo.	No	30 accounts	$20/yr; $10/yr. for redirect service
	Professional: $149.95/mo.	350 MB	20 GB/mo.	No	60 accounts	
NetNation http://www.netnation.com	Quickweb: $10.52/mo.	30 MB	1 GB/mo.	Yes	2	$9.95/yr.
	StarterPlus: $13.16/mo.	150 MB	5 GB/mo.	Yes	10	
	Pro: $20.20/mo.	300 MB	10 GB/mo.	Yes	40	
	Economy Std: $30.76/mo.	400 MB	12 GB/mo.	Yes	50	
	Power: $43.96/mo	500 MB	15 GB/mo.	Yes	70	
	Economy Adv: $57.16/mo.	800 MB	20 GB/mo.	Yes	100	

E-commerce options	Notes
	$40 setup fee for Starter and Basic plans; $50 for everything else, including e-commerce. E-commerce Premium has $125 setup fee.
15-product catalog, $29.95/mo.	
	Optional services: visitor counter, message boards, guest book, wireless domain, additional storage, additional data transfer, additional email addresses
$74.95/mo. All features of Enhanced plan plus unlimited number of products and pages, real-time credit card processing, "on sale" product model, product search	
$119.95/mo. All features of Premium plan, plus coupons, digital downloads, product searches, discounts, inventory tracking	
20-product catalog	Both e-commerce plans include: catalog manager, automatic tax and shipping calculations, integrated shopping cart, and are PayPal compatible.
100-product catalog	
50-product catalog, $10/mo.	$25 setup fee; $50 setup fee for e-commerce packages. All e-commerce plans include: real-time credit card payments, inventory-tracking tools, mailing-list manager, UPS shipping calculations.
100-product catalog, $15/mo.	
Unlimited-product catalog, $15/mo.	Additional 5 MB, $4.95/mo.; additional 1 MB traffic, $0.10/mo.
	Domain pointing service (register multiple domains, redirects to one page): $25 setup fee, 4.95/mo.
All include mailing-list organizer. Add-ons:	$29.95 setup fee
Miva Merchant ($8.95/mo.), includes real-time credit card processing, inventory-tracking tools, mailing-list manager, UPS shipping calculations	Additional 10 MB, $10/mo.; additional 1 GB/mo. traffic, $25/mo.; 5 more mailboxes, $5/mo.
Verisign ($34.95/mo.), 350 secure transactions	
Thawte ($150/yr.), secure transactions	
$29.95/mo. Online catalog with 10,000 products, secure ordering, customer order status, shopping cart, customized FrontPage add-in, PayPal support.	$35 setup fee
Miva Merchant comes with Economy Standard and Economy Advanced.	$14.95 setup fee
Real-time credit card processing, $19.95/mo.; Quick SSL certificate, $165/yr.; True Business SSL, $199/yr.	$19.95 setup fee
	$49.95 setup fee
	$49.95 setup fee
	$99.95 setup fee
	$99.95 setup fee
	Add-ons: additional 5 MB of storage, $5/mo; 1 GB of traffic, $20/mo.; extra email account, $2/mo.

	Price (Base cost)	Storage (MB)	Bandwidth/ month	CGI–bin access?	# of email accounts	Domain name hosting?
Verio *http://www.verio.com*	Bronze: $24.95/mo.	250 MB	7.5 GB/mo.	Yes	20	$9.95/yr. with 10-year purchase; free domain forwarding
	Silver: $49.95/mo.	300 MB	10 GB/mo.	Yes	30	
	Gold: $99.95/mo.	350 MB	12.5 GB/mo.	Yes	40	
	Platinum: $129.95/mo.	12 GB	Unlimited	Yes	50	
ValueWeb *http://www.valueweb.com*	Standard: $24.95/mo.	250 MB	10 GB/mo.	Yes	20	$17.50 for 2 years
	Commerce: $49.95/mo.	1 GB	50 GB/mo.	Yes	50	
	Professional: $99.95/mo.	5 GB	200 GB/mo.	Yes	200	
	Enterprise: $199.95/mo.	10 GB	500 GB/mo.	Yes	500	
Yahoo! GeoCities *http://geocities.yahoo.com*	Plus: $4.95/mo.	25 MB	5 GB/mo.	Yes	None	No
	Pro: $8.95/mo.	25 MB	10 GB/mo.	Yes	5	Yes
Yahoo! Small Business Web Hosting *http://smallbusiness.yahoo.com/ webhosting*	Business Starter: $11.95/mo.	2 GB	25 GB/mo.	Yes	25	Free
	Standard: $19.95/mo.	4 GB	75 GB/mo.	Yes	50	
	Pro: $39.95/mo.	10 GB	200 GB/mo.	Yes	100	

E-commerce options	Notes
15-product catalog, various e-commerce frontends, $29.95/mo.	
All of the above, plus 100-product catalog, $74.95/mo.	
All of the above, plus unlimited catalog, $124.95/mo.	
Web site promotion software	$19 setup fee
Includes above, plus Miva Merchant and My SQL as well as online catalog.	$29 setup fee
Includes above, plus automatic credit card processing and Thwarte security certificate.	$39 setup fee
Includes above, plus enough space to stream sound and video.	$49 setup fee
None	$10 setup fee
None	$15 setup fee
Merchant Solutions plans range from $39.95 to $299.95 per month. Cheapest plan includes a shopping cart with security features, a product catalog, and order-management tools; $99.95 plan includes all of the above, plus advanced merchandising and order-management tools and more reporting features; $299.95 plan includes all of the above, plus integration with your existing business systems and more ways to customize your store.	

STOP SENDING SITE VISITORS INTO OBLIVION

The Annoyance: I have broadband access and I host my own web site, but it's almost impossible for people to visit it—because my broadband ISP uses DHCP, my site's IP address changes all the time. That means whenever someone types in my site's URL, they can't find my server. How can I bring them back from oblivion?

The Fix: The problem, as you've surmised, is that because your IP address constantly changes, there is no way for people to connect to your site—one day its IP address might be *66.31.42.96*, and the next it might be *66.41.42.136*. Getting your own domain name doesn't solve the problem, because the Internet's DNS servers can't keep track of your changing IP address, either.

You can solve the problem by turning to a free redirection service such as No-IP.com (*http://www.no-ip.com*), which constantly tracks your current IP address and automatically sends visitors to it whenever they try to surf to your web address. When you sign up, choose a name for your server, such as *grallas*. The service will then add a *.no-ip.com* to the end of it—for example, *www.grallas.no-ip.com*. Give this new URL to people you want to visit your site.

Part of the signup process is downloading a program that continually monitors your IP address. Whenever the IP address changes, it tells No-IP.com. When people try to visit your site, they're sent to a No-IP.com server, which looks up your server's current address and then redirects them to your web server, based on your current IP address. The visitors don't see any of this happening, of course; they just end up at your site. Note: if you want visitors redirected to your own domain instead of a No-IP.com address, you'll have to sign up for the company's Plus service, for $24.95 per month.

Another solution is to see if your ISP can offer you a static IP address. You typically pay extra for this service, but it may be the only way to get your site—with your custom domain name—online.

Before you host a server of any kind, check with your ISP. Most cable and DSL providers won't let you host a web server on your home account. Some providers may not allow you to host a web server in any fashion, but that's changing. For example, cable provider Comcast offers domain name hosting, 100 MB of space, and 3 GB of monthly data transfers for as little as $24.95 per month.

DESIGN AND MAINTENANCE HELP

MAKE WEB PAGES THE EASY WAY

The Annoyance: I don't have the time to learn HTML tricks, but I'd like to build a web site that's more exciting than a dead fish. Help!

The Fix: Your best bet is to use a graphical web-site creation program that lets you build pages without writing (or editing) a lick of HTML code. You do everything visually, from pasting in graphics to creating input fields to setting text. The program generates the appropriate HTML, which you then post as your web site.

A good basic, free program is Netscape Composer (*http://wp.netscape.com/communicator/composer*). The program sports some notable niceties, such as automatically converting graphics to a web-friendly format. However, it doesn't include many advanced features, such as any interactivity—it focuses on straight HTML.

A much more comprehensive, and expensive, program is the $199 FrontPage 2003 (Figure 4-2). It also lets you build web pages visually, but it includes some sophisticated features for e-commerce, building very large web

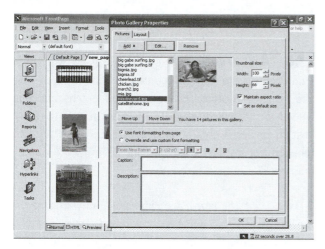

Figure 4-2. A program like FrontPage makes it easy to build web pages without knowing much HTML—you can even build online photo galleries, as shown here.

sites, integrating web sites with databases, and more. If you're building relatively simple web pages, it's overkill. But if FrontPage came with your copy of Microsoft Office, using it is worth your while. (For some caveats about FrontPage, see "Why Won't FrontPage Work with My Host?" later in this section.)

FIND OUT WHO'S LINKING TO YOUR WEB SITE

The Annoyance: Last week, for no apparent reason, my web site got a huge jump in traffic. I have to pay my ISP extra if I exceed a certain amount of traffic, so this huge increase has put me in a financial hole. I figure all the extra traffic probably came from someone linking to me. How can I find out what web sites have linked to mine, so I can stop it?

The Fix: Google, the master of all trades, can show you all the sites that link to your site. Head to *http://www.google.com*. In the search box, type `link:www.<sitename>.com` (where `<sitename>` is the name of your site), and press Enter. Google will list all the sites linked to yours in its normal search format, and show you a grand total.

WHY ARE THERE SO MANY TOP-LEVEL DOMAINS?

You've no doubt noticed that domains end in more than just *.com*—they can end in *.net*, *.org*, *.edu*, *.mil*, *.biz*, and many others as well. Each of these domains is supposed to be for a different purpose, although the conventions aren't always strictly adhered to. So which can you use, and for what? The *.com* domain is supposed to be for businesses and individuals; *.net* for network organizations (an ISP, for example); *.org* for organizations, primarily non-profits; *.edu* for educational organizations; and *.mil* for the military.

Theoretically, there should be limits on who can use *.net* and *.org*, but in practice, that's not the case. Registrars do not ask for documentation when you register these domains, and there is no Internet police force making sure domains are used properly. Also, keep in mind that when you search via a registrar to see which domains are taken, it may not

search through all top-level domains. In particular, many won't search for available *.edu* and *.mil* names.

Since the original top-level domains were created, there has been such a huge demand for fresh names that new top-level domains have been introduced (such as *.biz*, which is aimed at businesses). But these new domains really haven't caught on, and most Internet users still don't know they exist. (By the way, if you see a domain ending in *.tv*, it's not what you think—that's not actually a top-level domain created for television. Instead, it's the domain of the tiny country of Tuvalu, a Pacific Island nation that has tried to capitalize on its fortuitously named domain. In fact, it's been fairly successful—in 2000 Tuvalu licensed the domain for $50 million to a VeriSign-owned company.)

WHY WON'T FRONTPAGE WORK WITH MY HOST?

The Annoyance: I used FrontPage 2002 to build my web site, but when I uploaded my files to my hosting service, all the best features that I built in the wee hours of the night wouldn't work. What's the deal?

The Fix: Chances are your hosting service doesn't support FrontPage extensions. FrontPage extensions are a set of scripts that add all sorts of cool features to your web site, from secure user-input forms to pulling in live views from external databases. But the extensions must live on the server hosting your web site for these features to work. If your host doesn't support the extensions, only your web site's basic features will work.

Try asking your hosting service if it will install the extensions. If it won't, start looking for a new host—and this time, ask about FrontPage extensions right up front. Another possibility is to check whether your hosting service supports SharePoint services (see "Goodbye to FrontPage Extensions"). If so, upgrade to FrontPage 2003, because you'll be able to use SharePoint services to do everything FrontPage extensions can do, and more.

FRONTPAGE EXTENSIONS GONE BAD

The Annoyance: I've been using Microsoft FrontPage for the last two months to build my web site, and yes, my hosting service supports extensions. But when I tried to upload the latest version of my site to my hosting service, I got the error message "FrontPage Extensions Not Installed." Is FrontPage having some kind of brain lock?

The Fix: The FrontPage extensions on your area on the host's servers have been corrupted. Unfortunately, this is a frequent occurrence. The only fix is to reinstall them from your PC to the server. How you do this depends on the hosting service. Sometimes it's as simple as clicking a Set up FrontPage Extensions button, and then clicking an Install/Reinstall Extensions button. Other times, it requires a relatively lengthy procedure. Check with your hosting service.

When you reinstall the FrontPage extensions, you'll lose your themes and shared borders, so before reinstalling, make sure that the copy of your site on your PC is current, including themes and shared borders. After you've reinstalled the extensions, upload your entire web site again. This will replace the default themes and borders with your custom ones.

FIX TYPOS IN URLS

The Annoyance: For some reason, many of my site's visitors seem to have dyslexia. They frequently misspell the addresses of individual pages on my site, so they can't get to them. Short of buying them all spell-checkers, what can I do? I use Internet Information Services (IIS) to host my web site. (Hey, it came with XP Professional, OK?)

The Fix: Mistyped URLs are the bugaboo of every web site administrator. When someone mistypes a URL, he gets the dreaded "404. The page cannot be found" error and you lose a visitor.

Since you run your site with IIS, you can solve the problem with URLSpellCheck for IIS (*http://www. port80software.com/products/urlspellcheck/*)—it redirects misspelled URLs to the proper pages, so your visitors don't get error messages. URLSpellCheck catches extra, transposed, missing, and just plain wrong characters in URLs. It also catches incorrect extensions (for example, *.htm* rather than *.html* or *.asp* rather than *.htm*). In essence, it creates an index of your site with all the correct URLs, compares entered URLs to the correct ones, and makes the appropriate corrections.

> ### t i p
> URLSpellCheck can't correct a mistyped domain name, such as *http://www. microoft.com* rather than *http://www. microsoft.com*. Domains are handled by the Domain Name System (DNS), which add-in software can't touch.

You can download a fully working 30-day trial of URL-SpellCheck; after that, expect to pay $49.95 for a single server license. (At press time, the package didn't work with Windows Server 2003/IIS 6.0, but the developer expects to port it over.)

If you use Apache as your web server, you can correct typos in a similar fashion, for free. Get a copy of the Apache module mod_speling at *http://httpd.apache.org/ docs/mod/mod_speling.html*.

FIX YOUR SPELLING ERRORS

The Annoyance: I'm a great web designer, but a dismal speller. I don't want visitors to think I'm an ignoramis—or is that ignoramus? How can I spell-check my site?

The Fix: First, see if there's a spell-checker in your HTML editor and, if so, use it before posting any pages. If there isn't, get a standalone spell-checker, or use a free online service that can spell-check text or even entire web pages.

To spell-check a posted web page, go to Free URL (*http:// spellcheck.freeurl.com*) and type in the URL of the page you want checked. In a few seconds, a page will appear that highlights potentially misspelled words (Figure 4-3). You can also paste text into a form and have it checked. Note: Free URL will check only the first 6,144 characters on a page.

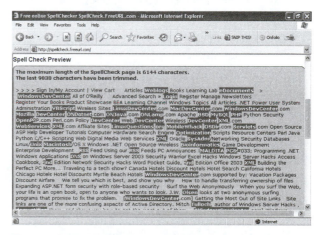

Figure 4-3. Worried your web page is riddled with misspellings? Free URL can find 'em fast.

If you find Free URL's length restriction too limiting, you can try SpellCheck.net (*http://www.spellcheck.net*). It will spell-check up to 20,000 characters, but it won't check live web pages. Instead, you must paste the page text into a box.

Another option is Spell Check Anywhere (*http://www.spellcheckanywhere.com*), a program that will spell-check inside any application, including HTML editors. Unlike the online services, Spell Check Anywhere will also correct the errors for you. It can even work inside Internet Explorer, so you can spell-check your web site after you've posted it. After a 15-day free trial, the program costs $29.97.

HELP YOUR HTML

The Annoyance: I'm no HTML master—in fact, quite the reverse. Broken tables, bad syntax... you name it, and I've done it. Why don't HTML doctors make house calls?

The Fix: They do—well, virtual doctors do, that is. There are a number of programs and web sites that will make your HTML turn its head and cough, and recommend treatment. Here are two good options:

- The CSE HTML Validator (*http://www.htmlvalidator.com*) does a thorough job of checking your web site for many errors. It checks your HTML coding for errors in syntax and inefficient code, does automatic spell-checking, checks for stylesheet errors, alerts you to dead links and missing graphics, offers advice for improving your site, and more. The free "lite" version does basic syntax checking, but not much else (it won't check for bad links, for example). For-pay versions range from $69 to $129, depending on how thoroughly you want the software to check your HTML. If you only build basic web pages that don't use CSS, XHTML, and JavaScript, and you don't need a link checker, the free version will be all you need.

- The NetMechanic site (*http://www.netmechanic.com*) checks for broken links, finds and fixes HTML errors, makes sure pages are compatible with multiple browsers, spell-checks your site, checks the download

times for your pages, and recommends how to optimize page loading, among other features. Just type in your URL, and the site goes to work (see Figure 4-4). It costs $60 per year for a single site with up to 100 pages, and $200 per site with up to 400 pages. Skeptical? You can scan up to five pages for free.

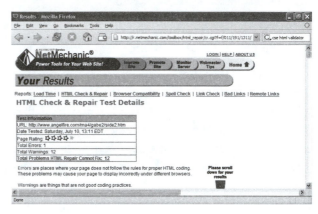

Figure 4-4. This page needs some help, says NetMechanic. The site can fix the one true HTML error it finds, but it can't repair warnings.

CAN'T VIEW SOURCE IN IE

The Annoyance: I know basic HTML, and as a way to learn more, I often look at the actual HTML used to build the page that I'm viewing. I do it in the usual way—in Internet Explorer, I choose View → Source, and the HTML page opens in Notepad. But for some reason, Notepad now refuses to launch!

The Fix: For some inexplicable reason, a setting has been changed in your Windows Registry that has disabled the View Source function in Internet Explorer. But it's simple to fix. First, close Internet Explorer. Then launch the Registry Editor by selecting Start → Run, typing regedit in the Open box, and pressing Enter. Go to the key HKEY_CURRENT_USER\Software\Policies\Microsoft\Internet Explorer\Restrictions and find NoViewSource. Double-click it, change its value from 1 to 0, and exit the Registry. Then relaunch Internet Explorer. (You may also need to restart your PC.) Now when you choose View → Source, Notepad will launch, with the HTML for the current page inside it.

BANISH BAD LINKS

The Annoyance: I have about 75 links on my site, and every day I get complaints from visitors who say that some of them point nowhere. Life's too short to be tracking down dead links, and I don't want to pay for software or a service to do it for me. What's a cheapskate like me to do?

The Fix: Download a copy of the free Windows program REL Link Checker Lite from *http://www.relsoftware. com/rlc/downloads*. It'll check up to 1,000 links per site for free. For more heavy-duty sites, get the company's Link Validator, which can check 100,000 links (including to HTTPS and FTP sources), examine password-protected pages, and confirm Internet Explorer Favorites. It also comes with tech support. Pricing ranges from $27 for a personal, 500-link license to $495 for a corporate, unlimited license.

GET CENTERED

The Annoyance: I'm trying to place some pictures and text right in the middle of my web page, sort of like a splash screen, but no matter what I do the positioning is always off. How can I get it dead center?

The Fix: The trick is to place all of the page content in a table set to be 100% high and 100% wide. (As you can guess, this tip works best for something like a splash screen or on pages where there isn't much content.) The table should have only one cell, which holds the text or picture, and must be set to be vertically and horizontally centered (see Figure 4-5).

Figure 4-5. Can't center text or images on your web page? Create a single-cell table and center that.

You should also set the page margins to 0, because some browsers take the margins into account when calculating that 100% height and width and consequently may add unnecessary scrollbars. Strictly speaking, the *height* attribute for tables is no longer part of the HTML specification, but this trick will probably work with most browsers, including IE.

Any text in the table will be center-aligned. If you want more control over the layout, place your text and graphics inside another table and place that inside the centered table (in effect, nesting one table within another). The following code (also available at *http://www.oreilly. com/catalog/internetannoy/downloads.csp*) incorporates this extra trick:

```
<html>
<head>
<meta http-equiv="Content-Type" content="text/
html; charset=iso-8859-1">
<style type="text/css">
<!--
body {
margin-left: 0px;
margin-top: 0px;
margin-right: 0px;
margin-bottom: 0px;
}
body,td,th {
font-family: Verdana, Arial, Helvetica, sans-
serif;
font-size: small;
}
a:link {
color: #000000;
}
a:visited {
color: #000000;
}
-->
</style><body>
<table width="100%" height="100%" border="0"
cellpadding="0" cellspacing="0">
<tr>
<td align="center" valign="middle">
<table width="300" border="0" cellspacing="5"
cellpadding="5">
<tr bgcolor="#FF0000">
<td colspan="2" style="color:#FFFFFF">Choose your
connection speed:<br>
<span style="font-size:xx-small">Choosing your
bandwidth setting will give you a version of the
site optimized for your connection.</span></td>
</tr>
```

```
<tr align="center" valign="middle">
<td bgcolor="#999999"><a href="fast.html">
Fast</a></td>
<td bgcolor="#999999"><a href="slow.html">
Slow</a></td>
</tr>
</table>
</td>
</tr>
</table>
</body>
</html>
```

WHAT HAPPENED TO MY COOL FONTS?

The Annoyance: I designed my site using some very cool-looking fonts, but visitors tell me they see plain-Jane ones.

The Fix: If you use fonts on your web page that aren't found on a visitor's computer, the visitor won't see them. Instead, they'll see those "plain-Jane" fonts.

If you want to be sure you're using fonts that most people

Table 4-1. Fonts typically found on Windows computers

Arial	Courier New
Arial Black	Garamond
Arial Narrow	Georgia
Book Antiqua	Helvetica
Bookman Old Style	Microsoft Sans Serif
Century Gothic	Times New Roman
Comic Sans	Verdana

have, stick to the basic set commonly found on Windows systems (see Table 4-1).

Of course, using just these fonts limits the kinds of designs you can do. Fortunately, there's a way around the problem: you can list several fonts with the *<FONT>* tag's *FACE* attribute. If the visitor's system doesn't have the first font, the browser will try to display the text in the second font on the list, and so on. So, for example, if you use the following HTML tag in your web page:

```
<FONT FACE="tahoma, arial, helvetica">
```

a visiting browser will display the designated text in the Tahoma font if it's available or, if not, in Arial; if Arial isn't available either, it will display the text in Helvetica. You can list as many fonts in a row as you'd like.

Of course, there's no guarantee that the fonts you list will be on everyone's computers, so you can also specify a general typeface "style" as the last choice. For example:

```
<FONT FACE="tahoma, arial, helvetica, sans-serif">
```

The browser will display a font in that style if it can't find any of the fonts you specified. The typeface styles you can choose from include serif, sans-serif, monospace, cursive, or fantasy. Serif fonts are fonts that have extra vertical or horizontal strokes on their letters to aid readability. One very common serif font is Times New Roman. A sans-serif font, such as Helvetica, lacks these strokes. The characters in a monospace typeface, such as Courier, have a fixed width—that is, each character takes up the same amount of space. Cursive typefaces look like script, and fantasy typefaces are those that use some kind of special effect.

USE WEB-SAFE COLORS

The Annoyance: When I design a site, the colors I choose aren't the ones that show up when people visit. What gives?

The Fix: When you choose a color for your web site, there's no guarantee that your visitors' computers can display the exact color you want. That's because different video cards and monitors handle colors differently.

But you can come pretty darn close if you use the *web palette*, an industry-standard collection of colors that all browsers will display the same. The web palette is made up of colors. When you use a web authoring program such as FrontPage, by default you'll be offered colors from the web palette, so if you stick to these, you should be fine. However, if you custom-mix colors, you'll be creating colors outside the web palette, so all bets are off.

HOW MONITORS DISPLAY THE WEB PALETTE

Contemporary monitors combine three basic colors—red, green, and blue—to produce every single color they display. A monitor can display 256 shades of each color, and any of those shades can be mixed with any of the shades of the other two colors. So, the total number of colors that your monitor can theoretically display is 256 X 256 X 256, or 16,777,216.

This system of displaying colors is commonly referred to as *RGB color* (R for red, G for green, and B for blue). You can refer to any of the 16,777,216 colors in numeric fashion using the RGB system, by assigning the R, the G, and the B each a value from 0 to 255, where 0 is no color and 255 is the most saturated color. So, for example, dark green would have a value of R:0 G:255 B:0—in other words, no red or blue and a completely saturated green. A slate-blue color would have a value of R:106 G:90 B:205.

That probably sounds complicated enough, but in the real world, it's even messier. As it turns out, some computers can't display all 16,777,216 colors—so that vermillion ad banner you spent days getting just right on your fancy monitor could look like chartreuse on someone else's. To get around the problem, computers use *palettes*—standardized collections of colors that are displayed the way designers (including you) want them to be displayed. A computer's operating system has its own palette, as may programs that run on the computer. And web browsers have what is called the *web palette*—a collection of colors that all browsers should display the same. When you choose a color from the web palette, you know that visitors will see the color that you want them to see.

If you aren't using a web authoring program, another way to choose colors from the web palette is to buy a web color wheel, which is a nifty little gizmo that displays all the web-safe colors, tells you their RGB and hexadecimal codes, and organizes them into color groups so that you can see which colors work well with, or contrast with, other colors. You can often find the wheels for under $10 at local art supply stores. You can also order a Web Wheel from the Color Wheel Company: *http://www.colorwheelco.com*.

CREATE THUMBNAILS ON WEB PAGES

The Annoyance: My web site takes two eternities to load. I know the problem is that my pictures are too large, but I don't want to give up their high quality. What can I do?

The Fix: Your best bet is to use small, thumbnail-sized graphics that, when clicked, load the larger, high-resolution graphics.

The first step is to create the thumbnail-sized graphics using a program such as Paint Shop Pro or Adobe Photoshop Elements. Then you'll need to add the appropriate HTML for displaying the thumbnails and linking them to the larger image files.

Let's look at how to do this in Paint Shop Pro. Let's say that you have a JPEG that's 110K and 800 by 456 pixels. You want to boil it down to a GIF of about 10K that will be 205 by 117 pixels. When you click on the thumbnail, the larger, original 110K graphic will appear. Here are the steps:

1. Open the large picture.

2. Choose Image → Resize. The Resize dialog box, shown in Figure 4-6, will appear.

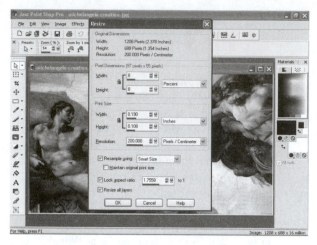

Figure 4-6. The Paint Shop Pro Resize tool makes it easy to create thumbnails from larger graphics.

3. The Pixel Dimensions drop-down boxes let you do the actual resizing of the big picture into a thumbnail. You can resize the image either by scaling it down to a percentage of the original size or by specifying a size in pixels. In the drop-down box on the far right of the Pixel Dimensions dialog box, choose either Percent or Pixels.

4. If you've chosen Pixels, click the down arrows in the Width and Height drop-downs until you've resized the picture to the right number of pixels (in this instance, until it is 205 pixels wide and 117 pixels high). If you've chosen Percent, click on the down arrows in the Width and Height drop-downs until you've resized the picture to your liking. As you change the percentage, you're shown how many pixels that will make your new, resized picture.

5. You'll have to experiment a little to figure out the right size for your thumbnails. They should be as small as possible to minimize loading time, but large enough so that they're legible. In our example, the 205-by-117-pixel picture still retains details, but is only 9K.

6. Ignore the Print Size dialog box; that's relevant only when you're resizing a picture that will be printed, not posted online.

7. Check the "Resample using" box, and choose Smart Size from the drop-down to the right. That ensures that when your picture is resized, it will use the best possible color settings.

8. Choose File → Save As, and specify a filename for the smaller picture. Make sure you save the thumbnail with its own name—don't overwrite the original graphic!

9. Now that you have the thumbnail-sized graphic, place it on the web page so that when it's clicked, it loads the larger picture. Let's say that the thumbnail is called *smallcreation.jpg*, the large original is called *creation.jpg*, and they're both found in *http://www.gralla.com/art/*. Here's what the tag for creating the thumbnail would look like: *<a href="http://www.gralla.com/art/creation.jpg"><img src="http://www.gralla.com/art/smallcreation.jpg"></a>*. The *<img src="http://www.gralla.com/art/smallcreation.jpg">* section tells the web page to display the thumbnail picture, and the rest of the coding tells the web page to display the larger picture when the thumbnail is clicked.

When you create a thumbnail, maintain the relative proportions of the original or it will appear distorted. Most graphics editors offer this option. For example, in Adobe Photoshop Elements, make sure that the "Constrain Proportions" box is checked. In Paint Shop Pro, check the "Lock aspect ratio" box.

QUICK-AND-EASY IMAGE CONVERSION

The Annoyance: I have a slew of TIF images that I'd like to post on my web site, but the files are huge—easily 2 MB apiece. Please don't tell me I have to load them one at a time into Photoshop Elements and then convert each one to JPEG or GIF. It'll take forever!

The Fix: You need a good batch image-conversion tool, and there are plenty out there. The best free one I've found is IrfanView, available at *http://www.irfanview. com*. To convert a file from one graphics format to another, open the desired file, choose File → Save As, click the Options tab, choose the output format, give the file a name, and click Save. When you're converting to *.jpg*, you'll see a slider on the Options tab that lets you adjust image quality. The lower the quality, the smaller the file.

To convert an entire group of graphics, choose File → Batch Conversion, select the files, choose the output format and any other relevant options, and click Save.

Another good bet is ImageConverter .EXE, available at *http://www.stintercorp.com/genx/imageconverter.php*. This free program ($35 if you register) offers much more control over the size and quality of the images you convert. It even shows you a side-by-side comparison of the before and after versions, complete with file sizes, so you can balance size versus image quality (see Figure 4-7). It also does batch conversions, lets you edit files, and can add a wide variety of special effects.

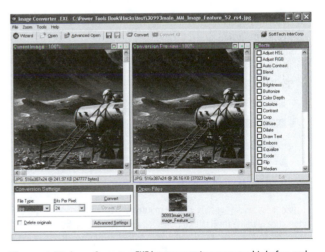

Figure 4-7. ImageConverter .EXE lets you preview your graphic before and after compression. The file on the right is 85% smaller than the original on the left, but you can barely tell the difference in quality.

GET A FREE PAGE COUNTER

The Annoyance: I don't have the time to write some fancy code that will count all the people who visit my web site. How can I get one of those cool counters I see on other web sites?

The Fix: You can get free counters of all kinds for your web site, without having to learn any onerous scripting techniques. Code for various counters is freely available all over the Internet. You create a counter on your site by pasting the HTML code for it into a page.

To find the code, start off with your web hosting service or ISP. Many of them offer free code for counters. Other places you can go to get counters include:

- *http://freelogs.com/create.php*
- *http://easy-hit-counters.com* (Figure 4-8)
- *http://www.inteliture.com*

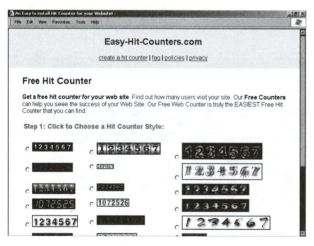

Figure 4-8. Pick your style of page counter, and Easy-Hit-Counters.com will automatically create the HTML you need to plug it into your web site.

BLOGGING

WHAT IS BLOGGING?

The Annoyance: The world needs saving, and I'm the man to do it. I've heard about "blogs" and would like to share my ineffable wisdom with the world through one. But I don't want to host my own web site—I want to blog as simply as possible.

The Fix: A webblog, or blog, is a public diary kept on the Web. They're typically updated daily or several days a week, and blog postings can range from mundane "I brushed my teeth today" jottings to reportage from political conventions. As I write this, an estimated 8.4 million Americans have created blogs. Ever on the cutting edge, even Bill Gates is contemplating writing a blog that one source says would "share personal details, such as tidbits from recent vacations." I can't wait.

There are many ways you can blog, but the simplest is to use a free web site that hosts and lets you quickly and easily create a blog. The leader in the field is Blogger, at *http://www.blogger.com*. (It's owned by Google.) Just register at the site, fill in some basic information about your blog, and use simple forms to create one. After you register, you give your blog a name and choose a URL for it. (The URL will end in *blogspot.com*, so your URL might be something like *http://www.prestonsposts.blogspot.com*.)

After you've chosen a name and URL, pick a template for it, and you're ready to start posting. To post, click the Start Posting button that appears after you choose your template, and you'll come to a page that looks like the one shown in Figure 4-9. Type in your musings, and use the HTML-formatting tools if you want to add fonts and colors. Click the Publish Post button at the bottom of the page, and you'll create your first post. Your blog will now be live at the URL you chose during setup. To post again to your blog, log in at *http://www.blogger.com.* You'll come to your Dashboard page, which is command central for your blogging. Click your blog name, and on the page that appears, click "Create a new post." You'll again see a page like that shown in Figure 4-9, where you can once again share your incisive thoughts with the world.

Figure 4-9. Blogger offers easy-to-use tools to create blogs.

t i p

If you're a webmaster and you want server software to host a blog on your site, your best bet is to get Movable Type from *http://www.movabletype.org.* You can download a free version that limits you to one blog author and a total of three blogs, or for $69.95, you can get a version that allows five authors and an unlimited number of blogs. For $99.95, you can have an unlimited number of authors and blogs.

WHY CAN'T I USE PICTURES IN MY BLOG?

The Annoyance: I used the Blogger site to build my blog, but I can't seem to post any pictures there. Doesn't Blogger know that a picture is worth a thousand words?

The Fix: Blogger doesn't host any pictures. But you can still post pictures to your blog—you'll just have to serve them up from another site, and point to them from your blog. The simplest way to do this is to use the BloggerBot web site (*http://hello.com/how_bloggerbot_works.php*). Download the Hello applet at *http://hello.com/download.php and* use it to resize your pictures, upload the pictures, and format your blog posts so that your pictures are "live."

You can, of course, host your pictures elsewhere, such as at your ISP or another third-party host. Once you've uploaded your pictures to your hosting service, you can include an image in a specific post or in your template by using the following tag:

```
<img src="http://www.myhost.com/pictures/
mypicture.jpg">
```

where *http://www.myhost.com/pictures/* is the location of your picture and *mypicture.jpg* is the name of your picture.

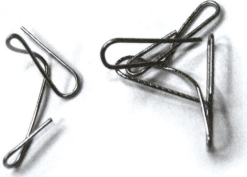

MOBLOG WITH TYPEPAD

The Annoyance: I use the TypePad blogging service (*http://www.typepad.com*) for my blog, and I'd like to post photos I take with my cell phone. But for the life of me, I can't figure out how to do it.

The Fix: It's easy—you just need to know where to look to set it up. From your TypePad home, click the Control Panel tab, then choose Mobile Settings. When you moblog, you can send text or photos via your cell phone. From the "When I send text messages via email" drop-down, choose which of your blogs should post text messages from your cell phone, and from the "When I send photos via email" drop-down, select which blogs should receive pictures sent from your phone.

When you've done that, fill in the box that indicates the email address from which you'll be sending photos and messages. Type in your cell phone's email address, and pick a verification method that will confirm you are the actual sender of the message. If you choose the "Confirmation Message" method, an email message will be sent to your cell phone asking if you want to post the message you've just sent; reply to this message to confirm the posting. Another option is to send messages to a unique TypePad email address that only you know, in which case you won't need to confirm the post. You can also elect to send messages using PGP encryption, but because as a rule mobile phones don't use PGP encryption, this method probably won't work.

When you're done, click Save. To moblog with your cell phone, just send the photo or text that you want posted, reply to the confirmation message (if necessary), and your post will appear.

BUST BLOG BLOCKAGES

The Annoyance: I like using Blogger's tools for building a blog, but I don't want my blog hosted on the Blogger site. Instead, I want to publish my blog on my web site. I've discovered that Blogger will indeed let me publish the blog to my site. The problem? My hosting service won't let Blogger in. What can I do?

The Fix: When Blogger tries to publish your blog to your site, it uses its IP address, not yours. That's why your hosting service is saying "no way!" The solution? Tell your hosting service to let through Blogger's IP addresses, which are *66.102.15.83* and *216.34.7.186*. Once your hosting service lets them through, your blog should work fine.

> **tip**
>
> Make sure that your hosting service enables ports 1024 and up for the IP addresses, so that you can post live updates via FTP.

BUILD AN AUDIO BLOG

The Annoyance: Call me lazy, but I'd like to post streaming audio files on my blog—why should I force people to read my posts, when they can instead listen to my sweet tenor? But it seems like too much trouble to record the sounds, find a hosting service, upload the files, and do all the coding to make it live.

The Fix: Here's a service just for you: Audioblog.com, at *http://www.audioblog.com*. It's an all-in-one tool that lets you record your musings over the Web using its BlogRecorder, then upload them as MP3 or WAV files to your existing blog on Movable Type, TypePad, Blogger, or LiveJournal (with support for more blog sites and software to come). You can even create audioblogs with playlists. The service isn't free, however; you'll have to pay $4.95 per month.

COMMENT ON WEB SITES

The Annoyance: In my blog, I frequently comment on other web sites and blogs. But referring to another site's URL and citing its (often half-witted) opinions is a total pain. When I find a site I want to comment on, I keep that site open, open up a second instance of Internet Explorer, log into *http://www.blogger.com*, and then create my post, switching back and forth and cutting and pasting text and URLs. There's got to be an easier way!

The Fix: There is—use Blogger's BlogThis! feature, available from *http://help.blogger.com/bin/answer.py?answer=152*. Drag the BlogThis! link to your browser's Links bar, and it will appear as a link. Then, whenever you're at a web page you want to comment on, just click the link. A small window will open, containing the URL of the page as well as any text you've highlighted (Figure 4-10). Type in your blog posting, then click the Publish button, and it'll be posted on your Blogger page. If you want to save it as a draft, click the Save as Draft button instead.

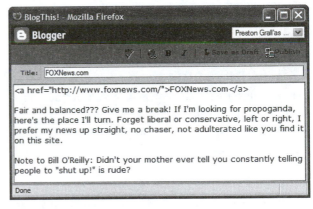

Figure 4-10. Blogger's BlogThis! feature makes it easy to comment on a web site and post that comment to your blog in one simple step.

If you blog using TypePad, you can do the same thing, but with a TypePad-specific tool. Visit the Your Weblogs screen in TypePad. Click the "Set up QuickPost bookmarklet" link in the blue box in the top-right corner of the content area, and follow the installation instructions. In your browser's menu bar, a TypePad QuickPost button will appear. When you're on a web site that you want to comment on, highlight the text you want to quote, click the TypePad QuickPost button, and fill out the form for commenting on the site and posting your comments to your blog.

If you use the Firefox browser, you can take advantage of its BlogThis feature for several different blogging sites, including Blogger, TypePad, Technorati, BlogHarbor, Bloglines, and LiveJournal. Download and install the free Firefox Toolbar from *http://www.firefoxtoolbar.com/ download*. When you're at a site you want to cite, click the BlogThis button in the Toolbar, and follow the blogging instructions.

SYNDICATE YOUR BLOG

The Annoyance: I want to syndicate my Blogger blog using RSS, so that people can get automatic feeds of it. But I can't find a way to do this—instead, I have to use a syndication feature called Atom. Why can't I use RSS on Blogger?

The Fix: Ah, the Internet. You've just been caught in the middle of another food fight over competing standards.

As you've noted, RSS is a syndication standard that lets any site publish a feed. Users who subscribe to the feed get postings or news automatically delivered to them. Atom is a competing standard that works essentially the same way as RSS. You also subscribe to and read Atom feeds using an RSS reader.

As you've discovered, Blogger's free service only lets you syndicate your blog using Atom. To syndicate using Atom, log into your blog, click the Settings tab, and click the Site Feed link (see Figure 4-11).

In the Publish Site Feed drop-down, choose Yes. In the Descriptions drop-down box, choose Full if you want your entire posts to be published, or Short if you want only the first paragraph or 255 characters (whichever is shorter) to be published. Click Save Settings, and people will be able to subscribe to your feed using Atom.

Figure 4-11. To syndicate your blog using Atom on Blogger, just fill in the information on this page and click Save Settings.

If you subscribe to Blogger Pro, you'll be able to syndicate using either RSS or Atom. But if using RSS is your only reason for subscribing to the Pro service, there's another option: turn to the FeedBurner service at *http://www. feedburner.com*, which will let you publish your blog as an RSS feed, even on Blogger. The service is free.

POST TO YOUR BLOG VIA EMAIL

The Annoyance: Why should it take so much work to post to my blog on Blogger? I'm just entering a bunch of text. Rather than going to the trouble of visiting the site, logging in, then creating my post, why can't I just send a post via email?

The Fix: With the right settings, you can post via email, with no muss or fuss required. To do it, you'll have to configure your Mail-to-Blogger email address. Then you can simply send an email containing your post.

Log into Blogger and go to your blog. Click the Settings tab, then the Email link (Figure 4-12). In the Mail-to-Blogger Address box, enter the address to which you want to send your posts. The format of the address is *username.secretword@blogger.com*. Your username is already filled in for you; it's your Blogger login name. You just need to create and type in your secret word. Enter your secret word to create it, click the box next to Publish, and click Save Settings.

Figure 4-12. To post to your blog via email on Blogger, fill out this form, and you're ready to go.

To post something, send it via email to the *username. secretword@blogger.com* address. The post will immediately be made live.

Make sure that you keep your secret word secret, and don't use one that's easy to guess. If your secret word becomes public, anyone will be able to post to your blog, and it may quickly become a spam magnet.

MAKE YOUR BLOG PRIVATE

The Annoyance: I don't want to share my innermost secrets with the entire world—just a few good friends and family members. But the great unwashed are always visiting my site. Isn't there a way I can discourage them, or even keep them out?

The Fix: Strangers are most likely finding your blog via search engines, so your first step is to tell search engines not to index your blog's contents. Paste the following tag into your blog's template's *<head>* section, and search-engine robots will be told not to index your site:

```
<META name="ROBOTS" content="NOINDEX,
NOFOLLOW" />
```

If you publish your blog on your own web site, or have access to the root of its server, create a text file called *robots.txt*, containing only these two lines, and put it in the root:

```
User-agent: *
Disallow: /
```

That will also tell search robots to stay away.

Of course, the best way to make sure no one except friends and family can read your blog is to password-protect it. How you do this varies from blog service to blog service and from hosting service to hosting service.

WHY CAN'T I GET PAST THE MOVABLE TYPE LOGIN SCREEN?

The Annoyance: I use Movable Type on my server for creating and maintaining blogs. But whenever I log in and click any link in the main menu, I'm sent back to that same, annoying login screen.

The Fix: Movable Type uses cookies, and if you don't have them enabled in your browser, you'll be sent to a login prompt any time you try to do anything with it, including clicking any link. To make it work, you need to enable cookies in your browser. How you do this varies from browser to browser. In Internet Explorer, choose Tools → Internet Options, click the Privacy tab, make sure that the slider is set to Medium-High or lower, then click OK. For more on allowing and disallowing cookies, see Chapter 5.

You should also make sure that you've set your character encoding on LiveJournal properly. Go to your Personal Info settings at *http://www.livejournal.com/editinfo.bml*, scroll down, and choose your default text encoding. Choose Western European (Windows) if you're a Windows user, and Western European (ISO) if you use a Mac.

UPLOAD A USER PICTURE TO LIVEJOURNAL

The Annoyance: I'm a big fan of LiveJournal's feature that lets you use pictures as icons to represent your mood. But no matter how hard I try, LiveJournal won't let me upload my pictures. What gives?

The Fix: There are a few reasons why you might be having this problem. First, LiveJournal won't accept any picture more than 100 pixels wide or 100 pixels high, and it won't accept any picture larger than 40K. So check your picture size, and resize it if it's too large.

LiveJournal also only accepts pictures in GIF, JPG, or PNG format, so if you're trying to upload a picture in a different format, you'll get an error. Keep in mind that just changing the file extension won't put the picture in a different format—you need to convert the graphic to the proper format, using a tool such as IrfanView (available at *http://www.irfanview.com*).

Goodbye to Google

If you want your blog removed from Google's index immediately, so that no one can use Google to find it, head to this page: *http://services.google.com:8882/urlconsole/controller?cmd=reload&lastcmd=login*. Then follow the instructions for removing your blog from Google.

GET RID OF ODD CHARACTERS IN LIVEJOURNAL

The Annoyance: I use LiveJournal (*http://www.livejournal.com*) for my blog, but question marks and other odd characters sometimes show up randomly in my posts. Is there some way I can remove these unwanted intruders?

The Fix: The characters may be showing up for a variety of reasons. If you write your posts in Microsoft Word and then paste the text into your blog, that may be the source of the problem. In Word, if you use "smart quotes" instead of regular straight quotation marks, when you post your blog, all your quotation marks and apostrophes will show up as question marks. So before writing in Word, turn off smart quotes by choosing Tools → Auto-Correct, clicking the AutoFormat As You Type tab, unchecking the "'Straight quotes' with 'smart quotes'" box, and clicking OK.

5

Browser
ANNOYANCES

For most people, the Web *is* the Internet. And the window into the Web is your browser. And a very annoying window it can be.

Head to your favorite site. Oops! There are six pop-up windows that must be swatted down. Go to another site—an animated ad the size of Arnold Schwarzenegger covers the page. Great. Still another site has jumping, singing ads accompanied by eardrum-bending music. Oh wait…that e-commerce site just hijacked your browser, opening window after window after window.

These and other annoyances galore face every web surfer: from pop-ups to web sites that don't print properly to cookies that report your movements to nefarious marketers who want to send you even *more* ads!

In this chapter, you'll learn how to deal with all these and many other annoyances. You'll find out how to kill pop-up and pop-under ads, and how to flatten the most annoying ads of all time—animated Flash ads. In fact, you'll learn how to turn the Internet into an ad-free zone by killing all ads.

POP-UPS, ADS, AND FLASH

POP AWAY POP-UPS

The Annoyance: Browsing the Web these days feels like cruising a carnival midway, with pop-up ads screaming their messages at me everywhere I turn. If I wanted bright, flashing lights, I'd visit Las Vegas. How can I kill these digital carnival barkers?

The Fix: The Web's all-time great search tool, the Google Toolbar, kills pop-ups from directly within Internet Explorer. Get it at *http://toolbar.google.com*. Another good free pop-up killer is EMS Free Surfer mk II, available from *http://www.kolumbus.fi/eero.muhonen/FS/fs.htm*. Also popular (and, I think, superior) is iHatePopups, available for $9.95 from *http://www.sunbelt-software.com/product.cfm?id=935*. It can distinguish between "good" and "bad" pop-ups, and it lets you add specific pages to a "whitelist" so that it knows which pop-ups you want to let through. (What's "good" and what's "bad"? Any window that opens without your instruction is considered a "bad" pop-up window. A window that opens after you click a link or press Enter is considered a legitimate new window. Pop-up ads typically aren't triggered by clicking a link, but editorial pop-ups generally are.)

If you have Windows XP's Service Pack 2 (SP2), your updated version of Internet Explorer already includes a built-in pop-up killer. To make sure it's working, choose Tools → Pop-up Blocker, and make sure that "Turn off Pop-up Blocker" is unchecked. Both Opera and Netscape Navigator have built-in pop-up killers, too. In Opera, choose File → Preferences → Refuse pop-up windows. You can even tell Opera to allow pop-up windows but to open them in the background, instead of on top of your browser.

To enable Netscape's pop-up killer, choose Edit → Preferences → Privacy & Security → Popup Windows and check the "Block unrequested popup windows" box.

I WANT MY POP-UPS! (WELL, SOME OF THEM)

The Annoyance: I use the pop-up blocker in the SP2 version of Internet Explorer, and now I can't log into my favorite web site, because it uses a pop-up box for entering the password and username. I hate pop-ups, but this is one pop-up I need!

The Fix: Whenever Internet Explorer blocks a pop-up, you hear a little "pop" sound, and the new Information Bar appears underneath the Address Bar, telling you a pop-up was blocked. To let the pop-up through, click the Information Bar and choose "Show Blocked Pop-up" (Figure 5-1). If you'd like all pop-ups from the site to be let through, choose "Allow Pop-ups from This Site."

Figure 5-1. If there's a friendly pop-up you'd like to let through, click IE's new Information Bar and let it know.

You can also tell Internet Explorer to let through pop-ups from other sites, or, conversely, stop them cold in their tracks. To let 'em through, right-click the Information Bar, choose "Pop-up Blocker Settings," and type in the relevant URLs in the "Allowed sites" part of the dialog box (Figure 5-2). Want to stop accepting pop-ups? Select a listed site and click the Remove button.

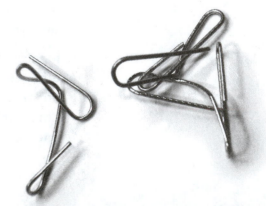

Figure 5-2. Here's where to tell Internet Explorer which sites' pop-ups to allow.

MAKE THE INTERNET AN AD-FREE ZONE

The Annoyance: In all my years of web surfing, I figure I've seen approximately 65,438 ads, and I have yet to click a single one. Isn't there some way I can turn off these annoying annoyances?

The Fix: There are plenty of ad blockers out there. My favorite free one is WebWasher Classic (Figure 5-3), which is available for download from *http://www.webwasher.com/client/download/private_use/windows/index.html?lang=de_EN*. It lets you block ads on a site-by-site basis; will kill only from specific ad servers; and will kill pop-ups, animations, cookies, and other annoyances.

WebWasher Classic is not the easiest program in the world to use, so check out the tips at *http://www.pacific-net.net/~bbruce/workshop.htm*. An excellent paid ad blocker is AdSubtract, which kills ads, banners, pop-ups, cookies, JavaScripts, Java applets, animations, and background music. With AdSubtract you can create profiles for different sites, so that, for example, you allow only animations and background music through on one site, and only animations and Java applets on another. A free

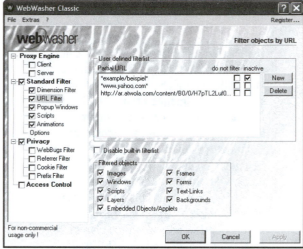

Figure 5-3. From WebWasher's main configuration screen, you can customize how to block ads—the Partial URL section is the filter list.

version is available at *http://www.adsubtract.com/se/features.html*, but it only blocks web banner ads. For the real deal, pony up the $30 for the full package (a free 30-day trial is available from *http://www.adsubtract.com*).

Figure 5-4 shows a typical web ad. Figure 5-5 shows what you'll see when you've successfully blocked the ad.

Figure 5-4. Tired of seeing big fat ads across the top of your browser?

Figure 5-5. Ad begone! It's now replaced by a soothing white box.

NEWS FLASH—I HATE FLASH!

The Annoyance: I like animations, movies, and sound as much as the next guy, but the overuse of Macromedia Flash and other "rich media" ads that include sound and animation is completely out of control. How can I turn off all this multimedia junk?

The Fix: Your first impulse might be to uninstall the Flash player on your PC, but this is easier said than done—Flash isn't listed in the Add or Remove Programs control panel, and there's no uninstall program anywhere else on your hard drive. However, Macromedia has posted an uninstaller at *http://www.macromedia.com/support/flash/ts/documents/remove_player.htm*.

There's one problem with this solution, though—sometimes you *want* to see Flash animations. A better solution is TurnFlash, available at *http://www.pcworld.com/downloads/file_description/0,fid,22947,00.asp*. When you visit a site with an annoying Flash animation, click the TurnFlash icon in the Windows System Tray, and the animation will be killed. (If you go to another page on the site and then return to the first page, you'll have to turn off the Flash animation again.)

That still may not quite solve your problem, though, because you may want to see Flash animations when they're part of the actual content of the page, but not see annoying Flash and animated GIF pop-up ads.

Most pop-up blockers don't block rich media ads, which are often built using Macromedia Flash and sometimes with animated GIFs. One that does is the free Pop-Up No-No!, available at *http://www.popupnono.com*. It runs in the System Tray and will block Macromedia Flash ads, background sounds, animated GIFs, normal pop-ups, and Windows Messenger Service spam. It works with Internet Explorer, Netscape, Mozilla, Firefox, and Opera, and it lets multiple people using the same computer customize their own settings. To change your settings, right-click its icon in the System Tray and make your choices (Figure 5-6).

For details on WebWasher Classic, AdSubtract, and Pop-Up No-No!, see Table 5-1.

Figure 5-6. Pop-Up No-No! lets you choose which types of rich media ads, pop-ups, and other annoyances to kill, and which to let through.

Table 5-1. Ad-blocking software features

	WebWasher Classic	AdSubtract Pro	Pop-Up No-No!
Static banners	✔	✔	
Animated banners	✔	✔	
Pop-ups	✔	✔	✔
Pop-unders	✔	✔	✔
Flash ads	✔	✔	✔
Flashing GIF/other multimedia ads	✔	✔	✔
Messenger Service ads			✔

WHO CLICKS RICH MEDIA ADS?

If rich media ads seem to be everywhere these days, that's because they are. In February 2004, the largest distributor of web ads, DoubleClick, said that rich media ads made up almost 40 percent of all of the ads it distributed. That number was up by 60 percent compared to 2003.

Who clicks on rich media ads? Most likely you do, or someone you know. DoubleClick also reported that rich media ads were a whole lot more effective than static ads and banners. The company said that one in 79 Internet users who saw a rich media ad in February 2004 clicked it, compared to only one in 370 for other types of ads. The company even claims that even those who didn't click were more likely to head off to the advertisers' web sites or buy their products.

Proxomitron Kills Flash, Too

Another tool that will kill Flash animations is Proxomitron. When you run it, instead of seeing a Flash element, you see a link. Click the link to play the animation; leave it alone if you don't want to play it. Proxomitron does a lot more as well, including blocking pop-ups. It's no longer in development, but you can still download it from *http://www.proxomitron.info*.

FIND THAT FLASH FILE!

The Annoyance: I sometimes come across Flash animations on web sites that I'd like to save, but there doesn't seem to be any way for me to do it. Are the files lurking somewhere on my PC?

The Fix: You bet they are. Go to *C:\Documents and Settings\<Your Name>\Local Settings\Temporary Internet Files* (where Your Name is your XP account name) and look for the most current files with a *.swf* extension—the extension for Flash movies. Copy the SWF files to another location on your PC, and you can play them whenever you want. (Just double-click a file and it will load in your browser.) Another solution is to get Cool Flash Player, which lets you save Flash animations to your PC, turn SWFs into executable files, and convert Flash files to screensavers or Windows wallpaper. Download the program and the first 20 "executions" are free; after that, you'll have to $29.95 if you decide to keep it. Get it from *http://www.siskinsoft.com/downloads.html*.

FAVORITES AND BOOKMARKS

WHERE'D MY COOL FAVORITES ICONS GO?

The Annoyance: When I add a web site to IE's Favorites menu, a cool icon often comes along for the ride, such as the red Y! logo for Yahoo! The icons stay on my Favorites menu for a while and then suddenly disappear, never to return. How can I make them stay?

The Fix: Every time you add a site to your Favorites list, Internet Explorer sees whether the site has defined a *favicon* for itself (like the red Y!). If the favicon is there, Internet Explorer stores it in your temporary Internet files cache, and it shows up on your Favorites list.

BETTER FAVORITES AND BOOKMARK MANAGEMENT

If you use more than one browser and you want to keep all your bookmarks in one place, try Powermarks. It does more than just keep them in one place, though. Want to search through your bookmarks to quickly find the one you want? When you add a bookmark, Powermarks automatically grabs keywords and the description field for it from the Web site in question, and you can then search through the keywords and descriptions for the site you want. It will also automatically notify you when any bookmarked page has new content on it, and it lets you rate bookmarks on a scale of 1 to 10 so you can easily see which sites are your true favorites. You can also copy and paste bookmarks to the clipboard. Your bookmarks appear in a separate window, so you can drag and drop them for easy organization. A free 30-day trial is available at *http://www.kaylon.com/power.html*; after that, you'll have to pay $24.95 to use the program.

If you clean out your Internet cache, or your cache fills up to the brim, the icon is pushed out and vanishes. To keep that favicon, you must associate it permanently with the right Favorite. Here's how:

1. To find the favicon for a site, go to *http://www.<website>.com/favicon.ico*. For example, go to *http://www.oreilly.com/favicon.ico* for the O'Reilly icon. Keep in mind that not all web sites have favicons, so you won't be able to do this for every site.

2. Once you find the *favicon.ico* file, right-click it, choose Save Picture As, and save it on your hard disk.

3. Add the web site to your Favorites.

4. Right-click the web site in Favorites and choose Properties → Change Icon.

5. Navigate to where you've stored the *favicon.ico* file, select it, click OK, then click OK again (Figure 5-7).

You're done—the icon will now be associated with your Favorite forever.

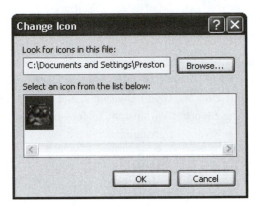

Figure 5-7. Want to keep a site's icon associated with a Favorite? Once you find it, a few clicks can make it permanently yours.

If you can't find a favicon at a site, but you can see the icon associated with the site in your Favorites list, it may be hiding on your hard disk in *C:\Documents and Settings\ <Your Name>\Local Settings\Temporary Internet Files*. Look for files with the *.ico* extension, copy them to another location, and permanently associate them with the desired Favorite.

> **t i p**
>
> If you don't want to go through the trouble of finding and copying favicons manually, there's a utility that will do it for you automatically—grab a copy of FavOrg at *http://www.pcmag.com/article2/0,1759,13999,00.asp*.

MOVE FAVORITES AND BOOKMARKS FROM HERE TO THERE

The Annoyance: Bookmarks, Favorites, whatever you call them, are driving me crazy! I want to be able to transfer my IE Favorites from one computer to another, make my Netscape bookmarks available in IE, and so on. Why is this so hard to do?

The Fix: It's not as hard as you think. To copy Favorites from Internet Explorer to another computer running Internet Explorer, or to Netscape or Opera, choose File → Import and Export. In the Import/Export Wizard that launches, tell IE you want to export your Favorites. You'll be able to save your entire Favorites list, or just a selected folder, to your hard disk, a removable disk, or a network drive.

To import your faves into Internet Explorer on another computer, choose File → Import and Export and tell the Wizard where the exported Favorites from the first computer are saved (i.e., point to the correct CD, floppy disk, or network directory). That's it; they'll now appear in Internet Explorer, appended to your existing list of Favorites.

To import your Favorites into Netscape, select Bookmarks → Manage Bookmarks. In the Bookmark Manager that appears, choose Tools → Import and navigate to where you stored the Internet Explorer Favorites. In Opera, choose Bookmarks → Manage bookmarks. Then, from the Bookmark toolbar that appears, choose File → Import Internet Explorer favorites, and navigate to the Favorites folders you want to import. In both cases, the imported Favorites are appended to your existing set.

You can, of course, export bookmarks from Netscape or Opera to Internet Explorer as well. In Netscape, choose Bookmarks → Manage Bookmarks, and in the Bookmark Manager, choose Tools → Export. Save the bookmarks file, and then use Internet Explorer's Import/Export Wizard to import them. In Opera, choose Bookmarks → Manage bookmarks, then choose File → Export as HTML from the Bookmark toolbar that appears. Save the bookmarks file, and then use Internet Explorer's Import/Export Wizard to import them.

SEARCH YOUR FAVORITES

The Annoyance: I've got hundreds of Favorites, and trying to find the one I want *now* is impossible. There's absolutely no search feature in Internet Explorer at all!

The Fix: Ah, Windows Explorer to the rescue. Fire it up, go to the Favorites folder at *C:\Documents and Settings\<Your Name>\Favorites*, and click the Search button on Explorer's toolbar (look for the magnifying glass). Click the "All files and folders" link, enter your search terms in either the "All or part of the file name" box or the "A word or phrase in the file" box, and click the Search button. Chances are your search phrase will be in either the name you gave the Favorite or the site's URL.

An easier, faster way to track down your Favorites is to download the freebie DzSoft Favorites Search (*http://www.dzsoft.com/favseek.htm*). Just click the new Favorites Search button on Internet Explorer's toolbar, and a handy vertical search window appears, splitting the screen. Type a word or letters that are part of the URL or site name, click the Find button, and the Faves are listed, lickety split. Click a link, and the site is displayed on the right. Neat.

ALPHABETIZE YOUR FAVORITES

The Annoyance: Whenever I add a new Favorite or create a new Favorites folder in Internet Explorer, it adds it to the bottom of the list. Call me old-fashioned, but I like to organize things alphabetically. Don't tell me I have to manually alphabetize the entire list!

The Fix: It's a mystery why Internet Explorer doesn't do this automatically, but it doesn't. (Does someone need to teach Microsoft the alphabet?) To alphabetize your Favorites, right-click a folder or a Favorite that is not within a folder, and select Sort by Name. They'll be alphabetized automatically (for the moment, anyway—you'll need to do this regularly as you add new favorites and folders to keep them in alphabetical order). Note that Favorites within folders won't be sorted alphabetically; this trick only alphabetizes the order of folders and Favorites that aren't in folders.

If you want to alphabetize Favorites within a folder, select the folder so that all of its Favorites are displayed. Then right-click any Favorite within it, and choose Sort by Name. The Favorites within that folder—and only within that folder—will be alphabetized.

JUMP THROUGH YOUR FAVORITES LIST

The Annoyance: I have a list of Favorites that's about a mile long, which means scrolling to the bottom or the top takes forever. How do I jump quickly to the top or bottom of the list?

The Fix: You can do it, but you'll have to first display your Favorites in Internet Explorer's Favorites pane on the lefthand side of the screen (see Figure 5-8). Press Ctrl-I to make this pane appear. To jump to the bottom of the list, press Ctrl-End; to jump to the top, press Ctrl-Home.

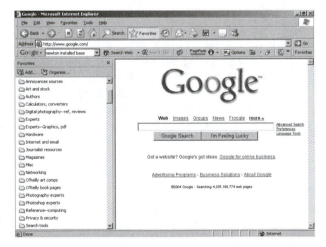

Figure 5-8. To jump quickly up and down the Favorites list, open the Favorites window and use Ctrl-End and Ctrl-Home.

WHY CAN'T I PRINT MY IE FAVORITES?

The Annoyance: I'd like to print out all my Favorites, organized by folder and name, but there doesn't seem to be a way to do it. Did Microsoft really leave something this simple out of its supposedly world-class browser?

The Fix: Yes, Microsoft did leave it out, but you can print out your Favorites if you follow this workaround. You'll first export your Favorites to an HTML file, then print *that*. Here's how:

1. In Internet Explorer, choose File → Import and Export. The Import/Export Wizard will appear. Click the Next button.

2. In the screen that appears, choose Export Favorites and click Next.

3. If you want to print out all of your Favorites, highlight Favorites at the top of the screen, and click Next. If you only want to print out a single folder, highlight that folder, then click Next. (Alas, it's all or one; you can't print out a select number of folders.)

4. In the screen that appears, select the "Export to a File or Address" radio button, then click the Browse button and select the destination where you want your Favorites list (as an HTML file) stored. Supply a name, click Save, and then click Next.

5. Click the Finish button, then OK, then OK again. The HTML (*.htm*) file is now saved on your hard disk.

6. In Internet Explorer, choose File → Open, and open the HTML file.

7. A list of all your Favorites (by name, organized by folder) will appear in IE. Choose File → Print, and you're done!

Alas, this won't print out the actual web addresses. If you want the URLs, here's a semi-successful workaround: perform steps 1 through 6, then choose File → Print, click the Options tab, check the "Print table of links" box, and click the Print button. This will generate the folder/Favorites listing you got above, followed by a table that lists the Favorites' names on the left and the actual web addresses on the right. The downsides: the folder names aren't printed in the table, and really long web addresses may be truncated.

THE LINKS FOLDER: THE MOST ANNOYING FAVORITE

The Annoyance: I like to keep my Internet Explorer Favorites list lean and clean, so I deleted the pointless Links folder by right-clicking it and choosing Delete. That did the trick—at least until the next time I started Internet Explorer. Then it returned, like Dracula rising from the dead. What's the silver bullet for killing this annoying folder?

The Fix: Put away the revolver. To remove this Folder of the Undead, exhume the Windows Registry Editor. First, exit Internet Explorer. Then select Start → Run, type `regedit` in the Open box, and press Enter. In the Registry Editor, navigate to `HKEY_CURRENT_USER\Software\Microsoft\Internet Explorer\Toolbar`. In the righthand window, double-click the `LinksFolderName` item. In the "Value data" box, delete the word "Links," and leave the box blank. Click OK and exit the Registry Editor. Restart Internet Explorer and delete the Links folder. No more rising from the grave; it'll stay deleted.

If you hate mucking around in the Registry, simply hide the Links folder. In Internet Explorer, right-click the Links folder, choose Properties, check the Hidden box, and click OK. The folder still exists; you've just made it invisible. To make it visible again, uncheck the Hidden box. You can also hide it by running Windows Explorer and going to *C:\Documents and Settings\<Your Name>\Favorites*. That's the location of your Favorites folder. You'll find a subfolder underneath it named Links. Right-click it, choose Properties, check the Hidden box, and click OK.

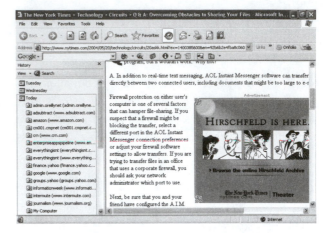

Figure 5-9. Go back to where you once were, using Internet Explorer's History pane.

DON'T KNOW MUCH ABOUT HISTORY?

The Annoyance: Several days ago I visited a web site and found a piece of information I'd been looking for. But I've forgotten the information—and what's worse, I can't remember the web site where I found it! How can I retrace my steps?

The Fix: Internet Explorer includes an easy-to-use History pane feature that lets you browse through the pages you've visited recently and, more to the point, lets you search them as well. Click the History button in Internet Explorer (look for the round clock with a green arrow moving counterclockwise), and the History pane will open on the lefthand side of the browser (see Figure 5-9).

You'll be able to go back through pages you've visited for up to the last 20 days, depending on how much memory you've devoted to your Internet cache.

To make it easier to find the site you're looking for, you can sort the pages in your History list in several ways. Click View, and then choose By Date, By Site, By Most Visited, or By Order Visited Today.

If that still doesn't help, you can search through your History pages. Click the Search button, type in a search term, and then click Search Now. A list of sites that match the term will be displayed.

You can control how many days Internet Explorer tracks in the History list. Choose Tools → Internet Options, and click the General tab. In the History section, change the "Days to keep pages in history" setting, and click OK.

WORKING THE INTERFACE

FILL FORMS FASTER

The Annoyance: I hate filling out forms on the Web. Internet Explorer helps some—as I start to type my name or a phone number into a field, it pops up a list of past entries, which I can stick in the field with a click. But it's a field-by-field chore. Why can't I fill out the entire form all at once?

The Fix: IE can't do it, but other tools can. The all-purpose Google Toolbar also includes a very handy form-filler that works with the click of a button. Simply fill out the Toolbar's form first, with your name, address, and any other info you'd likely have to enter at a web site. (You can even save your credit card number—password-protected, of course.) When you get to a site with, say, a registration form, click a button, and wham! The form is filled out. The free RoboForm does an even better job, automatically logging you into many sites, remembering much more information (it functions as a password manager, too), and working with any browser, not just Internet Explorer. Get it at *http://www.roboform.com*.

Beware of Gators

If anyone offers you a free form-filler called Gator eWallet, think twice. Considered adware/spyware by many, the program, as the company admits, "occasionally displays pop up ads on your computer screen based on your online behavior…" but "only your first name, postal/zip code, and country are sent to [the company]." Is that all? We'll pass. Caveat downloader!

STOP DEBUGGING ME!

The Annoyance: When I browse the Web using Internet Explorer, I am constantly assaulted by error boxes that say "A Runtime Error has occurred. Do you wish to Debug?" As far as I can tell, this note serves no purpose other than to annoy me. How can I stop this?

The Fix: That error message (see Figure 5-10) is designed to help developers fix problems, and you're right—it's of no use to you. You can easily turn it off. Choose Tools → Internet Options, click the Advanced tab, check the "Disable script debugging" box, uncheck the "Display a notification about every script error" box, then click OK.

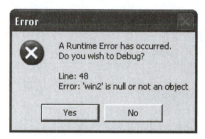

Figure 5-10. Say goodbye to this most annoying of Internet error messages when you configure Internet Explorer properly.

END TOOLBAR MADNESS

The Annoyance: I'm just a boy who can't say no—every time I see a toolbar or ActiveX control I can use for Internet Explorer, I download it. The Google Toolbar, Ask Jeeves Toolbar, Yahoo! Toolbar… you name it, I've got it. But now Internet Explorer crashes almost every time I load it. I'm sure it's due to all the toolbars and ActiveX controls I'm using. Do I have to remove these digital helpmates?

The Fix: If you have Windows XP SP2, Internet Explorer offers a simple way to disable toolbars, ActiveX controls, and browser extensions. Choose Tools → Internet Options, click the Programs tab, then click the Manage Add-ons button. Select the toolbar, ActiveX control, or add-on you want to turn off, choose Disable, and click

OK (Figure 5-11). You'll have to restart Internet Explorer for the changes to take effect.

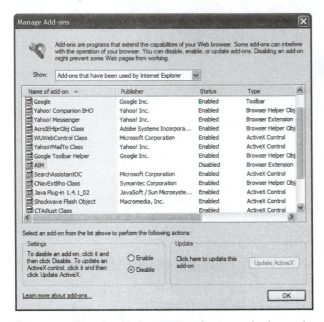

Figure 5-11. Upgrade to Windows XP SP2, and you can easily take control of unruly Internet Explorer add-ons.

If you don't have SP2, you can still uninstall ActiveX controls and toolbars, but it takes a bit more work. First, try to uninstall them as you would any other program, by opening the Add or Remove Programs control panel. Scroll to the ActiveX control or toolbar you want to uninstall, and click the Change or Remove button. It will be uninstalled. Not all ActiveX controls, toolbars, and browser extensions will show up, though. If the one you want to uninstall doesn't appear, open Windows Explorer and go to \Windows\Downloaded Program Files. Right-click the one you want to delete, and choose Remove.

TEACH ADOBE ACROBAT READER SOME MANNERS

The Annoyance: What's with Adobe Acrobat? Whenever I click a PDF file on a web site, it opens right in my browser. I want it to open in a separate window. Worse, when I close the PDF file, Acrobat keeps running in the background, sucking up RAM. How can I teach it some manners?

The Fix: Simple—force Acrobat to open in a separate window. Run Adobe Acrobat and choose Edit → Preferences. Select Internet from the list on the left, uncheck the "Display PDF in browser" box, and click OK (Figure 5-12). From now on, when you click a PDF file, you'll get the File Download box. Choose Open, and Acrobat Reader will display the file in its own window. Better yet, when you close the Reader, it'll close properly and won't live on in memory.

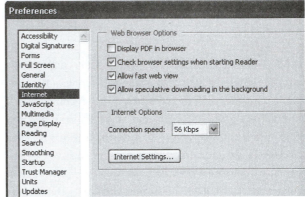

Figure 5-12. Stop the Adobe Acrobat Reader from launching in your browser, and living on in memory, from this screen.

If you like viewing PDFs in your browser, you can easily banish Acrobat from memory when you're done. Just right-click the Windows Taskbar at the bottom of the screen and choose Task Manager. On the Processes tab, select Acrord32 or acrobat.exe, and click the End Process button.

OLD NEWS IS NOT GOOD NEWS

The Annoyance: I'm a news junkie, but sometimes when I'm on a news site and I refresh the page, nothing changes, even though I know there's new news. Has Internet Explorer gone senile?

The Fix: Normally, when you click the Refresh button (or press F5 or Ctrl-R), Internet Explorer reloads the page. You would think it would reload the newest page from the server, but that's not always the case. Internet Explorer always checks the timestamp of the web page on the server, and if it matches the timestamp of the page that's already stored in your browser cache, it reloads the page from the cache, not from the web server. The result: old news.

For a true refresh, press the Ctrl key when you click the Refresh button, or press Ctrl-F5, and you'll reload the latest page from the server.

ZAP ZIP

The Annoyance: I downloaded a Zip file the other day and accidentally unchecked the "Always ask before opening this type of file" box. Now whenever I download a Zip file, WinZip jumps up and extracts it. It's a real pain in the neck—most of the time I just want to download the file and open it later. How can I stop this annoying behavior?

The Fix: In Windows Explorer, choose Tools → Folder Options, and click the File Types tab. Scroll to the bottom of the list and find "ZIP WinZip File." Click the Advanced button, check the "Confirm open after download" box, click OK, and then click OK again. The annoyance is now banished!

FIND THE HIDDEN BUTTON

The Annoyance: Internet Explorer toolbars drive me up the wall. For no reason I can figure out, the Print button has simply vanished, and I can't figure out where it went. How can I find it again and put it back on the toolbar?

The Fix: If you cram a lot of buttons onto the toolbar, some buttons may disappear. They're not gone; they've just been pushed offstage. Look for a double-sided arrow and click it, and a list of buttons that can't fit on the toolbar will appear. Click on any button to use it.

A better solution is to reorganize your toolbar so that the ones you use most often are visible. Right-click an empty part of the toolbar and choose Customize. In the Customize Toolbar dialog box that appears (Figure 5-13), you can add and delete icons. To add one, highlight it on the left

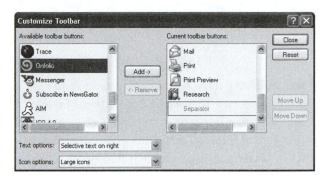

Figure 5-13. Make the IE toolbar your own by picking which buttons you want on the toolbar.

(in the "Available toolbar buttons" list) and click the Add button. To delete it, highlight it on the right (under "Current toolbar buttons") and click the Remove button.

To move the buttons around, alas, you can't just click and drag them. Instead, you must open the Customize Toolbar dialog box and drag them up and down in the "Current toolbar buttons" list. You can, however, drag and drop the toolbars to move them around (within limits). First, unlock the toolbars. Right-click on an empty area of a toolbar, and uncheck the "Lock the toolbars" option. A series of vertical lines, called "handles," will appear at the left end of every toolbar.

You can now resize and move a toolbar, by grabbing a handle and dragging it (and the attached toolbar) up and down in the stack of toolbars at the top of the IE screen. When you're done, lock the toolbars in place by right-clicking on an empty area of a toolbar and checking the "Lock the toolbars" option. Note: you can't truly "undock" IE's toolbars and move them to the bottom of the screen, or flip them 90 degrees and store them vertically on the right or left side of the screen.

The Links toolbar may be the most misunderstood part of Internet Explorer. Why is it there, and what do you use it for? It's a way to give you one-click access to your favorite web sites, quicker than using Favorites. When you're at a web site, drag its URL to the Links toolbar, and a button will appear that, when clicked, jumps you to that site.

SAVE DOWNLOADS WHERE YOU WANT

The Annoyance: I want to download all files to the same directory: *C:\Download*. But Internet Explorer is a poor learner; it insists on first trying to download them to the default directory, and I then have to navigate to get to *C:\Download*. Can't I teach it to obey?

The Fix: Internet Explorer is stubborn about such things, but you can force it to download files to whatever folder you want by tweaking the Windows Registry. Run the Registry Editor and go to HKEY_CURRENT_USER\ Software\Microsoft\Internet Explorer. Double-click the "Download Directory" item in the righthand window, and enter the desired destination folder in the "Value data" box. Exit the Registry, close Internet Explorer, and restart, and the changes will take effect.

PRINT THAT WEB PAGE—ALL OF IT!

The Annoyance: Before traveling to a hotel in an unfamiliar town, I always print out driving directions from the hotel's web site. But the printout invariably looks like this:

```
Proceed for five miles until you come to a
on the right. One and a half miles later, and
continue on. Drive until you see Exi
```

Why does this happen? The pages are perfectly (and completely) readable online. Why don't they print properly?

The Fix: You can tell your browser that when it prints out a web page, it should devote more of the space to text and pictures, and less to the right and left margins. Here's how to do it in Internet Explorer, Netscape Navigator, and Opera:

Internet Explorer

Choose File → Page Setup, and in the "Margins (inches)" section at the bottom of the dialog box, reduce the right and/or left margins. The default is 0.75 inches, so try 0.5 inches for the right margin, and see if it helps. Click OK once you've made your changes.

You can check whether it will print properly by previewing the page (File → Print Preview). Keep changing the margins until the entire page prints out correctly.

Netscape Navigator

Choose File → Page Setup → Margins & Header/Footer, reduce the right and/or left margins, and click OK. As with Internet Explorer, preview the page before printing by choosing File → Print Preview, and then redo the margins until you get the settings right.

Opera

Choose File → Print options, reduce the right and/or left margins, and click OK. Note that Opera's measurements are in centimeters, not inches. The default is 1.5 centimeters, or about .6 inches. A centimeter equals about .4 inches, so make your changes accordingly. As with Internet Explorer and Navigator, preview the page by choosing File → Print Preview, and then redo the margins until you get the settings right.

If this technique doesn't work with the page in question, print out the page in landscape mode.

One More Way to Fix the Problem

If you don't want to fiddle with browser margins or landscape mode, there's another simple solution: use a screen-capture program. It will capture your browser screen and send that screen to the printer as-is, so your whole page will print. An excellent option is Snag-It, available as try-before-you buy software at *http://www. techsmith.com*. Use it for free for 30 days, then pay $39.95. An especially useful feature is its ability to capture only text from a web page, so you won't print distracting ads.

BYPASS WEB SITE LOGINS

The Annoyance: It drives me crazy that so many sites require that I register before I use them. It's bad enough spending my precious time registering, but they also ask for private information. Then, to add insult to injury, they send me spam! Is there some way I can get around the registration process?

The Fix: Help is on the way. The site BugMeNot (*http://www.bugmenot.com*) will give you usernames and passwords for many sites that require registration. When you want to log in, just use the username and password that BugMeNot provides. That way, you'll be able to log in, but you won't be annoyed by the registration process, and you won't get sent irritating spam.

The site claims to have usernames and passwords for 14,000 different web sites that require registration. Using the site is simplicity itself: just type in the name of the site that you want to visit without registering, and BugMeNot supplies you with a username and password you can use for the site.

PLUG-INS MAKE IT EASIER TO USE BUGMENOT

It can be a bit of a pain to use BugMeNot. When you come across a web site that requires registration, you have to head over to BugMeNot, get a username and password, head back to the site, and then type in the information.

There's a faster solution: run a plug-in right inside your browser that fetches the username and password from BugMeNot behind the scenes. When you're at a site that requires registration, right-click in your browser, choose BugMeNot from the menu, and a username and password for the site will pop up. Copy and paste them into the site, and you're ready to go.

For the plug-in for Internet Explorer, head to *http://www.unixdaemon.net/zips/bugmenot.exe*. If you use the Mozilla or Firefox browsers, head instead to *http://extensions.roachfiend.com/index.html#bugmenot*.

ORGANIZE YOUR WEB CLIPPINGS

The Annoyance: As I browse the Web, I like to collect snippets of information and even entire web pages. I cut and paste them into Microsoft Word documents, which is worse than useless, since there's no simple way to organize them or find them. Is there a better way of storing the information?

The Fix: Forget Word. You need Onfolio, a nifty Internet Explorer add-in that lets you save entire web pages, or snippets of web pages, in browsable and searchable collections. You can have one collection for recipes, for example, and then organize that collection into separate folders for pasta, chicken, and so on. You can create as many collections and folders as you want, and then not only browse quickly through them, but also search through them for text. You can even save text from other programs, such as Word, in your collections.

Onfolio installs directly inside Internet Explorer and sits in the lefthand pane (Figure 5-14). When you want to add pages or snippets to it, just click a button. You can do a full-text search on the text, searching for a word or

Figure 5-14. Capture web snippets and entire web pages and organize them in searchable collections with Onfolio.

phrase, using Boolean operators such as AND and OR. Searches are lightning fast and span multiple folders. You can even quickly create a report or set up an RSS feed.

The newest version of the program works as an add-on to Internet Explorer and Firefox, but you can use the stand-alone Onfolio Deskbar with other browsers. The only difference is that you drag the URL from the browser into the Deskbar; then you use the Onfolio tools in the same fashion. You can try Onfolio for free for 30 days; if you keep it, you'll have to pay $49.95. Get it from *http://www. onfolio.com.*

KEEP INTERNET EXPLORER MAXIMIZED

The Annoyance: Sometimes, for no reason at all, when I launch Internet Explorer it opens as a small window. I always want it maximized when I launch it—how can I teach it to remember to start big?

The Fix: One reason Internet Explorer opens in a small window is because it remembers the window size and position from the last time you closed it. So if you close it and it's not maximized, the next time you launch it, it won't open maximized.

One simple fix that should work is to always make sure the window is maximized when you exit IE. If it opens minimized, maximize the window, exit IE, then open it again. It should now be maximized and stay that way, unless you shrink the window and then close the browser.

If this doesn't work, turn to the free utility IE New Window Maximizer, from *http://www.jiisoft.com/iemaximizer.* It will force Internet Explorer (and Outlook) to always launch maximized. You can also use it to launch new Internet Explorer windows in the background, and close or hide all Internet Explorer windows by pressing a hotkey.

t i p

Some people are fans of Internet Explorer's full-screen mode (toggled by pressing F11), in which it takes up the entire desktop, to the point of hiding the menu and address bars. If you want it to always open that way, close Internet Explorer, then run the Registry Editor and go to HKEY_CURRENT_USER\Software\ Microsoft\Internet Explorer\Main. Double-click the FullScreen item in the righthand pane, change the value in the "Value data" box to Yes, and exit the Registry. The next time you start Internet Explorer, it will open in full-screen mode. Change the value to No if you want to return to IE's default.

TRACK DOWN THE GOOGLE TOOLBAR

The Annoyance: I installed the Google Toolbar, but when I go to View → Toolbars, the Google Toolbar isn't listed—which means there's no way to turn it on or off. Instead, I see two menu entries labeled Radio. What gives?

The Fix: You're not alone—a number of people have reported this bug. There's a simple fix, however. Just choose the second Radio entry—that's the Google Toolbar.

PUT YOUR BRAND ON INTERNET EXPLORER

The Annoyance: I own a small company and I want to brand Internet Explorer by putting my company logo and name on it, but I can't figure out how.

The Fix: There's not much you can alter—just Internet Explorer's title bar and the IE logo in the upper-right corner. (If you're using Windows XP Pro, see the sidebar "Easier Way to Change Logos"). Here's how to change the title bar and logo.

Change Internet Explorer's title bar

The title bar in Internet Explorer says—surprise!—Microsoft Internet Explorer. Accurate, but rather dull. Here's how to change it to say anything you want:

1. Run the Windows Registry Editor.

2. Go to `HKEY_CURRENT_USER\Software\Microsoft\Internet Explorer\Main`.

3. In the righthand window, right-click in a blank area and select New → String Value. Type `Window Title` in the box and press Enter. Now double-click the Window Title item and, in the "Value data" box, enter what you want to appear in IE's title bar—for example, `Mr. Bill's Browser`. (If the Window Title item is already in your Registry, just double-click it and add your custom title.)

4. Exit the Registry Editor.

5. When you start Internet Explorer, your text will appear in the title bar after the name of the web site you're visiting (Figure 5-15).

Figure 5-15. Oh, no, Mr. Bill! Your name's in the browser title bar! It's easy to use the Registry to change IE's title bar to anything you want.

Change Internet Explorer's logo

This takes a bit more work, especially if you want your own animated logo. Before you make the change, here's a bit of background on logos. Internet Explorer has both a static logo and an animated logo. The static logo is what you see when the browser is just sitting there. The animated logo flutters when the browser is doing something, such as downloading a page from the Web. There are two sizes of static and animated logos: small and large. (You can display either large or small icons on the Internet Explorer toolbar. To switch between the two logo sizes, choose View → Toolbars → Customize, and select the desired size from the Icons drop-down.)

The static and animated logos you create for Internet Explorer will also appear in Outlook Express.

Your first step is to create the new logos. You'll have to create two sets of icons in *.bmp* format—one set for the smaller logo and one set for the larger logo—each with a static and animated version. The static logos should be 22 by 22 pixels for the small icon and 38 by 38 pixels for the large icon. The animated logos must be animated bitmaps and should have a total of 10 frames, no more, no less. Internet Explorer cycles through those 10 frames, which is how it creates an animated effect. The small animated bitmap should be 22 pixels wide by 220 pixels high, and the large animated bitmap should be 38 pixels wide by 380 pixels high.

You can create the static bitmaps with any graphics program, including the Paint program that comes with XP. Unless you're a pro at this kind of thing, however, it's easiest to use an icon-creation program such as Microangelo Toolset, available at *http://www.microangelo.us*. It's free to try, but expect to pay $54.95 if you want to keep it. A specialized tool like Microangelo will also make it easier to create the animated bitmaps.

Easier Way to Change Logos

If you're running XP Professional, you can change IE's logos without editing the Registry. Instead, turn to the all-purpose Group Policy Editor. Select Start → Run, type `gpedit.msc`, and press Enter. Under User Configuration, open *\Windows Settings\Internet Explorer Maintenance\Browser User Interface*. In the window on the right, double-click Custom Logo, and in the dialog box that appears, supply the locations of the large and small static and animated logos you've created.

Now that you've created the icons, you're ready to plug them into Internet Explorer. Here's how:

1. Run the Registry Editor and open HKEY_LOCAL_ MACHINE\SOFTWARE\Microsoft → Internet Explorer\ Main. This key contains many important Internet Explorer settings. You're going to create new settings here to tell Internet Explorer to display the static logos.

2. In the righthand window, right-click in a blank area and select New → String Value. Type SmallBitmap in the box and press Enter. Then create a second String Value the same way, and name it BigBitmap. These values will tell Internet Explorer to display the static logos. Double-click the SmallBitmap item, and enter the path and filename of the small bitmap you created in the "Value data" box (for example, C:\ Windows\IEsmalllogo.bmp). Then do the same for the BigBitmap item, specifying the path and filename of the big bitmap (for example, C:\Windows\IEbiglogo. bmp).

3. Now it's time to tell Internet Explorer to use your animated logos. Go to HKEY_LOCAL_MACHINE\SOFTWARE\ Microsoft\Internet Explorer\Toolbar. Create two String Values, named SmBrandBitmap and BrandBitmap. These values will tell Internet Explorer to display the animated logos. Double-click the SmBrandBitmap item and enter the filename and full location of the small animated bitmap you created in the "Value data" box (for example, C:\Windows\ IEsmallanimatedlogo.bmp). Then do the same for the BrandBitmap item, specifying the location and filename of the big animated bitmap (for example, C:\ Windows\IEbiganimatedlogo.bmp).

4. Exit the Registry.

You'll have to restart Internet Explorer for the changes to take effect and for the new logos to be displayed. To go back to the original Internet Explorer logos, simply delete the Registry entries you created.

KEEP TABS IN INTERNET EXPLORER

The Annoyance: When will Internet Explorer join the 21st century? Any other browser worth its salt uses tabs for easy browsing.

The Fix: Tabs let you keep multiple sites open at the same time, so that you can jump back and forth between sites with just a click. Both Netscape and Opera use tabs, but for reasons known only to Microsoft, Internet Explorer doesn't. However, WebTools, available from *http:// www.microgarden.com/webtools*, adds them into Internet Explorer (see Figure 5-16). Download and install the utility, close and restart Internet Explorer, and voilà—instant tabs. It's shareware, so you can try it for free. If you keep it, the registration fee is $14.95.

Figure 5-16. Look just underneath the Address Bar and you'll see multiple open sites, represented by tabs.

Another excellent bet is Maxthon (né MyIE2), a browser based on Internet Explorer that uses tabs and adds other goodies as well, such as a "mouse gestures" features that lets you navigate the Web and issue commands just by moving your mouse. Get it for free at *http://www.max-thon.com*.

If you really dig tabs, drop IE and turn to Firefox, the best tabbed browser around. This free browser, based on Mozilla, is available at *http://www.mozilla.org/products/ firefox*. In addition to using tabs, it loads more quickly than Internet Explorer and has a lot of extras, such as extensions that give it all kinds of new features. (See the next annoyance for details.)

BETTER TABBED BROWSING IN FIREFOX

The Annoyance: I love Firefox's tabs, but one thing annoys me. When I click a link that opens a site, I'd rather have it open as a tab than a new window. After all, what's the point of a tabbed browser if you have a zillion windows open? But I can't seem to make Firefox do this.

The Fix: Firefox lets you install "extensions" that add extra features to the browser, and I've got an extension just for you. You want to open a site as a tab? Install the Single Window extension. Choose Tools → Extensions and click Get More Extensions. You'll be sent to a web site with dozens of extensions, organized by category. Scroll until you see the Tabbed Browsing category on the lefthand side of the page, and click it. On the page that appears, scroll down until you see Single Window, then click Install.

PAGES DON'T DISPLAY PROPERLY IN FIREFOX

The Annoyance: I'm a big Firefox fan, but the world revolves around Internet Explorer. So I sometimes come across sites that have been built specifically for IE and look kind of screwy in Firefox—the fonts are tiny, or the graphics are misplaced, or the page looks just plain weird. Help this Firefox fanatic!

The Fix: Until web designers all adhere to HTML standards, rather than building sites specifically for Internet Explorer, you'll be faced with this problem. Your best bet is to install IEView, a Firefox extension that allows you to instantly open any page you're visiting in Internet

> ### IS FIREFOX THE BEST ALTERNATIVE BROWSER?
>
> **If you're looking for an alternative to Internet Explorer, consider Firefox, a new browser that has developed a cult following because of its speed and extra features (such as tabbed browsing, which lets you store multiple open sites on different tabs). People claim that it's noticeably faster than Internet Explorer, and it's safer as well, because it's not prone to the same security holes. Firefox is open source and is based on Mozilla. It's free, it includes a pop-up blocker and a built-in Google search function, and it's a svelte download at only 4.7 MB. Get it from *http://www.mozilla.org/products/firefox*.**

Explorer. Get it from *http://ieview.mozdev.org*. After you've installed it, right-click any page you're on, and choose "View this page in IE." The page will launch inside a new Internet Explorer window.

WHY CAN'T I USE WINDOWS UPDATE WITH OPERA OR NETSCAPE?

The Annoyance: I'm not a big fan of Internet Explorer and its security vulnerabilities—in fact, I refuse to use it and instead use Opera or Netscape. But when I try to get Windows patches and updates at the Windows Update site (*http://windowsupdate.microsoft.com*), the site doesn't work. Is Microsoft so hard-core about its competitors that it blocks them from using its update site?

The Fix: The problem is that Windows Update uses ActiveX, and neither Opera nor Netscape (or Mozilla) supports ActiveX. That means they aren't capable of using the site, or other sites that use ActiveX. Several plug-ins have been developed that purportedly allow Netscape, Mozilla, or Opera to use ActiveX controls, but at press time they were still works in progress—you're better off staying away from them until they're more solid.

For now, either use Internet Explorer for Windows Update, or use Windows's built-in automatic update capabilities. In Windows XP, right-click My Computer, choose Properties, and click the Automatic Updates tab. If you want Windows to automatically download and install updates, select Automatic, and choose a schedule. If you'd prefer that XP automatically download updates but tell you when they've been downloaded so that you can install them manually, select "Download updates for me, but let me choose when to install them." And if you only want to be notified when updates are available, so you can download and install them yourself, select "Notify me but don't automatically download or install them." When you're done making your selection, click OK.

SPEEDUPS AND SHORTCUTS

INSTANT INTERNET SPEEDUP

The Annoyance: My life has three speeds: fast, faster, and fastest. I'll do anything to juice up my browsing speed. I've heard about some obscure file called a *HOSTS* file that can get me to sites super-quickly—how do I use it?

The Fix: Yes, a *HOSTS* file can speed up access to certain web sites, if you set it up correctly. But first, a bit of background. You navigate the Web by typing a site's name (called a hostname), such as *www.oreilly.com*, into your browser. But web servers and Internet routers can't understand English—they need those URLs translated into numeric IP addresses (such as *208.201.239.37*). DNS servers do this automatically behind the scenes as you surf the Web.

However, it takes time to send your request to a DNS server, have the server look up the proper IP address, and then send the IP address back to your PC. You can eliminate that delay by creating or editing a local *HOSTS* file on your PC that contains the hostnames of sites you frequently visit and their corresponding IP addresses. Windows will first look in the *HOSTS* file to see if there's an entry for the hostname. If there is one, it will grab the IP address from there instead of querying a DNS server. The *HOSTS* file is a plain text file that you can create and edit with a text editor such as Notepad. You'll find an existing *HOSTS* file in *C:\Windows\System32\Drivers\Etc.* (The file has no extension.) Open it in Notepad and enter the IP addresses and hostnames of your commonly visited web sites, like this:

```
208.201.239.37      oreilly.com
207.171.166.102     amazon.com
```

Each entry in the file should be on its own line. At least one space should separate the two columns. You can add a comment to the file by preceding the line with a pound sign (#), in which case the entire line is ignored by Windows; or by putting a # after the hostname, in which case only the comment following it will be ignored. For example, you might want to comment on individual entries, like this:

```
130.94.155.164      gralla.com      #still in beta
```

When you finish editing the file, save it to its existing location. From now on, you'll speed up browsing to the sites you've put into your *HOSTS* file.

SPEEDUP SOFTWARE KILLS WEB SITE ACCESS

The Annoyance: I installed a program that promised to speed up my Internet access. It didn't do much good, so I stopped using it. But now I can't get to certain web sites. What's the fix?

The Fix: Many Internet speedup tools add entries to your *HOSTS* file to speed up access. But your *HOSTS* file can easily become outdated, and if it contains old entries that are no longer valid, you won't be able to visit those web sites. To fix the problem, edit the *HOSTS* file as explained in the "Instant Internet Speedup" annoyance. Check the entries for sites you aren't able to visit, and either update the IP addresses or delete the entries. You'll be able to visit the sites from now on. You can also delete the entire *HOSTS* file—the next time you start Windows, a blank *HOSTS* file will be created.

REAL MEN DON'T USE MICE

The Annoyance: Real men (and women) don't use mice, and I'm a real man. I'm sick of having to constantly reach for the mouse to perform even the simplest tasks. Make my day—show me how to run Internet Explorer without a rodent.

The Fix: Here are two of my favorite mouseless timesavers: to quickly highlight the Address Bar (so you can type in an URL right away), press Alt-D. Once there, save your fingers some more—just type the core address (such as "oreilly") and press Ctrl-Enter. IE will slap on the "www." and ".com" and take you to the site.

IE has a gaggle of other keyboard shortcuts, too. F11 toggles between full-screen and normal-screen modes, Ctrl-N opens a new window, Ctrl-O lets you select and open a file, Ctrl-I opens the Favorites window, and so on. To get a complete list, venture into IE's help system. Select Help → Contents and Index, and click the Index tab. Type keyboard shortcuts in the "Type in the keyword to find" box, press Enter, and click the "Using Internet Explorer keyboard shortcuts" link. You'll see the keyboard shortcuts, broken down into a few categories. To see all of the shortcuts on a single page, visit *http://support.microsoft.com/default.aspx?scid=kb;en-us;306832*.

STOP AUTOCOMPLETE REMINDERS

The Annoyance: I'm not a big fan of Internet Explorer's AutoComplete function, which pops up a list of related words or URLs I can choose whenever I start typing in an address. So I turned it off. (The steps: Tools → Internet Options, click the Content tab, click the Auto-Complete button, and uncheck all the boxes.) But Internet Explorer is like a telemarketer when it comes to AutoComplete—it constantly asks me if I want to turn it on. How can I make it shut up?

The Fix: Internet Explorer does seem to love this feature. You can turn off the nagging, however, using the Windows Registry Editor:

1. Close Internet Explorer.

2. Launch the Registry Editor.

3. Go to HKEY_CURRENT_USER\Software\Policies\ Microsoft\Internet Explorer\Control Panel. If this key doesn't exist, go to HKEY_CURRENT_USER\Software\ Policies\Microsoft and create a new key underneath it called Internet Explorer. (How? Right-click Microsoft, select New → Key, and type Internet Explorer in the box. Now right-click the Internet Explorer item you just created, select New → Key, and name it Control Panel).

4. With the Control Panel item selected on the left, right-click in a blank area in the righthand window, select New → DWORD value, and name it FormSuggest. Double-click the FormsSuggest item, type 1 in the "Value data" box, and click OK.

5. Exit the Registry. Internet Explorer will no longer nag you to use AutoComplete.

PASSWORD HELP FOR THE MEMORY-IMPAIRED

The Annoyance: I recently revisited a web site that required a password. I'd created one months ago, but I couldn't remember it. Luckily, Internet Explorer automatically entered it for me—but it hid it behind a row of asterisks. I know this is a security feature, but is there any way to find out what's behind the asterisks?

The Fix: Download a copy of the free Asterisk Key utility from *http://www.lostpassword.com/asterisk.htm*. It'll show you the passwords hidden behind almost any row of asterisks.

WHY CAN'T I SAVE IMAGES AS GIFS OR JPEGS?

The Annoyance: Whenever I try to save a web page graphic in Internet Explorer by right-clicking the graphic and choosing Save Picture As, the only option I'm given is to save it as a *.bmp* file, even if the file is a *.gif* or *.jpg*. Has IE gone cuckoo?

The Fix: The most likely cause of the problem is that IE's Temporary Internet Files folder has gotten full. Clean it out by choosing Tools → Internet Options, selecting the General tab, clicking the Delete Files button, and then clicking OK. That'll clear out the folder, and you should now be able to save graphics in the appropriate format.

WHY WON'T INTERNET EXPLORER LET ME DOWNLOAD?

The Annoyance: I've just installed Service Pack 2 for Windows XP, and now Internet Explorer can't download files! I've heard that SP2's purpose was to beef up Windows security, but this is ridiculous.

The Fix: Microsoft seems to have a tough time balancing security and simplicity. By default, the new and improved version of Internet Explorer that SP2 installs (without asking you, of course) doesn't let you download any files from the Internet. To override this dumb default, choose Tools → Internet Options, click the Security tab, click the Internet icon, and click the Custom Level button. In the Downloads section, click Enable under "File download," and then click OK. You'll be able to download from anywhere now.

With this updated IE, you can choose to allow downloads only from certain sites. To use this feature, don't turn off download blocking. When you get to a site from which you want to accept downloads, click IE's Information Bar (which appears under the Address Bar when a download or pop-up is blocked) and choose "Allow this page to download files" (see Figure 5-17). You'll be able to download files from that site from now on.

Figure 5-17. Service Pack 2 for XP automatically blocks downloads, but you can tell it to let you download from specific sites.

TURN OFF THE NOTIFICATION BOX

Whenever you successfully download a file, Internet Explorer pops up a box giving you the news. But this reminder can be a real annoyance: it pops up over whatever else you're currently doing and won't go away until you click it. Here's how to stop the box from popping up:

1. **Run the Registry Editor.**

2. **Go to** `HKEY_CURRENT_USER\Software\` `Microsoft\Internet Explorer\Main`**.**

3. **Locate the NotifyDownloadComplete item in the righthand window. Double-click it and, in the "Value data" box, change** yes **to** no**.**

4. **Exit the Registry, and close and restart Internet Explorer. You may need to restart your computer for the change to take effect.**

COOKIES

TOSS YOUR COOKIES

The Annoyance: People complain about Internet cookies, but I figured it was much ado about bupkis. Then a friend showed me the directory where they're stored on my PC. Holy Moly! There were hundreds of them, a lot of them from ad sites that were most likely tracking my surfing activities. How can I toss these cookies?

The Fix: To send them all into oblivion, from IE simply select Tools → Internet Options, go to the General tab, click the Delete Cookies button, then click OK. (Netscape and other browsers have comparable tools for this.) However, this is an extreme measure, and it doesn't prevent future cookies from hiding out on your PC.

Keep in mind that cookies are both good and bad. These small text files planted on your PC by web sites can be used to track your Internet activity, or they can log you into web sites and allow you to customize the way you use the Web. Some sites require you to use cookies to work properly. For example, if you delete all your cookies, your Amazon.com wish list won't appear the next time you visit their site.

Still, they can be privacy invaders, too—the key in controlling cookies is distinguishing the good from the bad and then letting the good ones through and stopping the bad ones.

Internet Explorer lets you control cookies via six privacy settings, from Accept All Cookies to Block All Cookies. When choosing, keep in mind that some sites won't function well (or at all) at the higher privacy settings. The Medium High setting is usually a good compromise between protecting privacy and still being able to personalize web sites.

To customize your cookie settings in Internet Explorer, choose Tools → Internet Options, and click the Privacy tab (Figure 5-18). Then move the slider to the desired cookie setting. Table 5-2 describes each setting and what it does.

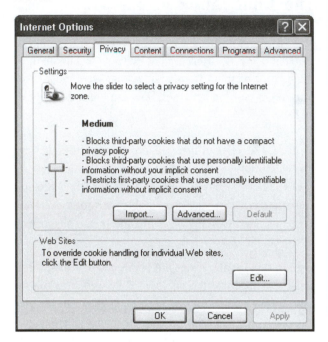

Figure 5-18. Move the slider to change Internet Explorer's cookie controls.

Table 5-2. Internet Explorer's privacy settings

Setting	How the setting affects your privacy
Block All Cookies	Blocks all cookies, without exception. Does not allow web sites to read existing cookies.
High	Blocks cookies from all web sites that don't have a compact privacy policy. (A compact privacy policy adheres to the standards set by the Privacy Preferences Project, or P3P, an industry standard for web privacy.) Blocks all cookies that use personally identifiable information without your explicit consent.
Medium High	Blocks third-party cookies from sites that don't have a compact privacy policy or that use personally identifiable information without your explicit consent. Blocks first-party cookies that use personally identifiable information without your implicit consent.
Medium (Default)	Blocks third-party cookies from sites that don't have a compact privacy policy or that use personally identifiable information without your implicit consent. Accepts all first-party cookies but deletes them when you close Internet Explorer.
Low	Blocks third-party cookies from sites that don't have a compact privacy policy. Accepts all other third-party cookies but deletes them when you close Internet Explorer.
Accept All Cookies	Accepts all cookies, without exception. Allows web sites to read existing cookies.

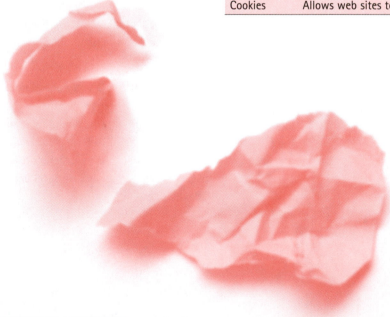

CUSTOMIZE INTERNET EXPLORER'S COOKIE HANDLING

The Annoyance: The cookie controls in IE are way too general. There's got to be a way I can dictate exactly which sites can cookie me and which can't.

The Fix: You can indeed. You can tell IE to accept or reject cookies from specific sites, or to accept or reject all first-party and/or third-party cookies.

To accept or reject all cookies from a specific site, choose Tools → Internet Options, click the Privacy tab, and click the Edit button. In the Per Site Privacy Actions dialog box (Figure 5-19), type the name of the site from which you want to accept or block cookies in the "Address of Web site" box, and click either Block or Allow.

Figure 5-19. The Per Site Privacy Actions dialog box lets you always block or always allow cookies from specific sites.

To customize how you handle first-party and third-party cookies, click the Advanced button on the Privacy tab, check the "Override automatic cookie handling" box, and click OK. Below, you can choose to accept or reject all first-party or third-party cookies, or be prompted whether to accept them. You can also decide to always allow *session cookies* (cookies that last only as long as you're on a specific web site and are deleted once you leave the site).

If you use Opera or Netscape, you aren't left out in the cold when it comes to handling cookies. In Opera, choose Tools → Preferences → Privacy and you'll be able to determine how cookies crumble. In Netscape, you can control cookies on a site-by-site basis. When you're at a site, choose Tools → Cookie Manager → Block Cookies from this Site. To unblock them, select Tools → Cookie Manager → Unblock Cookies from this Site.

A RARE COOKIE LOVER

The Annoyance: I just got a new PC, and now I can't automatically log into my favorite web sites, and sites that I've customized, such as My Yahoo!, don't remember me. I know it's because all my cookies are on my old PC. I actually *like* cookies. How can I move them to my new PC?

The Fix: It's easy to transfer cookies from PC to PC. On your old PC, open Internet Explorer and choose File → Import and Export. The Import/Export Wizard will launch. Choose Export Cookies and follow the directions. A single text file containing all your cookies will be created in *My Documents* (or a different destination of your choice, such as a removable disk or a network server). To import the cookies to your new computer, launch Internet Explorer, choose File → Import and Export to launch the Import/Export Wizard, choose Import Cookies, and browse to the location where you've stored the cookie file.

A BETTER COOKIE MANAGER

Better than browsers for handling cookies is Cookie Pal, available at *http://www.kburra.com*. Like Internet Explorer, it lets you easily dictate which sites you'll allow to place cookies on your PC and lets you accept or reject cookies on a case-by-case basis as you browse the Web. But wait, there's more! It has a cookie manager that lets you read and delete cookies, for example. It also lets you accept or reject cookies based on their expiration dates, lets you accept or reject cookies from a specific group of servers on the same domain, keeps a detailed list of all cookies accepted and rejected in a session, and more. If you don't use IE, though, you might be out of luck. As of this writing, Cookie Pal works only with Versions 3 and 4 of Netscape Navigator and Versions 4, 5, and 6 of Opera.

CAN I TRUST THIS WEB SITE?

The Annoyance: Many web sites don't date their pages or content, much less list their sources or even how to contact the site's authors. This makes it practically impossible to determine the validity of their information. What's a researcher to do?

The Fix: One way to find the date a page was posted is to look at the actual HTML file that creates the page. The date is often there. In Internet Explorer, choose View → Source. Notepad will launch, and in it will be the HTML code. Look through the file for a date—it's often at the bottom of the page. To view the HTML page in Netscape, choose View → Page Source. In Opera, choose View → Source.

To track down the owner of the web site, complete with contact information including name, address, phone number, and email address, do a Whois search. Head to *http://www.networksolutions.com/en_US/whois*, type in the name of the domain (such as *oreilly.com*), and you'll be shown the site's owner and contact information. Now it's up to you to make contact and determine whether the site is reputable or not.

Figure 5-20 shows the results of a sample Whois search. For more on Whois, see "Become Master of Your Own Domain" in Chapter 4.

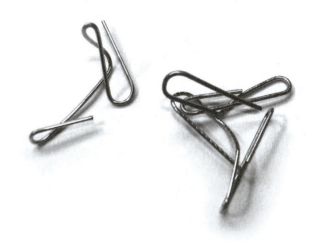

```
O'Reilly & Associates
1005 Gravenstein Hwy., North
Sebastopol, CA, 95472
US

Domain Name: OREILLY.COM

Administrative Contact -
DNS Admin - nic-ac@OREILLY.COM
O'Reilly & Associates, Inc.
1005 Gravenstein Highway North
Sebastopol, CA 95472
US
Phone - 707-827-7000
Fax - 707-823-9746
Technical Contact -
technical DNS - nic-tc@OREILLY.COM
O'Reilly & Associates
1005 Gravenstein Highway North
Sebastopol, CA 95472
US
Phone - 707-827-7000
Fax - - 707-823-9746

Record update date - 2004-05-19 07:07:44
Record create date - 1997-05-27
Record will expire on - 2005-05-26
Database last updated on - 2004-05-21 15:50:15
```

Run Whois from Your Desktop

Want Whois information right this second? Forget going to the Whois web site—download the free GeekTool Win32 Whois Client at *http://www.geektools.com/tools.php*. Double-click the GeekTool icon in the Windows System Tray, type in the name of the domain, click the Query button, and you'll get results, either in text or HTML, on the spot.

Figure 5-20. Do a Whois search to find out who owns a web site and to get contact information.

OPT OUT OF COOKIE-BASED AD NETWORKS

Online ad networks have the potential to create in-depth profiles of your web travels and personal interests. The trick? They place cookies on your hard disk that track you across multiple sites.

You can fight back by placing on your hard disk an opt-out cookie, provided by the ad network, that will tell the site to keep its nose out of your surfing habits.

To opt out of the DoubleClick online advertising network, go to *http://www.doubleclick.com/us/corporate/privacy/privacy/ad-cookie/* and click the "Ad Cookie Opt-Out" button at the bottom of the screen.

If you're using Internet Explorer, to see whether the opt-out worked, go to your cookies folder, which is typically C:\Documents and Settings\<Your Name>\Cookies. Look for a cookie that looks like <yourname>@doubleclick[1].txt, for example. The contents of thecookie—just double-click it to view it—should look something like this:

```
id OPT OUT doubleclick.net/ 1024 468938752
31583413 3447013104 29418226 *
```

If you use Netscape, the cookies.txt file is typically found in C:\Documents and Settings\<Your Name>\Mozilla\Profiles\default********.slt, where ******** is a random collection of numbers and letters (e.g., 46yhu2ir.slt). Look in the file for an entry that looks like this:

```
.doubleclick.net TRUE / FALSE 1920499138 id
OPT_OUT
```

You can use Netscape's built-in Cookie Manager to view the cookie, by choosing Tools → Cookie Manager → Manage Stored Cookies.

Some other advertising networks let you opt out as well. For details, go to *http://www.networkadvertising.org/optout_nonppii.asp* and follow the instructions for opting out. To confirm that you've successfully opted out of the other ad networks, click the Verify Cookies link in the toolbar on the left.

6

AOL
ANNOYANCES

AOL users, I feel your pain.

I feel it because I have been an AOL user for many years, and I have come across more annoyances than dandelions after an April shower.

I know that one of the greatest pleasures in any AOL user's life is venting about the service. So, please, feel free to continue venting—but let's go beyond our group hug (or group howl) and actually solve some of those annoyances. Sick of AOL screen clutter, the clueless email client, the grating "You've Got Mail!" greeting, and dozens of other annoyances? You've come to the right place.

GENERAL AOL ANNOYANCES

I DON'T CARE IF I'VE GOT MAIL!

The Annoyance: If I hear AOL's chirpy "You've Got Mail!" message one more time, I will pound my computer speakers into oblivion. How can I turn off this "Up with People" greeting?

The Fix: You're not alone in this desire, and fortunately the fix is simple. In AOL 9.0, sign in and select Settings on the AOL toolbar. Click the By Category tab and choose the A-Z tab. Then click N-S, select Sounds, and uncheck the "Enable AOL sounds such as the Welcome greeting and Instant Message chimes" box (Figure 6-1). Click Save, and the voice will disappear. In AOL 8, select Settings → Preferences, click the Toolbar & Sound link, and uncheck the "Enable AOL sounds" box.

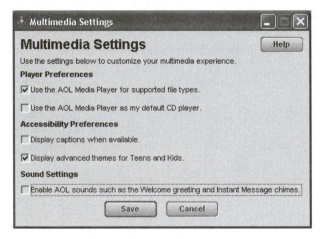

Figure 6-1. AOL, please shut up! Uncheck the box at the bottom of the screen to turn off the "You've Got Mail!" greeting.

I VANT TO BE ALONE

The Annoyance: With Version 8, AOL introduced a new annoyance—the AOL Companion. This pointless little applet launches whenever I connect to the Internet, whether I want it to or not. How can I send it away?

The Fix: It's easy to kill the little critter. Click the small X in the upper-right corner of the AOL Companion to close it. AOL will pop up a dialog box asking if you really want to close it. You do, of course, but before clicking Yes, make sure you check the "Do Not Show This Message Again" box (Figure 6-2). That way, you won't be annoyed by this annoyance's annoying pop-up again.

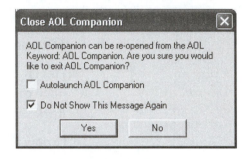

Figure 6-2. Applet begone! Close the AOL Companion, and tell it to never return.

WHO STOLE THE BACK AND FORWARD BUTTONS?

The Annoyance: Can we please take AOL's browser out into the cornfield and shoot it? The #@$@#$#!%! thing doesn't even have Forward or Back buttons! Can't I do something as simple as go forward and backward between sites?

The Fix: You're looking for buttons in all the wrong places. For some reason, AOL placed tiny forward and back buttons at the bottom of the AOL toolbar (just to the right of the QuickStart button), rather than in the browser window itself. You can also use Alt-Right Arrow and Alt-Left Arrow to move back and forth among pages you've visited.

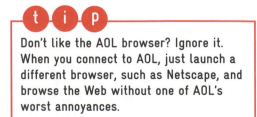

Don't like the AOL browser? Ignore it. When you connect to AOL, just launch a different browser, such as Netscape, and browse the Web without one of AOL's worst annoyances.

STOP AOL WINDOW OVERLOAD

The Annoyance: Windows, windows, and more windows! Whenever I use AOL, it seems to open about 537 windows, and I get completely lost navigating among them. The other day I even got an "open window limit" error message, and AOL wouldn't let me open any new windows. How can I close down all windows except one?

The Fix: It's easy. On the AOL menu, select Window → Close All Except Front. All the windows except the one on top will close. Unfortunately, this technique won't work on the AOL Welcome screen, because there's actually no way to completely close this screen. Even clicking the X in its upper-righthand corner doesn't close it; it only minimizes it.

CUT THE SCREEN CLUTTER

The Annoyance: At times, my AOL screen has more windows than a skyscraper. How can I shut these panes in the neck?

The Fix: AOL windows proliferate faster than rabbits, but there are a few ways to keep a lid on this population explosion. First, trim down the windows that open at startup. Like it or not, the Welcome screen and the AOL Channels bar on the left launch on startup, and there's nothing you can do to stop them. But you can stop other windows from launching. If you use AOL 9.0, go to Keyword: Start-up Settings. In the Additional Windows section, make sure that the None button is selected and click Save.

Next, tell your Buddy List not to load on startup. Go to the Buddy List setup screen (Keyword: IM Settings) and click the General Buddy tab. Uncheck the "Show me my Buddy List at sign-on" box, and click Save.

When you sign on, you'll only see the Welcome screen and AOL Channels. Close AOL Channels by clicking the X in its upper-righthand corner. You're now down to one window, the Welcome screen, which can't be closed. You can, however, minimize it by clicking the X in its top-right

corner. Do that, and you'll see one of the Seven Wonders of the Computing World: an almost completely bare AOL screen (see Figure 6-3). If you'd like your Welcome screen to start minimized every time, choose Window → Remember Window Size and Position.

Figure 6-3. Rarer than a dodo bird: an AOL screen almost completely free of windows.

> **t i p**
>
> It's easy to lose track of all the windows you have open. To keep them tidy, every so often choose Window → Cascade. This will line up all of your open windows, each one behind and slightly above the other. You can then move through them, closing any that you don't need. To close everything except the top window, follow the advice in the "Stop AOL Window Overload" Annoyance.

SPEED UP THE LONG GOODBYE

The Annoyance: Why does AOL take so $#@$# long to exit? And how can I speed it up?

The Fix: The most likely culprit is the amount of space AOL has set aside for temporary art files—that is, graphics used by your AOL software when you're online. (This is separate from the amount of space it sets aside for Internet Explorer temporary files.) By default, it sets aside 60 MB of space for its temporary art files; when you exit AOL, it deletes those temporary art files, which slows down your exit. So if you shrink the amount of space devoted to art files, you should speed up shutdowns.

To change the space allocation, click Settings on the AOL toolbar, click the A–Z tab, click N–S, and click Personal Storage Settings. The Personal Storage Settings dialog box will appear. In the Graphics Settings section at the bottom, select a number smaller than the default of 60 MB (for example, 20 MB), then click Save. That should solve the problem.

TURN OFF POP-UPS

The Annoyance: It's bad enough that AOL litters my screen with windows, but even worse are the pop-ups that AOL constantly throws at me. How can I turn these off?

The Fix: Luckily, it's simple to do. Go to Keyword: Popups, check the "Suppress AOL (R) member-only special offers" box, and click Save. While you're at it, check the "Suppress pop-ups from Web sites I visit using AOL (R) software" box, too (see Figure 6-4). When you visit web sites with the AOL browser, you'll eliminate their pop-ups, too.

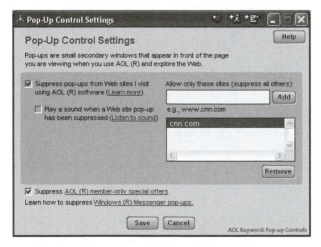

Figure 6-4. Pop-ups begone—put a stop to AOL and web pop-ups from this screen.

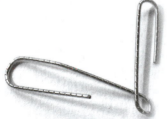

STOP USPS JUNK MAIL

The Annoyance: I recently subscribed to AOL, and now I'm getting tons of junk mail (the kind the postman brings to your door, not email) from AOL asking me to buy all sorts of stuff I don't need. How can I stop this flood of analog spam?

The Fix: Names and addresses are worth big bucks to advertisers, and AOL, like many other businesses, sends "special offers" to its subscribers. Turn off the spigot by going to Keyword: Marketing Preferences, clicking "U.S. Mail from AOL," selecting the "No, I do not want to receive special offers from AOL by mail" option, and then clicking OK. While you're here, you can turn off other ways AOL annoys you with its special offers by clicking the appropriate button (Telephone, for example) and then selecting the "No" option for each.

MOVE FAVORITES FROM AOL TO INTERNET EXPLORER

The Annoyance: I've finally had it with AOL's immensely annoying browser and am making the switch to Internet Explorer. But I've got over 100 Favorite Places in AOL, and I'd like to move them over to Internet Explorer. Why can't I do that?

The Fix: If you've got AOL Versions 4, 5, 6, 7, or 8, FavoRipper (Figure 6-5) will do the trick. (Version 9 users, see below.) Download it from *http://www.cablehead.com/downloads.htm*, and after you install it, log into AOL. Then run FavoRipper, select your version of AOL (if you have Version 8, select Version 7—it works for both), and click OK. Open your Favorites in America Online. Make sure all of your Favorite Places folders are open, then click OK, and they will be imported into Internet Explorer. They won't overwrite your existing Internet Favorites. Instead, they'll be placed in a new Favorites folder called Imported AOL Favorites. FavoRipper is shareware, and it will only import a limited number of Favorites unless you pay the $19.95 registration fee.

Figure 6-5. Export your Favorite Places from AOL to Internet Explorer, using FavoRipper.

If you have AOL Version 9, or if you want an all-around Favorites and bookmark organization tool in addition to one that will allow you to import your AOL Favorite Places into Internet Explorer, download URL Organizer 2 from *http://www.urlorg.com/urlorganizer2* (the program is shareware; registration costs $16.95). To import your Favorites from AOL into Internet Explorer using this tool, follow these steps:

1. In AOL, click the Favorite Places button.

2. Click the Save/Replace button at the bottom right of the Favorite Places window.

3. Select "Save My Favorite Places as a Favorites File on my Computer," and click OK.

4. Choose a location for saving the file (in PFC format, the only choice), and click Save.

5. Run URL Organizer 2, choose Lists → Import, locate the PFC file you saved, select it, and import it. Your Favorite Places will be imported into their own folder in Internet Explorer.

GET HELP FROM A LIVE HUMAN BEING

The Annoyance: I've tried using AOL's online help system—but then again, I've also tried winning the lottery and gotten the same results: zilch. Is there a way I can get a human being to walk me through my AOL problems?

The Fix: One of AOL's best-kept secrets is its surprisingly good help, available via live chat and via 24/7 telephone support. To get help via chat, go to Keyword: Live Help. Click the Get LIVE Technical Help button, then click the Go to LIVE Help button, and a chat screen will launch (see Figure 6-6). In the top box, type in the name you want to be called during your chat (your "handle"). Type your question in the box underneath, and click Chat Now. A chat window will open, and pretty soon a tech support person will log on and answer your question.

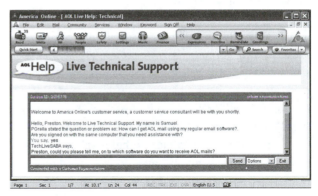

Figure 6-6. Holy cow, it's a live human being! Tech support via live chat on AOL is surprisingly helpful.

If you prefer Mr. Bell's invention, there's a list of AOL support numbers at Keyword: Call AOL. Scroll down to the "To contact AOL by telephone" section and you'll find a list of numbers for all kinds of problems, including tech support, billing, account cancellation, and others. But if you're in a hurry, here are the main tech support numbers right now: Windows users should call 888-346-3704 or 800-827-6364; Mac users can dial 888-265-8007.

SAVE TECH SUPPORT CHATS

The Annoyance: I've used AOL's chat help service, but I can't save the "conversation" from the session. If I highlight the text and press Ctrl-C or Ctrl-Insert, no text is saved. Nor can I choose Save from the File menu—it's grayed out. There's gotta be a way to save this text!

The Fix: AOL's chat support runs as an ActiveX control that lacks a save feature. However, if you select the text, right-click it, and select Copy, you can paste it into a program such as Notepad or Word and save it from there.

SAVE BETTER WEB GRAPHICS

The Annoyance: When I use AOL's browser to find and save pictures on the Internet, they're saved in a format I've never heard of, and that no graphics program I have can read. What can I do?

The Fix: In an attempt to speed up browsing, AOL uses the ART format, its own proprietary compression scheme for saving web graphics. But as you've discovered, almost no programs can read this format. One exception is Graphic Workshop Professional, available from *http://www.mindworkshop.com/alchemy/gwspro.html*, which can view ART and many other graphics file types, convert between formats, and do image editing. It's shareware; registration is $44.95. To look at ART files within AOL, choose File → Open and select the file.

> ### tip
>
> When you're browsing the Web with the AOL browser (or with Internet Explorer, on which the browser is based) and you find a picture that you want to save, right-click it and choose Save Picture As. Give the picture a name, select the format (whatever's available in the "Save as type" drop-down), pick a place to save it, and click the Save button.

If you don't want to download Graphic Workshop Pro, there's a simple fix: tell AOL not to compress graphics. Then, when you save a web graphic, you can save it in a standard format (usually *.jpg* or *.gif*). From the AOL 9.0 toolbar, choose Settings and click "Internet [Web] Options." (In AOL 8.0, select Settings → Preferences and click "Internet Properties (WWW).") Then click the AOL Browser tab, select "Never compress graphics," and click OK (see Figure 6-7).

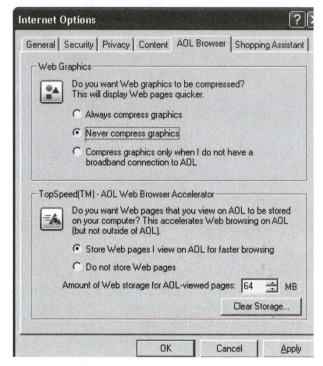

Figure 6-7. Tell AOL not to compress web graphics, and you'll be able to save them using a standard format.

Another benefit of turning off compression is that pictures on the Web will appear sharper—AOL's compression tends to make them fuzzy.

GET CALLER ID NUMBERS FOR DROPPED CALLS

The Annoyance: AOL's Voicemail system has caller ID built in, and if a message is left, the number is usually captured and saved as part of the email notification. But if a message isn't left—i.e., if the caller hangs up—the number is available only briefly, in a pop-up box. Once the caller hangs up, it's gone! Is there any way to retrieve this caller ID number?

The Fix: Go to Keyword: Voicemail and click the View Call Log button. The log maintains a record of the last 100 calls you've received, even if the caller hung up and never left a message. (Although naturally, if the caller has blocked her number, you can't retrieve any information about her.)

UNINSTALL PREVIOUS VERSIONS OF AOL

The Annoyance: The programmers who designed AOL must be packrats—whenever I install a new version, the old one stays on my system. How can I uninstall the old versions?

The Fix: At first this may seem impossible, since the Add or Remove Programs control panel only lists one AOL icon. But if you click the Change/Remove button next to the AOL icon, you'll get a list of all the AOL versions on your system, as you can see in Figure 6-8.

To delete them, highlight one or more versions and click the Next button. If there are any downloaded files, emails, or other files associated with that version stored in your filing cabinet that you want to save, make sure you check the "Downloaded files" and/or "Filing Cabinet files" boxes during the uninstall process.

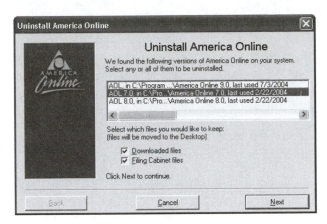

Figure 6-8. You can remove multiple versions of AOL, but make sure you keep copies of any data or downloaded files that you don't want to lose.

STOP AOL FROM BOOTING YOU OFF

The Annoyance: Last time I checked, the OL in AOL stood for "online"—yet half the time I'm quickly booted off after I connect. What gives?

The Fix: If you're using a dial-up connection and you have call waiting, an incoming call-waiting signal can kick you off AOL. Your best bet is to turn off call waiting for the duration of your AOL call. Here's how with AOL 9.0:

1. Sign off America Online.

2. On the Sign On screen, click the Sign On Options button.

3. In the Setup window, if you have only one location, click Edit Numbers. If you have more than one location, select a location and click Edit Numbers.

4. In the Edit AOL Access Phone Numbers window that appears, click Dialing Options.

5. In the Edit Dialing Options window, check the box next to "Dial *70." This will turn off call waiting for the duration of your connection to AOL.

6. If you use a code other than *70 to turn off call waiting, type that number into the box, then click OK.

7. Click OK to return to the Edit AOL Access Phone Numbers window, then click Next.

8. In the Summary window, click Sign On to AOL Now to sign on immediately.

In AOL 8.0, the sequence is a bit different: click the Setup button on the Sign On screen, click Edit Numbers, double-click the dial-up number you're using, and check the "Dial *70, to disable call waiting" box. Then click OK. From now on, call waiting will be disabled whenever you sign onto AOL, but it will turn back on after you log off.

For AOL 9.0 users, if call waiting isn't the problem, try using another AOL dial-in number:

1. On the Sign On screen, click Sign On Options, and then click Set Up Your Connection.

2. In the Setup window that appears, select a location and click Add Numbers.

3. Type in the area code from which you want to connect, and click Next.

4. In the Select AOL Access Numbers window that appears, select as many access phone numbers as you want from the list and click Next. (Insider tip: pick the numbers at the top of the list—they're usually the newest.)

5. Verify the information in the Confirm Your Selection window, and click Next.

6. In the Summary window, click Sign On to AOL Now.

In AOL 8.0, from the Sign On screen, click the Access Numbers button, enter the desired area code, click Next, and then follow steps 4–6.

Still no improvement? Try reducing the number of running programs before you sign onto AOL. Some modems are memory- and processor-dependent, and if your RAM and processor are busy with other programs, that may be the problem. If you're still having problems with your connection, get an updated driver for your modem. Check the manufacturer's web site, or go to AOL Keyword: Modem Software Update.

Even if a dial-up number is in your area code, you might be charged for a toll call. Check with your local phone company and make sure.

THE CASE OF THE $2,500 AOL CONNECTION

Some people complain that AOL charges too much. But how about a $2,500 phone bill for an AOL connection made over a single Christmas break? According to the Associated Press, when Elissa Walters was home from college on Christmas break, she connected to AOL using a phone number in her area code in Springfield, New Jersey. She didn't realize that because she had to dial a 1 she was making a long-distance call, so she left the connection open continually. Six weeks later, her father was hit with a phone bill for $2,500 from his long-distance carrier, Qwest. After complaining and haggling, Qwest agreed to drop the bill to $375—certainly not as bad as the original bill, but a whopper for merely connecting to AOL!

CHECK THAT LOCAL NUMBER!

The Annoyance: I just read your sidebar "The Case of the $2,500 AOL Connection," and I don't want *my* kids pulling this stunt when they come home. What can I do?

The Fix: First, reconfigure AOL to dial only truly local numbers. From AOL's sign-on screen, click the Sign On Options button, click Add Numbers, and then enter your local area code. Pick dial-up numbers in your exchange (the first three digits of your seven-digit phone number). Then call your local phone company and confirm that these are truly local numbers.

If you get it wrong (or someone else changes the access number) and the visiting kids rack up a big long-distance phone bill, don't bug AOL—it's not their fault. Contact your long-distance carrier and see if it will agree to eat the cost of the calls. Because of intense competition for customers, you can threaten to leave them for a competitor, and they may let you off the hook.

KEEP YOUR KIDS SAFE ON AOL

The Annoyance: AOL is so easy, even a six-year-old can use it (no wisecracks about it being *designed* for six-year-olds, please). AOL itself is pretty PG, but there's a lot of seamy stuff on the Internet that my kids could access via AOL's browser. What's a parent to do?

The Fix: AOL offers a set of built-in tools that stop kids from encountering objectionable material. To use them, go to Keyword: Parental Controls. Before you set the controls, you must create a separate screen name for each of your children.

When you set parental controls, you can block kids from going to certain potentially objectionable parts of the Internet and America Online, and you can restrict their access to certain services—such as chat and email—that could be gateways to the seamy stuff. As with any kind of parental controls, they're not perfect. They're not particularly flexible, so you can't filter instant messenger content, for example—you can allow your kids to use instant messaging, or stop them from using it, but you can't al-

low them to use it and filter out messages based on the message content or sender.

In Parental Controls, you can use a set of prefab controls, or you can mix and match to create customized controls based on what you want to let each kid do online. It's much simpler to use the built-in ones, but they're also less flexible.

When you go to the Parental Controls area, you'll see a list of all of the screen names in your account, as shown in Figure 6-9.

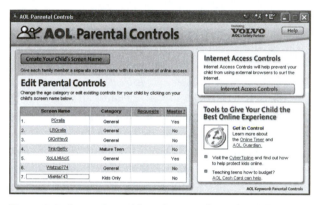

Figure 6-9. Command central for setting parental controls on AOL.

You set Parental Controls for each screen name individually. Click a screen name, and you'll see the controls in place for that user. The choices are General, Kids Only, Young Teen, and Mature Teen. (If you don't want any controls set for a screen name, leave it at General, the default.) America Online recommends that Kids Only be set for kids aged 12 and under, Young Teen be set for kids aged 13 through 15, and Mature Teen be set for kids aged 16 to 17.

To change the controls for the screen name, click the Edit Age Category button (see Figure 6-10), choose the category you want to use, click Save, and then click Close. Alas, it's not crystal clear what the individual controls actually do or represent. Just taking a look at a bar or slider won't tell you the specifics of how it controls a category (e.g., Web Browsing), but clicking the "More about these controls" link will give you some details.

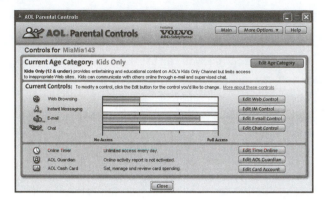

Figure 6-10. Uh, what exactly do these controls do? Click the "More about these controls" link to find out.

Here's the run-down of what the prefab Parental Controls settings do:

Kids Only

This setting lets kids (up to 12 years old) visit only one area of America Online—the Kids Only channel—and visit only web sites that are selected by AOL for age-appropriate content. All other content areas and web sites are blocked; nor can kids send or receive instant messages. They can't join member-created or private chat rooms either, although they can visit public chat rooms in the Kids Only area. They can send and receive mail, but they can't send or receive file attachments or pictures.

Young Teen

This setting allows teens to visit some chat rooms, but not member-created or private chat rooms. They can visit only web sites that have been judged appropriate for kids under 15. They're also blocked from Internet newsgroups that allow file attachments. There are no restrictions on IM and email.

Mature Teen

This restricts teens' access to certain web sites—they can only visit sites that have been judged appropriate for kids under. They're also blocked from Internet newsgroups that allow file attachments. There are no restrictions on IM and email.

Block That Access!

Certain areas of AOL cost extra—above and beyond your monthly fee. These premium areas, which up your monthly fees, offer such goodies as online gaming. You can imagine how quickly some kids would run up big bills playing games or visiting other premium areas. Luckily, Parental Controls block access to these premium services, which is a good idea if you're worried about your financial health.

Customizing Parental Controls

Parental Controls are one-size-fits-all. They treat all kids the same, and as any parent knows, no two kids are alike. Maybe you trust your kids to visit only appropriate web sites, but you're worried about their use of chat or email. America Online lets you mix and match controls any way you like. The controls offer broad ways to protect your kids—for example, by not allowing them to visit private chat rooms, or blocking them from receiving emails with attachments—and they let you create customized profiles (for example, limiting web access while providing unlimited email access). However, they offer only limited ways to customize each control. So, for example, you can either allow your kids to use instant messaging or block them from using it, but that's it—you can't block messages from specific people. (Although if you dig into AOL's mail controls at Keyword: `Mail Controls`, you can use the "Allow mail only from People I Know" to restrict messaging.)

t i p

Here's a Parental Controls annoyance: when you set them, they don't go into effect immediately. You must sign off the service, exit the America Online software, and then sign on again.

To customize controls, go to Keyword: Parental Controls, and click the screen name of the user in question. Click the specific control you want to customize, change the options for it, then click the Save button at the bottom of the screen—for example, click "Chat control"—to set controls for chat. (For once, logic from America Online!) Here's how you customize each control:

Web Browsing control

If you're worried that your kids are viewing inappropriate sites on the Web, use this control. You can limit them to sites appropriate for kids 12 and under, 15 and under, or 17 and under. However, you can't customize the control further—for example, you can't block access to specific web sites or domains, or, conversely, allow access to only specific sites or domains.

Instant Messaging control

You can completely block instant messaging, or limit it so that kids can't receive attached image, voice, or video files. You can't, as noted earlier, block IM by sender, or check a log to see whom your kids are sending messages to or getting them from.

E-mail control

This control is the same one you use when controlling spam and other email access. From here, for example, you can block mail containing files or attachments, block email by sender name, and even block mail by domain name. You can also create a list of people who are allowed to send your kids mail and block them from receiving mail from anyone else. (See the annoyance "AOL Chews Up My Email!" for more details.)

Chat control

You can block different parts of chat with this control. For example, you can block chat hyperlinks, so if someone sends your kid a link to an inappropriate web site, he can't click the link and go there. You can also block kids' access to chat rooms in the People Connection area, which is aimed at an older audience and includes a number of adult topics. Likewise, you can block access to member-created chat rooms in the People Connection area and block access to conference rooms (large chat rooms on America Online).

Report Inappropriate Sites

AOL's web-blocking software isn't perfect—there's no way it can know about every questionable site on the Internet. If you come across a site that you think should be blocked, go to Keyword: Report a Site. Then click the "Report a Site" button, supply the site's URL, and indicate which age range the site is really for. Click the "Recommend a Site" button if you think a site should *not* be blocked.

STOP AOL FROM DIALING UNNECESSARILY

The Annoyance: I have a cable connection to the Internet, but every time I try to connect to AOL, it insists on dialing my old analog modem. Why hasn't AOL figured out I've gone broadband?

The Fix: In spite of your new cable connection, AOL's software is still configured to dial your modem. To fix the problem, load the AOL software, and in the Location drop-down box, choose your cable modem connection rather than your dial-up connection. (The cable modem connection will most likely be labeled "ISP/LAN connection," or something similar.) Then click "Sign on," and you'll sign on using your cable connection, both now and in the future.

If you see only one connection in the Location drop-down box, you have a little more work to do. You're going to have to set up America Online to use your new cable modem. Here's how:

1. Click the Sign On Options button.
2. Click the Add a Location button.

3. Type in a name for the location (for example, "Home Cable"), and click Next.

4. A screen will appear telling you that America Online has detected that you have a broadband connection. Click Next.

5. If you want to sign onto America Online now, click Sign Onto AOL now. If not, click Make More Changes. You'll be sent back to the Setup screen. Click Close.

(The steps may vary, depending on your AOL version.)

EMAIL

KEEP YOUR SENT EMAIL

The Annoyance: Call me crazy, but when I use an email program, I actually like to keep old messages that I've sent. Why can't I do this with AOL? Even when I send mail and mark it "Keep As New," it automatically gets deleted. Can't AOL do this one simple thing?

The Fix: Mail you've sent is normally deleted after 27 days, but there's a way you can save it on your own PC, or on AOL's servers. If you save it on your PC, you can save as many messages as you want; if you save it on AOL's servers, you're limited to 140 MB of mail.

To save one or more emails that you've sent or read, highlight the message(s) on the Sent or Old tab, click the Save button, and choose "On AOL" or "On My PC." If you choose the former, the mail is taken off the Sent or Old tab and dropped into a "Saved on AOL" folder. If you take the latter course, you can save your mail in prefab folders, including Incoming/Saved Mail and Mail You've Sent, or in custom folders you create. If you want all of your sent mail saved automatically to your PC, from inside AOL choose Mail → Mail Settings. On the General tab, check the "Retain all mail I send in my Mail I've Sent Folder" box, then click Save. If you want to automatically save all received mail, check the "Retain all mail I read in my Saved Mail Folder" box.

To read the mail you've saved on your PC or on AOL's servers when you're online, just click the You've Got Mail button, then the Manage Mail tab. In the My Mail Folders box to the left, scroll down and select the "Saved on AOL" folder or any of the folders under "Saved on My PC" (see Figure 6-11). When you're offline, you can read mail saved to your PC by selecting Mail → Saved on My PC (Filing Cabinet) and clicking the Manage Mail tab.

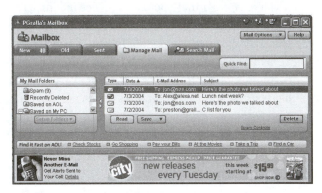

Figure 6-11. To make sure that sent and old emails don't vanish, save them on your PC.

FETCH AOL MAIL WITH YOUR OWN EMAIL CLIENT

The Annoyance: AOL's email software is pathetic. Why can't I use a third-party email program to send and retrieve my AOL email?

The Fix: Rejoice—AOL has seen the light, and it now lets you do that very thing. AOL doesn't go out of its way to let the world know about this option, but it's easily accomplished. In your email software, set up a new account as you would for any new email service. For the incoming mail server, choose the IMAP option rather than POP3, and use the address *imap.aol.com*. For your outgoing mail, use the SMTP server address *smtp.aol.com*, with the port number 587. For step-by-step instructions on how to access AOL email with your email client, go to AOL Keyword: Open Mail Access, then click the appropriate link for instructions.

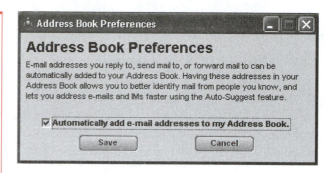

Figure 6-12. Uncheck this box to save yourself from address-book bloat.

In AOL 8.0 Plus, select Settings → Preferences, click the A–Z tab, click Address Book, and then uncheck the "Automatically add e-mail addresses to my Address Book" box.

STOP ADDRESS-BOOK OVERLOAD

The Annoyance: Whenever I read an AOL email message, the sender is automatically added to my address book. If this keeps up, I'll have an address book of about 5,000 names. How can I stop it?

The Fix: You'll have to dig deep into an unexpected place to turn off this feature. Here's how:

1. Click Settings on the AOL toolbar.
2. Click the A–Z tab.
3. Click Address Book Settings.
4. Uncheck the "Automatically add e-mail addresses to my Address Book" box (see Figure 6-12).
5. Click Save.

If you prevent AOL from automatically adding addresses to your address book, you can still easily add them on the fly. If you get an email from someone whose address you want to save to your address book, simply open the message, then click the "Add Address" button on the righthand side of the email form.

TELL AOL MAIL TO SEND YOUR FILE

The Annoyance: AOL is my only email program. But if I right-click a file in Windows Explorer and send the file to "mail recipient," nothing happens, even if AOL's client program is loaded. (If Communicator is installed, of course, it will pop up and attach the file to an outgoing message.) Why in the world can't AOL's built-in mail client do this?

The Fix: It can, but you must massage AOL a bit to get it working. First, select AOL as your default email program. In AOL 8.0 Plus, select Settings → Preferences, click the A–Z tab, select "AOL as Default," and click OK. In AOL 9.0, select Settings from the AOL toolbar, then click the A–Z tab, select "AOL as Default," and click OK.

SEND STALLED EMAILS

The Annoyance: When I tried to send an email the other day, AOL popped up a "This is not a known member" message. I was sending the message to someone with an Earthlink account, so how could this be an issue? I exited and restarted AOL, composed my message again, and voilà—my email was sent. Is AOL going senile?

The Fix: Nope—but you may be. (Kidding!) Chances are when you addressed the email, you entered a very tiny typo, probably in the Copy To box, as you tabbed down to the subject line. It's easy to accidentally enter a ' (left single quote) in this box, since it's right above the Tab key on most keyboards. AOL's email program isn't bright enough to realize this is a typo—it thinks it's a native AOL address. (Any address that doesn't have an @ in it is treated as an AOL address.) Naturally, AOL checked its secret member list, didn't find anyone named ', and balked. Next time this error pops up, carefully check the Send To and Copy To fields.

NO, AOL, I AM NOT A SPAMMER

The Annoyance: Forgive me, for I have sinned. I use AOL to send out my weekly newsletter, but because it goes out to several hundred people, AOL thinks it's spam and blocks it. How can I send out my newsletter without being labeled a spammer?

The Fix: Ask AOL to put you on its "whitelist," and your newsletter won't be blocked as spam. For details, head to *http://postmaster.info.aol.com/tools/whitelist_guides.html*. You'll have to follow a set of rules, including that your newsletter complies with the federal Can Spam Act, that valid contact information is included, that all of your subscribers have asked to receive the newsletter, and so on. (For more on newsletters and spam, see Chapter 1.)

GET AND SEND EMAIL IN A FLASH

The Annoyance: About all I use AOL for is sending and receiving email. Isn't there some way to do this without launching the full-blown, bloated AOL program?

The Fix: Someone deep inside AOL must have recognized how annoying the company's email software is, because there are not one but two fixes to this problem. One solution is to use AOL's "flash sessions" feature, which automatically grabs your email and downloads it to your PC so you can read and compose messages offline. It does load the whole AOL program, but at least it fetches mail quickly. The other solution is to use AOL Communicator, a powerful email client that lets you read and respond to messages without loading the whole AOL program.

Flash sessions

If you don't mind the normal AOL mail client, use the flash sessions feature to automatically send and receive mail. To set it up, go to Keyword: Flash Session and click the Continue button. You'll be asked several questions, such as whether you want AOL to automatically retrieve your mail, to automatically download any attachments, and to automatically send mail you've written offline. You'll also be asked about fetching newsgroup postings.

> **t i p**
>
> For safety's sake, don't automatically download file attachments. It's not a good idea to download files from people you don't know, because those files could contain viruses. You can always later manually download any attachments from people you know using AOL's mail client.

Once you've provided the basic information, you can schedule when to run flash sessions automatically. You can, of course, also run flash sessions manually at any time by choosing Mail → Run Automatic AOL. In the screen that appears, click Begin. If you want to automatically sign off AOL when you've downloaded all your mail, check the "Sign Off When Finished" box.

Once you've set a flash session, the Read and Write buttons will be available even when you're logged off AOL. You'll be able to read and write mail offline, but to send mail, you must log into AOL or run another flash session.

A flash session automatically downloads new, unread mail to the "Saved on My PC" folder, in *Incoming/Saved Mail*.

AOL Communicator

AOL Communicator (Figure 6-13) is a separate program from AOL. To use it, go to Keyword: Communicator and follow the download and installation directions. When you run it, it'll automatically grab all of your AOL email. With Communicator, you can do everything you can with AOL's built-in mail client, and then some. Aside from accessing your old, sent, and received mail, you can view mail from multiple screen names, send and receive email from your non-AOL email accounts (such as those you have with other ISPs), and more. Best of all, you don't have to run AOL to run AOL Communicator.

CHECK AOL EMAIL FROM THE WEB

The Annoyance: I sometimes need to check my AOL mail from a public computer at an Internet cafe, or from a friend's computer. These are people and places that do not look on AOL kindly—in fact, they stare bullets at me when I ask if they have AOL installed. Needless to say, they don't. Is there some way to check my AOL email when I'm away from my PC, without using AOL software?

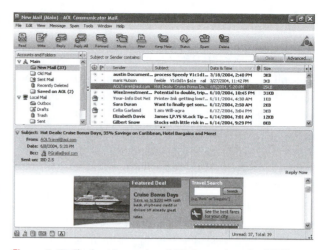

Figure 6-13. The Great Communicator? AOL Communicator is a full-blown email client that lets you send and receive mail without running AOL.

The Fix: Head to *http://webmail.aol.com*. Type in your username and password, then click Sign In, and you'll be able to check your mail, compose new messages, and send them (see Figure 6-14).

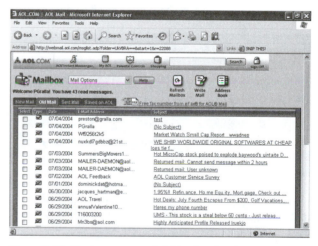

Figure 6-14. If you're at someone else's PC and need to check your AOL mail, you can run a webmail version of the AOL mail software.

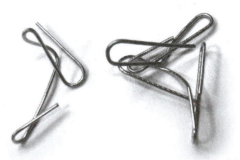

"UNSEND" AN EMAIL

The Annoyance: My anger-management classes don't seem to have taken hold. On more than one occasion I've sent off a flaming email to someone and then instantly regretted it. What can I do?

The Fix: Aside from taking another anger-management class? Well, AOL's got a feature that lets you take back an email after you've sent it—but only if you've sent the email to another AOL user, and the message hasn't yet been read. To find out if the message has been read, go to the Sent mail tab, select the email, and click the Status button at the bottom of the screen. If the pop-up box shows "(not yet read)," you can kill the message by closing the pop-up box, then clicking the Unsend button (see Figure 6-15). If it shows a date and time in the When Read column, your goose is cooked—you can't delete the message. If it shows "(you cannot check status of Internet mail)," the message was sent to a non-AOL email address and, alas, you don't have the option to unsend it.

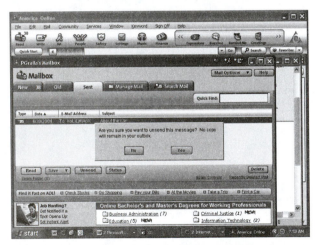

Figure 6-15. If you send an email you later regret, you can "unsend it"—if the message was sent to another AOL user and hasn't yet been read.

t i p

When you unsend a message, AOL completely blots it out—a copy of the message will not appear on the Sent tab. (For a related discussion, see "Stop That Email!" in Chapter 1.)

AOL CHEWS UP MY EMAIL!

The Annoyance: Four people in the last two weeks have complained that I didn't respond to their emails. But I never received them! What gives?

The Fix: It sounds like you set up your AOL spam filters improperly, to block almost all the mail sent to you. Go to your Spam folder and check the messages there—you'll probably find the mail from the people who couldn't reach you.

To change your settings and make sure that their mail isn't considered spam in the future, go to Keyword: Spam Controls. In the "Control Who I Get Mail From" section, make sure you've selected "Allow mail from all senders" in order to receive mail from the widest group of people. If you want to restrict incoming mail to only people in your AOL address book and Buddy List, choose "Allow mail only from People I Know." Here's the full range of spam controls:

Allow mail from all senders

You can get mail from anyone. With this and the other options, AOL will still filter out junk mail using its own built-in spam filters.

Allow mail only from AOL members

Only mail from other AOL members will get through to you.

Allow mail only from People I Know

You'll only get mail from people in your address book and Buddy List.

Block mail from all senders

Who would use this feature? Beats me, but if you want to be an email hermit, you can block all mail headed your way.

Use a custom sender list

Only people on a custom list you create can send you mail.

You can combine these choices with the "Block mail containing pictures or files" option in Mail and Spam Controls (Figure 6-16). For example, if you chose to receive mail only from AOL members, but an AOL member sent you mail with an attached picture or file, the mail would be blocked. Why do this? To make sure that viruses and objectionable pictures don't come your way.

Figure 6-16. Control who can send you mail, and how to stop spam, from this dialog box.

AOL'S SPAM CONTROLS

Because of its vast user base, AOL is the biggest spam magnet of all time. The service continually updates its anti-spam tools, so the spam you see in your inbox is only a small portion of the spam that's actually sent to you.

If you're getting too much spam on AOL (who isn't?), go to Keyword: Spam Controls and make sure you're using AOL's spam filters—the "Mail filtered by AOL's Advanced Spam Filter" box should be checked. Next, build your own custom spam list. Check the "Mail containing words and phrases on my Custom Word List" box. Then click the "Custom Word List" link and enter words commonly found in spam subject lines, such as "Viagra" and "refinance." All mail containing those words (note: it's not case-sensitive) will be considered spam.

You should also dictate how AOL will handle spam. You can tell the service to automatically delete all spam, or to move it to a spam folder so that you can examine the mail and decide whether it's spam or not. If you create your own custom spam list, it's a good idea to have the mail moved to the Spam folder, so you can double-check and make sure no legitimate mail is being blocked.

SORT MAIL BY PERSON AND DATE

The Annoyance: AOL's new/old/sent email boxes let you sort mail by type, date, email address, and subject—but only by one factor at a time. I want to find an email I sent to Ted on September 15, 2004, not all 3,000 messages I've sent him in the last 3 years. Why can't I do something as simple as sort by name *and* date?

The Fix: That would make too much sense. But there is a solution, if you use AOL 9.0. The trick? Use the search feature in combination with sorting and you can see all of your emails to Ted, sorted by date. Go to the Sent mail tab, and type in Ted's email address in the Quick Find box in the upper-righthand corner of the Mailbox screen. You'll get a list of all of your messages to Ted, sorted by date. You can now sort all of your emails to Ted by another category, such as Subject.

> **t i p**
>
> You can also see all of the mail you've sent to someone and they've sent to you, sorted by date—just click the Search Mail tab and type in the person's email address.

WHY CAN'T I REPORT SPAMMERS?

The Annoyance: I use AOL Communicator, and (no surprise) I get a ton of spam in my inbox. But I'm having a problem reporting emails as spam to AOL. When I read some emails, there's a big Report Spam button at the top of the email. But when I read others, that button isn't there. Why does AOL make it so tough for me to crack down on spammers?

The Fix: You've just found one of the eccentricities in AOL Communicator. Before you can report a piece of email as spam, you first have to *mark* it as spam. So when you come across spam, highlight it and click the Spam button at the top of the Communicator toolbar. When

you do that, a Report Spam button appears at the top of the email message. Click it to report the message as spam. If you come across a message marked as spam that you think isn't spam, click the This Is Not Spam button at the top of the email message.

FIX FLAKY FONTS

The Annoyance: I occasionally get emails that have all sorts of screwy fonts and colors in them, and sometimes I send messages that look like plain text to me and hear the same thing from the recipient. What's going on?

The Fix: The problem is due to the way AOL email handles HTML. Versions of AOL before AOL 9.0 didn't do a very good job of translating incoming HTML, or of sending out standard HTML messages. But the newest version of AOL seems to have fixed the problem. If you upgrade to AOL 9, the problem should go away.

If you don't want to upgrade, or if you still have the problem, you can use a workaround for sending messages. When you create a message, you can tell AOL to use only plain text, and no HTML or pictures. In the message you're creating, right-click on the white, blank portion of the screen in the message area. Choose "Compose as Plain Text," and your email will be sent as text only and won't include any flaky fonts.

There's no workaround for received messages, except to tell your correspondents to only send you plain-text mail in the future.

IM ANNOYANCES

Instant messaging—what could more useful? It lets you instantly get in touch with friends and family… and lets spammers from all over the world instantly get in touch with you, with fab offers for drugs, real estate, and diamond mines. It lets friends tell you about great sites you should visit… and lets malware writers plant Trojans on your PC.

If you'd like to reap all the benefits of instant messaging, and avoid the annoyances, this chapter is for you.

Note: throughout this chapter, you'll find coverage of the latest versions of AIM, Windows Messenger/MSN Messenger, Yahoo! Messenger, and ICQ Lite. (Covering past versions would require an entire book!) Most, if not all, of the solutions for ICQ Lite also apply to the larger (many would say bloated) ICQ Pro program, and the same goes for some older versions of the other IM apps covered here.

GENERAL INSTANT MESSAGING ANNOYANCES

SLAM IM SPAM

The Annoyance: I'm chatting with my daughter using AOL Instant Messenger (AIM). Suddenly, I get an instant message from Debby from Dallas, who has some not-so-kosher home videos she wants to sell me for $49.99. How can I stop this kind of stuff?

The Fix: IM spam has become an unfortunate way of life. Here's how to stop it in the major instant messaging programs:

AIM

Click the Prefs button at the bottom of the AIM screen, then choose Privacy. In the "Who can contact me" section (see Figure 7-1), select "Allow only users on my Buddy List" and click OK. That means any instant message from anyone not on your Buddy List will automatically be blocked, and you won't get any more IM spam. You can also block specific people from reaching you, block everyone from reaching you, and tap several other privacy-related options.

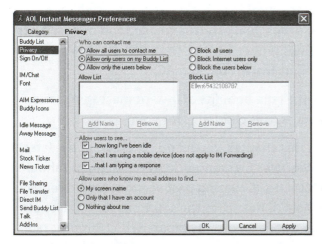

Figure 7-1. To stop spam in AIM, block anyone not on your Buddy List from sending you instant messages.

Yahoo! Messenger

To allow messages only from people on your Messenger list, go to Messenger → Preferences → Ignore list, choose "Ignore anyone who is not on my Messenger list," and click OK. Alternatively, you can opt to ignore specific people: choose "Ignore only the people below," and add them to the list.

Windows Messenger/MSN Messenger

To restrict who can send you messages, choose Tools → Options → Privacy, highlight "All other users in the My Allow List," click Block, then click OK. The "All other users" entry will be moved to the My Block List, so only your buddies can send you instant messages.

ICQ Lite

To set your privacy level in ICQ Lite, choose Main → Spam Control. For maximum privacy, check the "Accept messages only from users on my Contact List" box. If you don't check that box, you can still filter out spam: in the "Not in List Messages" area, check both the "Apply ICQ Anti-Spam filter when receiving messages from users not in my Contact List" box and the "Display the 'Accept Messages' dialog when receiving messages from users not in my Contact List" box. You should also check the "Do not accept World Wide Pager Messages" and "Do not accept Email Express Messages" boxes. Click OK when you're done.

Is That Spim or Spam?

You know what spam is. But do you know about spim? It's the name some use for IM spam, and its use is skyrocketing. According to the research firm Ferris Research, an estimated 1 billion spims were sent in 2003, up fourfold from 2002. An estimated 4 billion spims will be sent in 2004.

DUELING WINDOWS MESSENGER SPAMS

When it comes to instant messaging, Microsoft has done everything in its power to confuse the world—after all, it has two separate instant messaging programs, Windows Messenger and MSN Messenger, which are kind of the same but also kind of different. To make matters worse, there's also the Windows Messenger Service, which is another beast entirely. It's not an instant messaging program, but it is responsible for some of the most annoying spam on the planet. The Windows Messenger Service was originally designed for network administrators to send text-based messages over a network, such as "Network coming down in 15 minutes!" Unfortunately, spammers have used it to blast out millions of spams to poor, unsuspecting souls. For more about the Windows Messenger Service and how to turn it off, see "Kill the Windows Messenger Service" in Chapter 9.

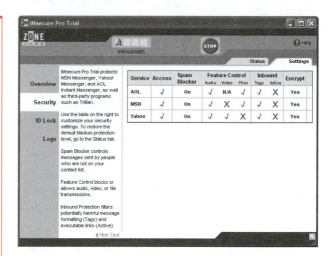

Figure 7-2. IMsecure offers the best all-around IM protection.

Service	Access	Spam Blocker	Feature Control			Inbound		Encrypt
			Audio	Video	Files	Tags	Active	
AOL	√	On	√	N/A	√	√	X	Yes
MSN	√	On	√	X	√	√	X	Yes
Yahoo	√	On	√	√	X	√	X	Yes

http://www.imsecure.com. There's a free version, but it only protects against buffer overflow attacks. For full protection, you'll need the Pro version. You can try IMsecure Pro for free for 15 days; after that, you'll have to pay $39.95 to keep it. Note that it works with AIM, Yahoo! Messenger, Windows Messenger/MSN Messenger, and Trillian, but not with ICQ.

GET ALL-AROUND IM PROTECTION

The Annoyance: My biggest IM gripe? No matter how hard I try to keep up-to-date, my IM program will always be vulnerable to viruses, Trojans, people stealing my personal information, and worse. Should I just give up on IM for good?

The Fix: Not at all. The threats you list affect email and any PC connected to the Net, not just IM programs. For IM users, the best all-around protector you can get is IMsecure Pro, from firewall maker ZoneLabs (see Figure 7-2). It protects you from a wide variety of IM attacks, such as so-called "buffer overflow attacks" that can be used to crash your system or install malware on it, Trojans, dangerous executable links, and more. It can also prevent your personal information from being sent out, and it lets you block specific features (such as file transfers) in different IM apps. IMsecure is available from

SEND TEXT MESSAGES TO CELL PHONES

The Annoyance: I have a friend who's always traveling and seldom takes a laptop along. I figure the best way to get his attention is to IM his cell phone—why can't I send him a text message with my IM program?

The Fix: All the major IM programs let you send text messages, but not all cell carriers/phones can receive them. Don't forget, also, that those people who can receive your messages may not be able to respond—again, it depends on the carrier and/or the phone. Check with your pal's cell phone provider, and while you're at it, try sending him a text message with your IM program. If you get a message telling you the service is unavailable, you're probably out of luck. (Of course, it could also mean that his phone is off, or that the carrier supports the feature but your pal didn't buy that package.) Here's how to send text messages (also called SMS messages) from the major IM programs:

AIM

With AIM, just add a mobile phone number to your Buddy List, and you can then send text messages to the cell phone in the same way you would IM any buddy. To add a number, click the Setup button near the bottom of the AIM window. The Setup Buddy List window will appear. Click the Add Mobile icon. In the form that appears (shown in Figure 7-3), select the appropriate country and enter the area code and phone number (don't enter a 1 or a country code, and don't use any characters such as dashes or parentheses). If you want a name rather than the cell phone number to appear in your Buddy List, type that in the appropriate box. Click OK.

Figure 7-3. When you add a cell phone as a buddy, type in the person's name so it will show up in your Buddy List instead of the cell phone number.

The cell phone number will show up in your Buddy List, and you can now send a text message to that phone. Note that AIM will show this buddy as online all the time, even if his phone isn't turned on. If your recipient can respond, his return address will be his phone number, not a buddy name (see Figure 7-4).

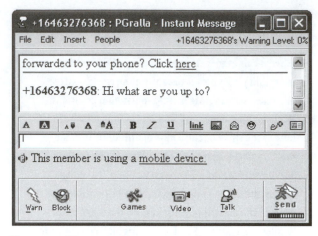

Figure 7-4. When you receive a text message from a cell phone in AIM, you'll see the sender's cell phone number, not his name.

Yahoo! Messenger

To send a text with Yahoo! Messenger, click the Text icon (the small cell phone). In the To box, type in the cell phone number, then type in the text message and click Send. If you want to add someone's cell phone as a contact, click the Text icon, enter the phone number, choose Contact → Contact Options → Add to Address Book, then fill out the form to add the contact, as you would any other.

Windows Messenger

There's no way to send text messages to cell phones using Windows Messenger. If you want this capability you'll have to install MSN Messenger. You can download it from *http://messenger.msn.com/*.

ICQ

To send a text using ICQ, click the SMS button. In the screen that appears, type in a name for the contact, type in the phone number, and pick the country. As with many things ICQ, the process is more confusing than it needs to be. (For example, you must type the cell phone number's area code in the Network # box.)

If you want this contact to always show up in your Contact List, check the "Add new SMS Contact to my Contact List" box. Click OK. ICQ will launch, and you can now send a text message to your contact's phone.

USE IM PROGRAMS ON A CELL PHONE

IM programs, including AIM, Yahoo! Messenger, and Windows Messenger/MSN Messenger, are becoming increasingly available on cell phones. The IM programs on phones often look and act very much like the ones on your PC, and generally they can use the buddy lists stored on your PC. However, this varies from phone to phone and IM service to IM service. On older phones, the IM program may not match the look or features of the PC-based IM program, and you may be limited in the number of buddies you can have. For example, older Nokia phones limit you to a total of 30 buddies; newer phones don't impose such a strict limit. Check with your cell phone provider for details. Most providers (including T-Mobile, Cingular, AT&T, Nextel, Sprint, and others) offer IM capabilities, and most newer phones (including those from Nokia, Motorola, Samsung, Sanyo, and others) will let you use IM programs.

PLUMB YOUR IM PROGRAM'S MEMORY

The Annoyance: I was IMing with my old college roommate late one night last week, and together we hatched a business plan that we're sure would reap us a bundle and lead to an early, lucrative retirement. We both went to sleep soon after, and now we can't remember the scheme! Is there some hidden log of the chat that I can unearth? And how can I save my brainstorms in the future?

The Fix: Almost all IM programs let you save your chats as text files—although there's no guarantee your midnight brainstorm won't seem like a slight drizzle the next day. Keep in mind, though, that with all the IM programs (except ICQ, as discussed below) you must save the chat session either during the session or at the end. If you end the session without saving it, your brilliant schemes and conversations will sadly be lost forever.

For future reference, here's how to save your chat sessions with the major IM programs:

AIM

At the end of your chat session, choose File → Save in your chat window, or press Ctrl-S. You can save the session as an HTML file (what AOL calls AOL Rich Text Format) or as a text file in the folder of your choice.

Yahoo! Messenger

In your chat window, choose File → Save or press Ctrl-S. You can save your chat only as a text file.

Windows Messenger/MSN Messenger

In your chat window, choose File → Save. You can save your chat only as a text file.

ICQ Lite

Alas, you can't save chats on a chat-by-chat basis with ICQ Lite—you must choose to save all of your chats or none of them. To automatically save all your chats, choose Main → Preferences and Security → Saving Options and check the Save History box (see Figure 7-5). To read any chat, double-click the contact whose chat history you want to read—even if the person isn't online—and then click the Message History button (the one with a large H on it). You'll see the transcript of that session, as shown in Figure 7-6. To delete a transcript, select it and press Delete. You can delete all of your chats by choosing Main → Preferences and Security → Saving Options, typing your password, and clicking the Clear History button.

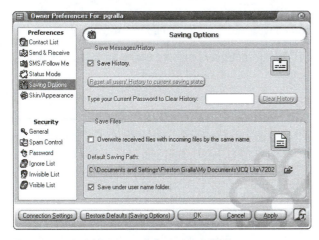

Figure 7-5. Here's how to save all of your chats in ICQ Lite.

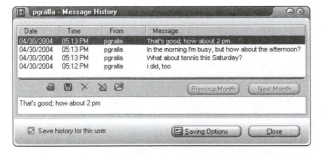

Figure 7-6. When you review your ICQ chats, you'll see each message sent in a chat, including the sender's name, the time, and the message itself.

IM AND JENNIFER ANISTON'S HAIRDO

The Annoyance: Whenever I open AIM, ICQ, or Yahoo! Messenger, a browser window appears with the latest useless "news." If I wanted the scoop on Jennifer Aniston's new hairdo, I'd pick up a supermarket tabloid. How can I stop this window from launching?

The Fix: That window is basically the IM app's welcome screen. Here's how to put the kibosh on it:

AIM

Click the Prefs button at the bottom of the AIM window, and choose Sign On/Sign Off. Uncheck the "Show AIM.com window at sign on" box, and click OK.

Yahoo! Messenger

Choose Messenger → Preferences → General, uncheck the "Show Yahoo! Insider when I login" box, and click OK.

ICQ Lite

Choose Main → Preference and Security → Contact List, uncheck the "Show the 'Welcome to ICQ' screen" box, and click OK (see Figure 7-7).

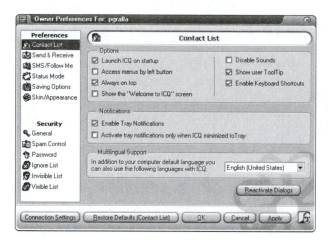

Figure 7-7. To stop ICQ from displaying its annoying welcome screen, just uncheck the "Show the 'Welcome to ICQ' screen" box.

PROTECT YOUR PRIVACY WHEN USING IM

The Annoyance: I received an IM yesterday from a complete stranger, wishing me a happy birthday and then trying to sell me a ring with my birthstone. How in the world did this scamster get my birthday? And how can I protect my privacy?

The Fix: The source of this grief was undoubtedly the personal profile you filled out when you registered your IM program. That profile is public, so anyone can read it, including people who want to sell you things you don't want.

If you're worried about your privacy, delete the profile or make it invisible. Here's how:

AIM

Choose My AIM → Edit Profile and uncheck the "Allow People to Search for Me" box (Figure 7-8). Make sure to keep clicking the Next button all the way through each screen; if you cancel at any point, your profile will still be public.

Figure 7-8. When you don't let people search for you, you essentially hide your AIM profile.

Yahoo! Messenger

Choose Messenger → Yahoo! Account Info. You'll be sent to a web page that asks for your password. Enter it, and you'll be taken to the Yahoo! Account Information page. This information is not public; only you can see it. Click Edit/Create Profiles. You'll be sent to a page that lists all your profiles. (Yahoo! lets you have more than one.) Click your profile, and you'll be sent to a profile page (see Figure 7-9). Other Yahoo! users *can* view this page. If there's any information here you don't want others to see, click the Edit Profile Information link near the top of the page. On the page that appears, delete any information you don't want made public and click Save Changes. Then, on the next page that appears, click Finished Editing.

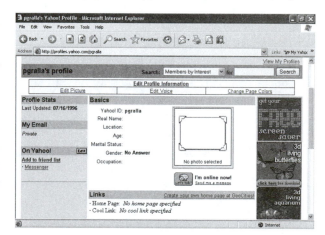

Figure 7-9. For maximum privacy, don't include any information in your public Yahoo! profile.

Windows Messenger/MSN Messenger

Choose Tools → Options → Personal → Edit Profile. If you haven't created a profile, you'll be asked if you want to download an add-in from the Web to do so. Since you haven't created a profile, your information isn't public, so there's no reason to download the add-in. If you have created a profile, you'll be sent to a page that has your public profile. Delete any information you don't want others to see, and click Save.

No More Windows Messenger Profile

If you install XP Service Pack 2 on your PC, you'll discover a new "enhancement" to your Windows Messenger account: your previous public profile has vanished. Nor can you create or edit one—the option is apparently no longer available in Windows Messenger.

ICQ

Choose Add/Find → View My Details. An Info Summary screen will appear that details all the information you've made public. Click each entry (Home, Work, Personal Info, and so on), and delete any information you don't want public. Click OK when you're done.

IM IS KILLING MY BUSINESS!

The Annoyance: I run a small business, and I'm worried that my employees are spending more time IMing than getting actual work done. I'm no Scrooge, but I really don't want them chatting on company time, much less exposing our network to dangers. How can I tell if they're chatting?

The Fix: If you're looking for snooping software, there are several programs that will do the trick. Most can report which port the user used, the number of logon attempts, the number of messages sent and received, and the number of files sent and received. IM Detector, for example, will scan your network, see if anyone is using AOL Instant Messenger, Windows Messenger/MSN Messenger, Yahoo! Messenger, or ICQ Lite or Pro. You can download a free evaluation version of IM Detector from *http://www.imlogic.com/resources_downloads.htm*. Such programs are useful, but they can be complex to set up, and ultimately you'll have to pay for them. If you're willing to do a little work, you can check for IM traffic yourself, using the outgoing traffic logs maintained by your router and looking for the ports and resources that all IM apps use. (Not all routers have this capability, though, and how you cull information varies from router to router and even among products from the same manufacturer.)

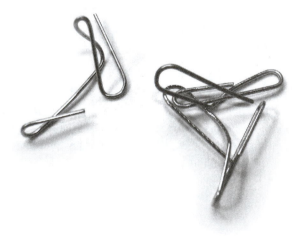

Note: with IM Detector or IM Guardian, you're automatically alerted when someone is using an IM program. With this do-it-yourself method, you'll have to regularly check the router's logs throughout the day. Here's how to check the logs of the popular Linksys BEFW11S4 router:

1. Log into your Linksys router's setup screen by going to *http://192.168.1.1* in your browser. Unless you've set it up with a username and a different password, leave the username blank and enter `admin` as the password.
2. Choose Administration → Log.
3. Make sure that the Yes radio button is selected, and click Save Settings.
4. Click the Outgoing Log button. A browser window will appear, listing all the outgoing traffic from your network to the Internet.
5. Examine the outgoing log for telltale signs of IM traffic in the Service/Port and Destination URL/IP columns. Look for these signs of IM use:
   - **AIM.** Port number 5190; URL *aim.aol.com* or *www.aim.com.*
   - **Yahoo! Messenger.** Port number 5050; URL *update.messenger.yahoo.com*, *update.pager.yahoo.com*, or *update.messenger.yahoo.com.*
   - **ICQ.** Port number 5140; URL *xtraz.icq.com.*
   - **Windows Messenger/MSN Messenger.** Port number 1863; URL *svcs.microsoft.com.*

If you see these port numbers or URLs repeatedly in the log, people on your network are instant messaging. To find out who is using IM, for any of the port numbers or URLs listed in step 5, write down the LAN IP address. Then go back to the Outgoing Log screen and select Status → Local Network. Click the DHCP Client Table, and you'll see a list of every IP address in use on your network, and the name of the computer tied to it (see Figure 7-10).

Outgoing Log Table - Microsoft Internet Explorer

Outgoing Log Table

Refresh

LAN IP	Destination URL/IP	Service/Port Number
192.168.1.100	205.188.5.100	5190
192.168.1.100	aim.aol.com	HTTP
192.168.1.100	205.188.6.206	5190
192.168.1.100	ar.atwola.com	HTTP
192.168.1.100	64.12.185.119	HTTP
192.168.1.100	www.aim.com	HTTP
192.168.1.100	64.12.24.189	5190
192.168.1.100	205.188.179.233	5190
192.168.1.100	66.151.150.16	2703
192.168.1.100	66.151.150.22	2703
192.168.1.100	pop3.catalog.com	POP3
192.168.1.100	bay1.oe.hotmail.com	HTTP
192.168.1.100	pop3.catalog.com	POP3
192.168.1.100	63.172.126.3	POP3
192.168.1.100	130.94.155.164	POP3
192.168.1.100	mail.comcast.net	POP3
192.168.1.100	bay1.oe.hotmail.com	HTTP
192.168.1.100	loginnet.passport.com	HTTP
192.168.1.100	bay1.oe.hotmail.com	HTTP
192.168.1.100	oe.hotmail.com	HTTP
192.168.1.100	services.msn.com	HTTP

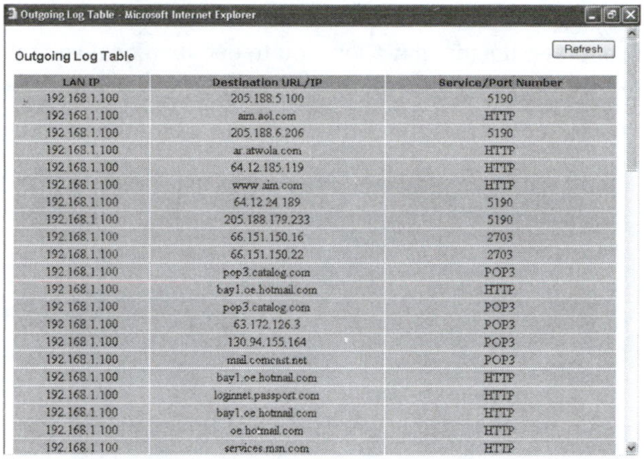

Figure 7-10. Looks like someone's been instant messaging on this network—the repeated use of port 5190 is a dead giveaway.

GET A UNIVERSAL INSTANT MESSENGER

The Annoyance: The inability of the major IM programs to talk to each other is a huge pain. It's like not being able to talk to a friend on the phone because her phone is made by a different manufacturer than mine! How do I topple this Tower of Babble?

The Fix: Get the free program Trillian from *http://www.ceruleanstudios.com.* It connects to all the major instant messaging programs, including AIM, Yahoo! Messenger, Windows Messenger/MSN Messenger, ICQ, and the original Internet chatting protocol, IRC (Internet Relay Chat).

To use it, you'll need accounts with each IM service. Run Trillian, enter the requested information about each of your accounts, and Trillian will automatically get your contact lists from each IM app. You'll then be able to see all your contacts from all of your instant messaging programs, and communicate with each from a single interface. Trillian lets you do most typical IM tricks, including sending and receiving messages and files, viewing profiles, and so on. It'll even tell you when you have email on AOL or Yahoo! and will launch you to their respective email web sites.

The basic version of Trillian is free; the $25 Trillian Pro supports plug-ins that allow you to get your local weather forecast piped into Trillian, do faster file transfers, and more (Figure 7-11).

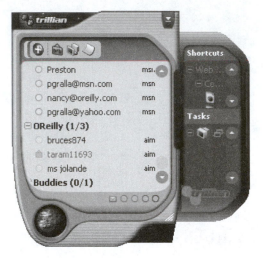

Figure 7-11. No need to run multiple IM programs—Trillian can communicate with all of them.

Other Universal Instant Messengers

Trillian is the most popular universal instant messenger around, but it's not the only one. Other notables are Gaim, an open source universal messenger for Windows, Linux, and the Macintosh (*http://gaim.sourceforge.net*), and Pandion (*http://www.pandion.be/rhymbox*) for Windows (formerly RhymBox).

TEACH TRILLIAN TO TALK AGAIN

The Annoyance: I thought Trillian was supposed to be a universal messenger, but two days ago it stopped connecting to AOL Instant Messenger. What's so universal about that?

The Fix: Every once in a while, the engineers at the IM vendors get tired of Trillian connecting to their instant messaging services, and so they block Trillian from getting through. But within a few days, Trillian's engineers figure out a workaround. If you run into an e-brick wall, look for the latest patch on the Trillian site at *http://www.ceruleanstudios.com*. You'll find instructions on how to download the update, or information on when one will be available.

HELP A MAC FRIEND

The Annoyance: My best friend is a Mac user. (I try not to hold this against him.) I'm a big IM fan and use ICQ, AIM, Windows Messenger, and Yahoo! Messenger. How can he IM me? Is there a Trillian for the Mac?

The Fix: The main free universal instant messaging program for the Mac is Fire, available from *http://fire.sourceforge.net*. It can communicate with AIM, ICQ, Windows Messenger, and Yahoo! Messenger, as well as with IRC and Jabber.

SEND FILES EASILY VIA IM

The Annoyance: I've tried sending a file to a coworker via email three times today, but each time my ISP rejected it, saying it was too large. There's gotta be some workaround.

The Fix: There is—use your IM app. No file size limits apply, because unlike with email, your attachments don't use up space on the ISP's server. As long as your company isn't blocking IM apps, you're home free. (If your company is, well, you're outta luck.)

Here's how to send files via the major IM programs:

AIM

Double-click the buddy you want to send the file to and, from the instant messaging window, choose File → Send File. Click the File button, browse to the file you want to send, and click Select. Click the Send button. Your buddy will be notified that you want to send a file. If he clicks OK, the file will be sent and you'll see the transfer status (Figure 7-12).

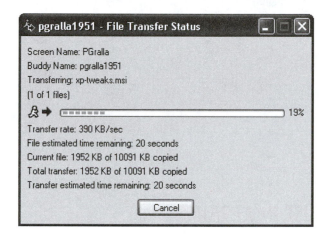

Figure 7-12. Gotta send big files? Forget email—IM is the way.

Windows Messenger/MSN Messenger

Double-click your buddy and, from the message window, click Send a File or Photo. Browse to the file you want to send and click Open. Your buddy will get a notification that you want to send a file. If he accepts it, the file transfer will start. You'll be able to see the transfer status at the bottom of the screen.

Yahoo! Messenger

Double-click your buddy and choose Contact → Send a File. Click the Browse button, choose the file you want to send, and click Open. In the Send a File dialog box, type a description of the file you want to transfer, and click Send. Your buddy will be asked whether he wants to accept the transfer. If he says yes, the file will be sent. You'll see its transfer progress and get a notification when the file transfer is complete (Figure 7-13).

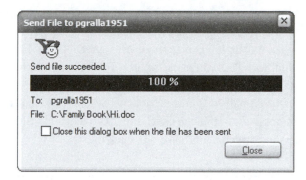

Figure 7-13. Unlike other IM apps, Yahoo! Messenger tells you when a file transfer is complete.

ICQ

Right-click the buddy you want to send the file to and choose Send File. Select the file you want to send, and click Open. The file will be sent.

STOP VIRUSES SENT VIA IM

The Annoyance: Gee, thanks for the advice on how to transfer files using IM. Now my computer is on the fritz, thanks to a virus I got via AIM. I thought my Norton AntiVirus would catch this!

The Fix: It sounds like you have an older version of Norton AntiVirus—versions prior to Norton 2003 didn't catch IM-borne viruses. Your best bet is to upgrade to the latest version of Norton (or get a comparable competing product). Even if you have the latest version, however, Norton won't necessarily protect you. It only catches files transferred with AIM Version 4.7 or later, Yahoo! Messenger Version 5.0 or later, and Windows Messenger/MSN Messenger Version 4.6 or later, so if you use ICQ or older versions of these IM apps, you're still at risk. Note: if you install Norton AntiVirus and then install an IM program, IM protection might not be enabled in Norton. To turn it on, choose Options → Instant Messenger, check the boxes next to your instant messaging programs, and click OK.

McAfee VirusScan will also catch viruses, but only those sent via AIM 2.1 or later, Windows Messenger/MSN Messenger 6.0 or later, or Yahoo! Messenger 4.1 or later. Again, with ICQ, you're out of luck. To make sure IM file-transfer protection is turned on, right-click the McAfee icon (the small "m") in the Windows System Tray, choose Options → ActiveShield, check the "Scan inbound instant message attachments" box, and click OK.

DOWNLOADED AND FORGOTTEN

Let's say you're sent a file via IM, but you don't immediately use it. The next day, you want to find it… but where in the world did it go? If you've saved it to a folder you've created, it should be easy to find. But if you used the default folder suggested by your IM program, you may have trouble tracking it down, because IM apps tend to keep these folders well hidden. Here are the default folders for the popular IM apps:

- ☒ **AIM:** *C:\Documents and Settings\<Your Name>\My Documents\filelib\<AIM Name>*, where *<Your Name>* is your XP account name and *<AIM Name>* is your AIM account name.

- ☒ **Windows Messenger/MSN Messenger:** *C:\Documents and Settings\<Your Name>\My Documents\My Received Files*. For a shortcut to get to the files, from Windows Messenger/MSN Messenger, choose File → Open Received Files.

- ☒ **Yahoo! Messenger:** *C:\Documents and Settings\<Your Name>\Application Data\Yahoo! Messenger\<Screen Name>\receive*, where *<Screen Name>* is your Yahoo! screen name.

- ☒ **ICQ:** *C:\Documents and Settings\<Your Name>\My Documents\ICQ Lite\<ICQ Number>*, where *<ICQ Number>* is your ICQ number, such as 7202344.

USE IM AT WORK

The Annoyance: I've been trying, to no avail, to convince my boss that we should use IM for our group. He tells me that the "powers that be" (whoever they are) have said that IM is too insecure to be used in our corporation. Is there a secure IM tool I can tell these dinosaurs to install?

The Fix: There are a variety of IM programs that can be used securely in corporations, but at the top of most everyone's list is Jabber Messenger, available from *http://www.jabber.com/index.cgi*. Jabber can't just be downloaded and installed by anyone at your company; your IT department will have to do some network and infrastructure configuration. (Tell them to head to *jabber.org* to get started.) With security in mind, the IT staff can disable certain Jabber features, create custom tabs, set up secure collaboration and text messaging, require authentication, and more. Once it's up and running, Jabber will do everything an IM program can do, and then some—and it'll do it securely, company-wide.

AOL INSTANT MESSENGER (AIM)

KISS OFF AIM ADS

The Annoyance: Those ads at the top of AIM are about to drive me around the bend. I do not want to search for homes for sale; I'm perfectly happy where I live. Isn't there some way to turn them off?

The Fix: There are a lot of free and commercial AIM ad-blockers out there, but the very best in my opinion is DeadAIM, available from *http://www.jdennis.net*. True, you'll have to pay $5 for it via PayPal, but this nifty little utility goes well beyond just blocking ads. With AIM, it's generally all or nothing—block all ads, or block none. With DeadAIM, however, you can let some through and not others, log everything from chats to events to sounds, customize your Buddy List, and more. You can even change the way AIM looks, turning it transparent by varying degrees so you can see right through it. Alternatively, if you're a real cheapskate, you can get the free AIM Ad Remover from *http://www.necrocosm.com*.

Fix DeadAIM Problem with AIM Upgrade

If you install DeadAIM and later upgrade AIM, DeadAIM may no longer work. There's an easy fix: shut down AIM and select Start → Programs → Repair DeadAIM. Sometimes rebooting will solve the problem, too.

DOES AIM INSTALL SPYWARE?

The Annoyance: I scanned my PC for spyware using Ad-Aware, and I found a program on it called Wild-Tangent, apparently installed along with AIM. WildTangent collects anonymous information about your computer, including what game components you have installed, your computer's CPU speed, and your video card configuration, and sends it to AOL. Is it spyware, and can it be removed?

The Fix: Here's an instance where spyware is in the eye of the beholder. AOL and WildTangent say that the information is not tied to your computer and is not shared with anyone else. That may be small solace; if you like, you can remove WildTangent with Ad-Aware, and AIM will still work just fine. (For details, see the "Spyware" section in Chapter 9.)

If you don't want to use Ad-Aware to remove WildTanget, you can do it yourself. Go to *http://wildtangent.custhelp. com* and select the Uninstallation item. (If it's not there, search the help system for "How do I uninstall the Web Driver and games?") For more information about Wild-Tangent, head to *http://www.kephyr.com/spywarescanner/library/wildtangent/index.phtml*.

tip

The newest version of AIM warns you before installing WildTangent. During installation, it asks if you want to play AIM-based games. If you say yes, it will install WildTangent.

BE INVISIBLE IN PLAIN SIGHT WITH AIM

The Annoyance: I use AIM at work, because I need to communicate with my coworkers quickly and we're in different locations. But I don't want to be bombarded all day with IMs from other people. How can I be online, but hidden?

The Fix: You can easily make yourself invisible to all AIM users except ones that you specify, so that only your coworkers can communicate with you. Simply click the Prefs button at the bottom of the AIM window (in some versions, you click Setup and then choose Preferences) and choose Privacy. Click the "Allow only the users below" radio button, type in the buddy names of your coworkers, and click OK. They'll be the only people who can "see" you. If, after work, you want to be open to the IM world, return to the same screen, click the "Allow all users to contact me" radio button, and click OK.

USE AIM AND AOL AT THE SAME TIME

The Annoyance: I often have AIM and AOL running at the same time. I didn't think this was a problem until I realized that if AOL is up and running, IMs sent to me go to AOL, not AIM! How can I stop this annoying practice?

The Fix: You can't directly fix this, as this is the way AOL is set up to work. The only solution is to create a new AIM account that isn't tied to your AOL account and use that for instant messaging. That way, any IMs sent to you will always show up in AIM, even when AOL is running. To set up a new AIM account, run AIM, but don't log in. From the AIM screen, click Get a Screen Name. You'll be sent to a web page where you provide basic information, such as the new screen name you want to set up, your password, and so on. After you fill in the form, you'll have a new AIM account. If you have more than one account, you can switch between them by choosing the account from the Screen Name drop-down box on the login window, entering your password, and clicking Sign On.

MY ROUTER BLOCKS AIM FILE TRANSFERS!

The Annoyance: I just installed a home network, and now I can't transfer files using AIM. What's going on here?

The Fix: Your router is blocking the AIM-to-AIM connection, so you need to reconfigure both AIM and your router to allow file transfers. With a Linksys router, for example, you'd follow these steps:

1. First, tell AIM what port to use for file transfers. Click the Prefs button at the bottom of the AIM window, and choose File Sharing. You'll see the screen shown in Figure 7-14. In the "Port number to use" box, type 2500. (If these steps don't work, try a higher port number.) Click OK.

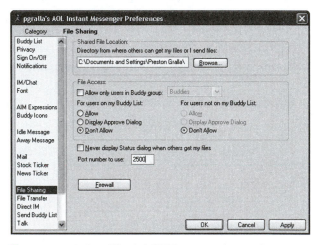

Figure 7-14. Can't send files with AIM? You may need to reconfigure your router.

2. Log into your Linksys router's setup screen by going to *http://192.168.1.1* in your browser and entering the necessary password and username (the default is admin for the password and no username).

3. Choose Applications & Gaming → Port Triggering.

4. Create an entry for transferring files via AIM. Type "AIM Transfer" in the Application box. In the Triggered Range section, type 5190 in the Start Port and End Port boxes. For the Forwarded Range, set the Start

Port and End Port to 2500 (see Figure 7-15). Click Save Settings. You'll be able to transfer files in AIM from now on.

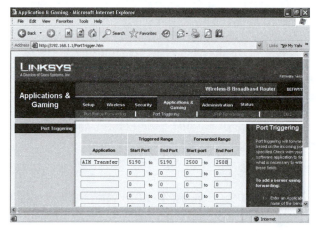

Figure 7-15. Force your router to accept AIM file transfers by turning on and configuring port triggering.

MAKE ICQ AND AIM TALK

The Annoyance: My best friend only uses ICQ, and I only use AIM. Even though America Online owns ICQ, the two IM apps apparently don't talk to one another. How can we bridge this gap?

The Fix: Actually, the two messengers can now talk to one another—AOL put them on speaking terms without any fanfare. Although it's not obvious how to do it, if you're an ICQ user, you can put an AIM friend on your Buddy List, be notified when he's online (and vice versa), chat, and so on. The same holds true for an AIM user.

In ICQ, to add an AIM user to your Buddy List, click Add/Find and go to the Add/Invite User tab. Select Add AOL Screen Name, type in your buddy's screen name, and click Add. Then add him to your Buddy List as you would any ICQ user.

In AIM, click the Setup button at the bottom of the screen, select Add a Buddy, then type in your friend's ICQ number. AIM will instantly recognize it as an ICQ member and will add it to your Buddy List, with the letters "ICQ" after the number. A dialog box will appear, letting you assign the ICQ buddy a name, so that instead of seeing 72020344 – ICQ, for example, you could see something like Joey-Boy.

SHRINK YOUR BUDDY LIST

The Annoyance: Maybe I'm just a popular guy, but I have a huge Buddy List. The problem is that every time I sign in, all of my Buddy Group lists expand, and the result is as long as the Dead Sea scrolls. I collapse the groups, but the next time I log in, there they are again, expanded.

The Fix: The solution lies in the Windows Registry. Here's what to do:

1. Exit AIM.

2. Launch the Registry Editor by selecting Start → Run, typing regedit in the Open box, and pressing Enter.

3. Go to the Registry key HKEY_CURRENT_USER\Software\ America Online\AOL Instant Messenger (TM)\ CurrentVersion\Users\<Your Name>\Buddy, where <Your Name> is your AIM username.

4. Right-click Buddy, then click New → DWORD Value.

5. A new item will appear in the righthand window. Name it AutoExpandGroups.

6. Press Enter to save the new key, and then exit the Registry Editor.

WHY CAN'T I RESIZE MY AIM SCREEN?

The Annoyance: I'm constantly fiddling with the size of my AIM window, and I think I've pushed AIM too far—now I can't change its size, no matter what I do. What happened? What's the fix?

The Fix: Sometimes, for no apparent reason, AIM suffers brain lock and refuses to let you change its window size. You'll have to edit the Windows Registry to fix the problem. Here's how:

1. Exit AIM.

2. Launch the Registry Editor by selecting Start → Run, typing regedit in the Open box, and pressing Enter.

3. Go to the Registry key HKEY_CURRENT_USER\Software\America Online\AOL Instant Messenger (TM)\CurrentVersion\Users\<Your Name>\WindowPos, where <Your Name> is your AIM username.

4. Right-click WindowPos, select Delete, and choose Yes in the confirmation dialog.

5. Exit the Registry. The AIM window will now be at its default size, and you can now resize it at will.

USE AIM WITHOUT INSTALLING IT

The Annoyance: I'm using a friend's PC, and he doesn't have AIM installed and won't let me install it on his computer. Is there another way I can keep in touch via AIM?

The Fix: There's a web-based version of AIM that looks and works just like the real thing. To use it, go to *http://www.aim.com/get_aim/express* and click the Start button. Then log in and use AIM as you normally would.

Note that if your friend has a pop-up blocker installed, you won't be able to use AIM—the pop-up blocker will stop various AIM windows from launching, including your Buddy List. To get around this problem, either disable the pop-up blocker or add *http://aimexpress.aim.com* to the list of allowed domains. (For information on adding domains to the list of allowed pop-ups, see "Pop Away Pop-Ups" in Chapter 5 and "I Want My Pop-Ups! (Well, Some of Them)" in Chapter 5.)

If you're an ICQ fan, its web equivalent is at *http://go.icq.com*.

TURN OFF AIM ANNOUNCEMENTS

The Annoyance: All day long, big, annoying windows pop up in the Windows System Tray, telling me whenever one of my AIM buddies has signed in, signed out, taken a break, come back from a break, or even taken a breath, it seems. How can I turn them off?

The Fix: Easy: choose MyAIM → Edit Options → Edit Preferences → Notifications, uncheck the "Show pop-up notifications" box, and click OK. If you want to be notified about only certain events—for example, when a buddy signs on—check the "Show pop-up notifications" box and the boxes next to the specific events, then click OK.

SHUT UP AIM

The Annoyance: If I hear one more sound effect from AIM, I am going to tear my speakers out of their jacks. I'd like a gentle audio notification when a buddy comes online, but I don't want a constant bombardment of sounds for other notifications.

The Fix: To stop the madness entirely, go to MyAIM → Edit Options → Edit Preferences → Buddy List → Sounds, choose "Do not play any sounds" from the drop-down box, and click OK. If you want to hear some sounds, but not others, choose "Play the sounds below" from the drop-down box and pick the desired events. You can also choose which sound plays for each type of notification. For example, if you click the Sound button next to "Play a sound when buddies sign on," you can then select the desired sound to play from the Sound drop-down box. Click the Preview button to hear it. If you want to use a sound other than one provided by AOL, click the Browse button and select the desired *.wav* file.

STOP OBNOXIOUS AIMERS

The Annoyance: I continually get obnoxious IMs from one person when I use AIM. I ended up blocking the person from sending me messages, but I'd like to warn others to beware of him. What can I do?

The Fix: You can issue an AIM warning about a user. Everyone in AIM-land can see the user's warning level and can decide whether to block messages from that user. The user's ability to send and receive messages is limited, too; with each new warning he can send and receive fewer and fewer messages, until ultimately he can't send or receive any messages at all.

You can only issue a warning when you're in an IM session with that user; you can't issue warnings after the fact. To issue a warning when you're in an IM session, choose People → Warn. A screen will pop up, noting that you're about to send a warning (see Figure 7-16). If you don't want the user to know that you're issuing the warning, click the "Warn anonymously" box. If you do this, however, the person's warning level won't be as severe. To send the warning, click the Warn button.

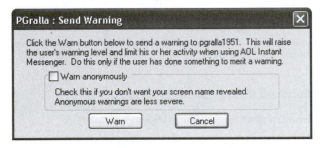

Figure 7-16. If someone is being obnoxious, issue a warning via AIM.

You'll get a notice that the person's warning level has been increased. For the first offense, the level is increased to 20%. According to AOL, each warning increases a user's warning percentage by 20%—so five quickly issued warnings could effectively shut down that person's ability to IM. (Note however, that each of those warnings

must come from a different person.) The offender will receive a notice that a warning has been issued, and unless you sent it anonymously he'll be told it's from you (see Figure 7-17).

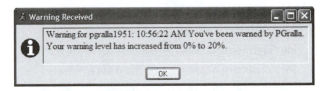

Figure 7-17. Here's the message a user receives when a warning is issued against him.

From now on, that person's warning level will appear next to his name in people's Buddy Lists, as shown in Figure 7-18, and in the upper-righthand corner of the chat window during any instant messaging session. There's no appeal procedure for the offender. Over time, the offender's warning percentage decreases, until he falls below a "critical" level (as AOL puts it) and can send IMs again.

Figure 7-18. Users' warning levels appear next to their names in other people's Buddy Lists.

BRAVE NEW AIMBOTS

The Annoyance: I had a thoroughly bizarre IM conversation with a stranger the other day on AIM—it was kind of like talking with a schizophrenic who was still learning English. I saved the log of the chat and showed it to a tech-savvy friend, who said I hadn't been talking to a person at all; it was an "AIMBot." What the heck is an AIMBot, and do they serve any useful purpose?

The Fix: AIMBots combine artificial intelligence with instant messaging; they're buddy-cum-computer programs that respond to you more or less like a sentient being. And as you've discovered, some are more intelligent than others. You talk with AIMBots as you would any other buddy. Put them on your Buddy List and start chatting; they'll respond, and the "conversation" is on its way.

Some AIMBots are designed to deliver information, and they do a surprisingly good job once you learn how to use them. The best of the bunch is SmarterChild (*http://www.smarterchild.com*), which can find news stories, gather stock quotes, and perform other research tasks. You can converse with SmarterChild like you would with any other AIMBot, but with a twist. If you want to see the latest news stories, type "Get the latest news," "news," or a similar variant. If you want to see news about a particular subject, type "news" followed by the subject, such as "news iraq." To get information about anything, type in a phrase. For example, type in "Romeo and Juliet," and you'll get a menu that will let you choose what kind of information you want about the play—you can opt to read the entire play, search the play for a word or phrase, and more.

To find an AIMBot, go to *http://runabot.com* and scan the lists of the most popular AIMBots, Editor's Picks, and so on. You can even create your own AIMBot using tools you can download from the site.

Many people believe that in the future, AIMBots and other instant messaging bots will be used for customer service—ask them questions, and they deliver answers. Given the current state of bot development, that sounds awfully optimistic, but considering the lousy state of customer service, we could do worse.

WINDOWS MESSENGER

STOP WINDOWS MESSENGER FROM AUTOSTARTING

The Annoyance: Every time I start Windows, an unwelcome visitor shows up in the Windows System Tray: Windows Messenger. I try to close it by right-clicking the icon and choosing Exit, but it behaves like a door-to-door salesman with his foot in my front door—it refuses to leave. What can I do?

The Fix: Once Windows Messenger is running, it's tough to shut down. First close Internet Explorer, Outlook, and Outlook Express, and then right-click the Messenger icon and select Exit. This keeps it out of the way until you reboot your PC or turn it off and then on.

A better solution, of course, is to keep Windows Messenger (and MSN Messenger) from loading in the first place. Load the IM app and select Tools → Options → Preferences. Uncheck the "Run this program when Windows starts" box, then click OK.

KILL WINDOWS MESSENGER FOREVER

The Annoyance: I never, ever, under any circumstances, want to use Windows Messenger. It was easy to remove from my work PC, but I couldn't even find it on my home PC. What's the scoop?

The Fix: The job is easy if your PC is using XP with Service Pack 1 or 2 installed. Just open the Add or Remove Programs control panel, click the Add/Remove Windows Components button on the left, and, in the Windows Components Wizard, scroll down and uncheck the Windows Messenger box. Click the Next button, and the job is done.

On the other hand, if you're using a pre-SP1 version of Windows XP, you'll have to force Windows Messenger to show up on the list of Windows components by editing the Setup Information file that controls what appears in the Windows Components Wizard.

Use Notepad or another text editor to open the Setup Information file, *sysoc.inf*, which is usually found in the *C:\Windows\inf* folder. For safety's sake, make a backup of the file before editing it. Keep in mind that *C:\Windows\inf* is a hidden folder, so if you want to view its contents, you will first have to make hidden folders visible by going into Windows Explorer, choosing Tools → Folder Options, clicking the View tab, and selecting "Show hidden files and folders."

Open the file and locate the line that looks something like this:

```
msmsgs=msgrocm.dll,OcEntry,msmsgs.inf,hide,7
```

This entry refers to Windows Messenger. If there is a hide command embedded in the string, it won't show up in the Windows Component Wizard. To force it to show up in the wizard, remove hide so that the line looks like this:

```
msmsgs=msgrocm.dll,OcEntry,msmsgs.inf,,7
```

Save the *sysoc.inf* file, then run the Windows Components Wizard. Windows Messenger will now show up, and you can remove it using the steps noted earlier.

One warning: on some systems, you simply won't be able to remove Windows Messenger—it won't show up in the Windows Components Wizard even after you edit the *sysoc.inf* file. The ultimate solution is to upgrade to the latest Service Pack. To find the newest Service Pack, go to *http://www.microsoft.com/windowsxp* and search for service pack.

FILE TRANSFERS FLAKE OUT

The Annoyance: Transferring files via Windows Messenger is a great alternative to email, because some versions of Outlook and Outlook Express won't let you accept certain kinds of files, and some ISPs block messages over a certain size. But it's only a great alternative if the file transfer actually works, and often it doesn't. How can I make sure my files will get through?

The Fix: The problem is that your firewall—or a firewall on the receiving end—is blocking the file transfer. Firewalls typically block ports 6891 through 6900—the very ports Windows Messenger uses for file transfers. How you open these ports varies from firewall to firewall, but if you use the Windows Firewall with XP SP2, here's how the process works:

1. Double-click the Security Center icon in the System Tray ot choose Security Center from the control panel. The Security Center will appear.

2. Scroll to the bottom of the screen, click the Windows Firewall button, and the Windows Firewall options dialog box will appear.

3. Choose the Advanced tab and click the Settings button in the Network Connections Settings area. The Advanced Settings dialog box will appear.

4. On the Services tab, click the Add button. The Service Settings dialog box will appear.

5. In the "Description of service" field, type in File Transfers via Windows Messenger.

6. In the "Name or IP address" field, type in your computer's IP address, such as 192.168.1.5. To find your computer's IP address, select Start → Programs → Accessories → Command Prompt, type ipconfig at the command prompt, and look for the IP address. Type exit and hit Enter to close the prompt.

7. In both the "External Port number" and "Internal Port number" fields, type 6891 (see Figure 7-19). Select TCP for the external port. Click OK three times to confirm your choices.

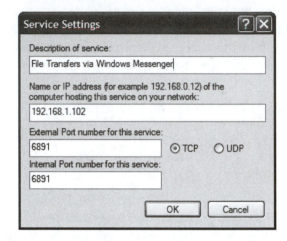

Figure 7-19. If you want to transfer files using Windows Messenger, you may need to punch a few holes in your firewall by opening specific ports.

8. Repeat steps 6 and 7 for every port between 6891 and 6900. I know—what fun!

What if You Don't Have SP2?

If you're running a pre-SP2 version of Windows XP, right-click My Network Places on the desktop and choose Properties. Then right-click your Internet connection, choose Properties, and follow steps 3 through 8.

STOP MESSENGER FROM LAUNCHING WITH OUTLOOK AND OUTLOOK EXPRESS

The Annoyance: Whenever I launch Outlook Express or Outlook, Windows Messenger launches as well. Make it stop!

The Fix: Ah, another brilliant Microsoft default. To stop this behavior in Outlook Express, choose Tools → Options, click the General tab, and uncheck the "Automatically log on to Windows Messenger" box. In Outlook 2002, choose Tools → Options, click the Other tab, and uncheck the "Enable Instant Messaging in Microsoft Outlook" box. In Outlook 2003, don't sweat—Microsoft has apparently eliminated this annoying habit.

SEND INSTANT MESSAGES FROM OUTLOOK

The Annoyance: I live in Outlook, but there are times when I'd rather grab someone for a quick IM session with Windows Messenger. Why can't I do everything from Outlook?

The Fix: You can, more or less. Both Outlook and Outlook Express can send instant messages to a Windows Messenger user. In Outlook Express, Windows Messenger contacts appear at the top of the Contacts pane. A green icon appears next to the name of each contact who is online. Double-click a contact name, and you essentially launch Windows Messenger and can send an instant message. In Outlook, if the contact is online, the green icon will show up in the Outlook InfoBar. To send an instant message, click the InfoBar, compose a message, and click Send.

YAHOO! MESSENGER

CLEAN OUT THE YAHOO! MESSENGER JUNK

The Annoyance: Surprise! When I downloaded Yahoo! Messenger, I didn't just install an instant messaging program. I also downloaded all kinds of add-ins, buttons, bookmarks and more—things like an annoying Yahoo! Companion Internet Explorer toolbar that shows up constantly, even after you shut it down. Not only that, but without telling you, Yahoo! sets your default Internet search site to Yahoo!, and it adds a set of bookmarks to Internet Explorer as well. How can I exorcise this junk?

The Fix: It'll take some work, but it's doable. First open the Add or Remove Programs control panel, then scroll down and locate Yahoo! Companion, Yahoo! Customizations, Yahoo! Internet Mail, and Yahoo! Messenger Explorer Bar. Leave Yahoo! Messenger alone. Select the other items in turn and click the Change/Remove button.

Here's how to get rid of Yahoo! search:

1. Open Internet Explorer and press Ctrl-E or click the Search button on the toolbar to open IE's Search pane.

2. Click the Customize button on the Search pane's toolbar, then click the Reset button. This will restore Internet Explorer's default search tool.

3. If you don't want to use the default search tool, click the Customize button again, pick the desired search engine from the scrolling list to the left, and click OK.

To axe the URLs Yahoo! snuck onto your Favorites list, jump to the bottom of the list, which is where you'll find them. Delete them as you would any other Favorites—right-click each, choose Delete, and then click Yes.

YAHOO! MESSENGER CRASHES WHENEVER I SEND A FILE

The Annoyance: Whenever I send a file using Yahoo! Messenger, it crashes. Needless to say, this defeats the entire purpose of instant communications. What's wrong?

The Fix: There's a corrupt file in the Yahoo! Messenger program directory. Uninstall the program with the Add or Remove Programs control panel. Make sure that the entire directory was deleted. (The default is *C:\Program Files\Yahoo!*.) Exit and restart Windows, reinstall Yahoo! Messenger, and the problem should go away.

CAN'T LOG INTO YAHOO! MESSENGER

The Annoyance: Whenever I try to log into Yahoo! Messenger, I get an "invalid cookie" error message. What's wrong? It worked fine last week!

The Fix: When you sign up for Yahoo! Messenger the first time, it plants a cookie on your system that's used for logging into your account. For some reason, the cookie's been corrupted and now doesn't match your Yahoo! ID. Here's how to fix it:

1. Go to *http://in.my.yahoo.com*, and sign in using your My Yahoo! ID and password. That will set your system's cookie correctly.

2. In the Messenger window, click Login and then choose Login/Change User. Make sure you use the same Yahoo! ID and password for Messenger that you use with My Yahoo!

3. Click the Login button. This will return you to Messenger. From now on, you'll be logged in correctly.

WHERE ARE MY MESSAGES?

The Annoyance: Whenever I send or receive an instant message, I don't see any text—just a blank screen.

The Fix: For Yahoo! Messenger to work, you must turn on scripting in Internet Explorer; yours has somehow gotten turned off. To turn it on:

1. Close Yahoo! Messenger. Then, in Internet Explorer, choose Tools → Internet Options and click the Security tab.

2. Click the Internet icon, then click the Custom Level button.

3. Scroll down a ways to Scripting, and make sure that "Active scripting," "Allow paste operations via script," and "Scripting of Java applets" are all enabled, as shown in Figure 7-20. Click OK, then OK again.

The problem should now be fixed, and you should be able to see your messages.

Figure 7-20. Turn on scripting to make sure that you can see messages in Yahoo! Messenger.

ICQ

MAKE ICQ A PRIVATE CLUB

The Annoyance: I'm tired of every Tom, Dick, and Harry being able to add me to their Contact Lists. Can I exercise some control over who considers me a buddy?

The Fix: Of all the instant messaging programs, only ICQ lets you control who adds you to their Contact Lists. Choose Main → Preferences and Security. In the screen that appears, choose General from the Security section. Check the "My authorization is required before users add me to their Contact List" box, then click OK.

STOP THE ICQ TYPEWRITER

The Annoyance: That echoey typewriter sound that ICQ makes when I type is driving me bonkers. One great thing about the death of the typewriter was the end of that #@#$@#$ clackety-clack. Help me send this sound effect to the bit bucket!

The Fix: Choose Main → Preferences and Security. In the screen that appears, choose Contact List from the Preferences section. Check the "Disable Sounds" box, and click OK.

GET ICQ OUT OF YOUR FACE

The Annoyance: ICQ reminds me of an overbearing aunt who talks at full volume about three inches from your face. After I launch ICQ, it always stays on top of every window on my screen. How can I stop this obnoxious behavior?

The Fix: This is ICQ's default setting. To make it go away when you switch to another window, choose Main → Preferences and Security. In the screen that appears, choose Contact List from the Preferences section. Uncheck the "Always on Top" box, and click OK.

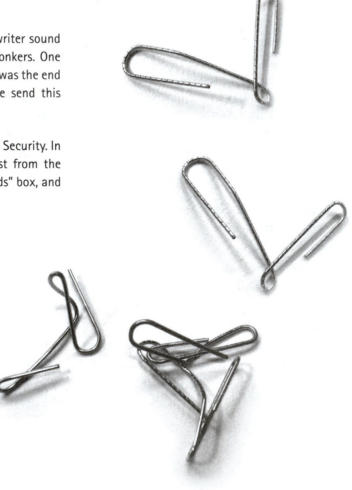

Searching
ANNOYANCES

8

Quick, answer this question: do you spend more time on the Internet searching for things or actually finding them?

I thought so—searching. After all, it's easy to type a few words into a search box, but it's tough to actually find anything you want. And that's no surprise. The Internet is a big, big place, filled with billions of pages of text, not nice, neat, indexable database records. Crafting the right search criteria for each different search engine, accommodating their quirks and limits, learning their arcane syntaxes, pawing through paid results looking for the real thing, is… well, bloody annoying. It's amazing we ever find anything! There's a wealth of information out there, though, and the tips within this chapter will show you how to bend the search engines to your will and track down whatever you're looking for.

GENERAL SEARCH ANNOYANCES

WEED OUT SPONSORED SEARCH RESULTS

The Annoyance: Call me an old fogey, but I remember the days when you used a search site and got back results based on relevance to your query. These days, the results are skewed—sponsors get top billing while everything else falls off the screen, and it's not always easy to tell sponsored results from really relevant results. How can I filter out these ads masquerading as search results?

The Fix: Use the AdSubtract utility's Search Sanity feature. AdSubtract's main job is to block ads while you surf the Web, but its Search Sanity feature is even more useful—it eliminates annoying sponsored and paid results (see Figure 8-1) so that you only see pages that really match your search.

You can get AdSubtract from *http://www.adsubtract.com*. (It's free to try for 30 days and costs $29.95 if you keep it.) When you install it, you'll have to turn on Search Sanity. Double-click the AdSubtract icon in the Windows System Tray, choose Search Sanity, and check the boxes next to the search engines whose results you want to filter (see Figure 8-2). Click OK, and sponsored results and ads will be banished! Figure 8-3 shows the results of a search with Search Sanity enabled.

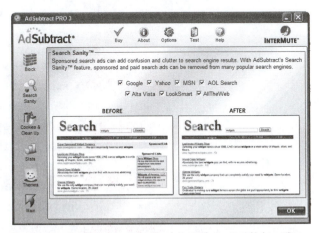

Figure 8-2. But if you turn on the Search Sanity feature in AdSubtract Pro...

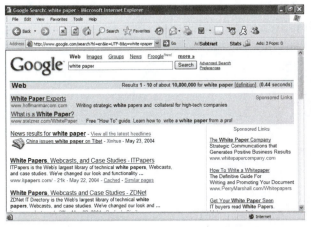

Figure 8-1. Even on Google, sponsored search results clutter up the page.

Figure 8-3. ...sponsored results vanish, making it easier find the most relevant results.

SEARCH THE PAST WITH THE WAYBACK MACHINE

The Annoyance: My favorite web site crashed and burned several years ago, never to be heard from again. I desperately need a piece of information on that site. Am I out of luck?

The Fix: Maybe not. The Internet Archive at *http://www.archive.org* has been saving web pages since 1996, and the site you're looking for might be there. Search the archive's Wayback Machine for any web site address or phrase, and you'll get a list of relevant pages, organized by year and month (Figure 8-4). Click the links to view the pages—well, at least what the Archive was able to get its hands on. Graphics are often missing, but the text is usually there. Links on retrieved pages don't always work, and occasionally you'll find a page that's largely blank. But when it comes to finding the remains of the Web, the Archive is about your only option.

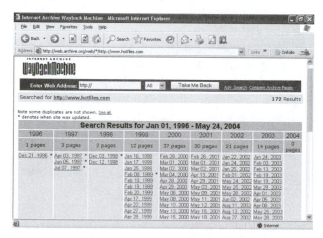

Figure 8-4. Get back to where you once belonged: you can find defunct web pages in the Internet Archive.

GOOGLE TOOLBAR ALTERNATIVES

The Annoyance: The Google Toolbar is way convenient—but I don't just use Google. Surely the competition has kept up! Do sites like HotBot and AltaVista have toolbars? Where can I get them?

The Fix: These days, any search site worth its salt has its own toolbar. Here are some of the notable ones:

- Ask Jeeves Toolbar: *http://sp.ask.com/docs/toolbar*
- AltaVista Toolbar: *http://www.altavista.com/toolbar/*
- Dogpile Toolbar: *http://www.dogpile.com/info.dogpl/tbar*
- HotBot Quick Search Toolbar: *http://www.hotbot.com/tools*
- Teoma Search Bar: *http://sp.ask.com/docs/teoma/toolbar*
- Yahoo! Companion Toolbar: *http://companion.yahoo.com*
- MSN Toolbar: *http://toolbar.msn.com*

These toolbars offer an array of features—some (such as Yahoo!'s) go in for pop-up blocking, while others (such as HotBot's) offer the ability to search files on your PC. They don't conflict with each other, either, so yes, you can pile 'em on.

CHANGE IE'S DEFAULT SEARCH ENGINE

The Annoyance: Whenever I search from Internet Explorer's Address Box, it always defaults to MSN Search—my least favorite search engine. Please tell me I can change this!

The Fix: You can indeed use other search sites, including Google and Yahoo!, among others. Here's how:

1. Click the Search button in the IE toolbar. A vertical Search window will open on the left.

2. Click the Customize button. In the Customize Search Settings dialog, click the Autosearch Settings button.

3. From the drop-down list in the Customize Autosearch Settings dialog box, shown in Figure 8-5, choose the search service you want to use. (If the search engine you want isn't on the list, check the next annoyance for a semi-fix.)

4. Click OK and OK again. From now on, when you search the Web from the Address Bar (or click IE's Search button), IE will use this service.

Figure 8-5. You can tell Internet Explorer to use a different search engine than MSN when you type in a search term in your Address Bar.

t i p

If you want, you can turn off searching from the Address Bar. Why would you turn off this feature? Beats me, but Microsoft lets you do it. At Step 3, when you're in the Customize Autosearch Settings dialog box, select "Do not search from the Address bar" from the "When searching" drop-down.

SUPER SEARCHES FROM THE ADDRESS BAR

The Annoyance: I know that if I type a word or phrase in IE's Address Bar, IE will search for those terms using the default search engine. But there are times when I don't want to use my default search engine—I might want to use, say, Yahoo! instead. Why isn't there a simple way to use any search engine from the Address Bar?

The Fix: There is—but it takes a bit of work. Once done, you'll be able to search via Yahoo!, for example, by typing something like yahoo stem cell in the Address

Bar. The trick requires the services of that great all-around tweaking tool, TweakUI. Here's how it works:

1. Download TweakUI from *www.microsoft.com/windowsxp/pro/downloads/powertoys.asp*. Installation is straightforward; just follow the instructions.

2. Run TweakUI and open Internet Explorer → Search in the lefthand panel. Click the Create button on the right.

3. In the Search Prefix dialog box (shown in Figure 8-6), you will tell Internet Explorer to search via another site rather than the default. You must create a separate entry for each search engine you want to use.

Figure 8-6. Create separate entries for each search engine you want to be able to search directly from the Address Bar.

4. What you type in the Prefix box is what you'll have to type in IE's Address Bar before your search term. For example, to search via Google, type Google in the Prefix box. Note: you don't have to use the exact name of the search engine. For example, instead of typing Google, you could enter gl in the Prefix box. When you later ran a search, you'd type something like gl stem cell. For the purposes of this example, though, enter Google.

t i p

You can only put one word in the Prefix box, or else the search won't work. So, for example, if you set up Internet Explorer to do a search via Ask Jeeves, you'll need to enter a single word in the Prefix box (e.g., Ask).

5. In the URL box, type the search engine's URL—in this case, `http://www.google.com/search?q=%s`. The exact URL will vary, depending on the search engine. For a list of the URLs to use for several of the most popular search engines, see Table 8-1.

Table 8-1. Search URLs for search sites

Site	URL
Google	*http://www.google.com/search?q=%s*
Yahoo!	*http://search.yahoo.com/search?p=%s*
Alta Vista	*http://www.altavista.com/sites/search/web?q=%s*
Lycos	*http://search.lycos.com/default.asp?query=%s*
Ask Jeeves	*http://web.ask.com/web?q=%s*

6. Click OK, then Apply, and then OK again. You'll now be able to search Google from Internet Explorer by typing `Google` and then your search term, like this: `Google stem cell`.

You can add as many search prefixes to Internet Explorer as you like.

When **searching**, you can use more than one search term, just as you would when you're at an Internet search site.

USE A UNIVERSAL SEARCH ENGINE

The Annoyance: So many search engines, so little time. Isn't there some way I can search with all of them at once? And I don't just want results; I'd like to see them sorted into tidy little categories.

The Fix: There's a great piece of free software that can do this for you—Copernic Agent Basic, available from *http://www.copernic.com*. It automatically searches through 90 separate search engines, including many specialized ones, and then groups your results into related categories. It also automatically kills any searches that lead to bad links, lets you search within your results, and

Freely Ferret Out Information

Another worthwhile free utility that searches through multiple search sites is WebFerret, available from *http://www.ferretsoft.com*. You can sort your searches by page name, address, source, and the page abstract; automatically remove duplicate results; and more. It's not quite as powerful as Copernic, but different people often like different interfaces, so give it a spin.

lets you save pages to your PC so that you can browse them offline. Its toolbar integrates into Internet Explorer so that you can search from wherever you are on the Web.

DO A REVERSE PHONEBOOK LOOKUP

The Annoyance: I have someone's phone number, but not his mailing address or last name. How can I find the address? And how can I find out who owns that phone number, short of hiring a detective?

The Fix: Turn to a reverse telephone book. Type in a phone number, and you'll find out who owns the phone number and that person's mailing address. You'll often have to try more than one site, because none of them lists *all* phone numbers. Here are some recommendations:

- AnyWho (*http://www.anywho.com/rl.html*)
- Langenberg Reverse Phone Directory (*http://reverse-directory.langenberg.com*)
- SuperPages.com (*http://yellowpages.superpages.com/yp.advanced.jsp?SRC=&STYPE=AP*)
- WhitePages.com (*http://www.whitepages.com/phone-lookup*)

If you type a phone number into Google using the format ###-###-#### (for example, 800-555-1212), Google performs a reverse phonebook lookup.

WHY CAN'T SEARCH ENGINES DO SCIENCE?

The Annoyance: I'm a scientist, and search engines like Google are just about worthless when I need to find good information. When I search for "Dolly," I don't want to know about Dolly Parton, Dollywood, or Dolly Magazine "for the fun-loving Australian girl"—I want solid, scientific information about Dolly the sheep. Where's a science geek like me to go?

The Fix: There are a variety of science-only search sites, but the best overall is Scirus, at *http://www.scirus.com* (Figure 8-7). The site combs through scientific journals, unpublished research, university web sites, conference minutes and agendas, mailing-list archives, corporate Internet sites, and more. It uses linguistic analysis to make sure that articles with the highest scientific value come up at the top of the rankings. And when you do your search, it will recommend more highly targeted terms that you can use to narrow the search; search for

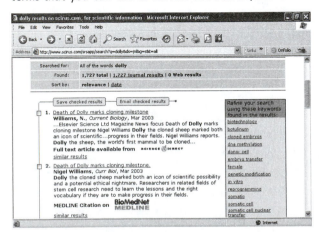

Figure 8-7. Hello Dolly, good-bye Dollywood! For science-related searches, head to http://www.scirus.com.

Dolly, and some of the more targeted searches it recommends are "somatic cell," "DNA methylation," and "transgenic." Click any of them, and you'll get results that include this term plus the initial term you entered.

PROTECT YOUR KIDS FROM SEARCH ENGINES

The Annoyance: I have a nine-year-old daughter, and she uses Google and Yahoo! to help her with schoolwork and, of course, just to have fun. But she accidentally came across a web page with some very objectionable content the other day. Is there a way that she can still use those search engines, but not get any results that lead to questionable sites?

The Fix: Both Google and Yahoo! offer kid-friendly filters that eliminate much of the toxic junk that you'd want to keep away from your daughter. In Google, click the Preferences link to the right of the Search button. In the SafeSearch Filtering section, select "Use strict filtering," then click the Save Preferences button. Her results will be filtered from now on.

In Yahoo!, click the Preferences link to the right of the Search button. On the page that appears, next to "SafeSearch Filter," click Strict, and then Save Preferences.

WHERE TO GET MEDICAL INFORMATION

Need to get information about health and disease? There's no dearth of web advice and database sites. For straightforward medical information, go to *http://www.webmd.com*. If you want in-depth information about more complex conditions and procedures, or you're looking for research, try MedHunt (*http://www.hon.ch/MedHunt/*) and Medline Plus (*http://www.medlineplus.com*). Medline Plus is run by the National Institutes of Health and the U.S. National Library of Medicine; it's a superb place to get in-depth information about medications, diseases, and conditions, as well as the latest medical news. You can even find information about clinical trials.

GOVERNMENT AND THE LAW

GET THE LOWDOWN ON CONGRESS

The Annoyance: I pay enough federal taxes every year to float a battleship. (Okay, maybe a destroyer.) So why is it so hard to track down information about bills before Congress? I've used the Thomas search site (*http://thomas.loc.gov*), but much of what I find is incomprehensible. What does "HJRes143" mean, for example?

The Fix: There's good news and bad news about Thomas, the federal legislative search engine that lets you find information about any bill before Congress. The good news is that it exists. The bad news is that it can be as confounding as an IRS form.

The aim of the site, of course, is to let people quickly find a bill, read the text, and find out where it is in the legislative process and who sponsored it. So here are some quick tips to find what you want, fast:

- When you're searching for a word or phrase, don't use the Bill Summary & Status link—instead, use the Word/Phrase search box (see Figure 8-8). If you search using the Bill Summary & Status link, you'll only search abstracts of the bills, not their full texts. For example, if you search for "spyware" using the Bill Summary & Status link, you'll find fewer bills than if you use the Word/Phrase search box.

- If you know the number of a bill, you can search for it in the Bill Number search box—and Thomas is positively open-minded about the format. For a House bill, all you have to do is slap an "HR," with or without periods, upper- or lowercase, before the bill number (for example, "HR 2929" or "h.r. 2929"). You don't even need a space between the HR and the number. To search for a Senate bill, preface the number with an "S," as in "S150" or "s 150."

- If you want to print out a bill, search for the bill, click the result you want to view, and then click the GPO's PDF Display link. Bills are normally displayed in HTML, but these pages don't print out well. The GPO link takes you to a neatly formatted PDF version of the bill—just like the one your Congressman sees.

GPO stands for Government Printing Office—it's the federal agency that prints out federal bills, reports, and so on.

- Learn the lingo. H.R. means that it's a bill before the House of Representatives. S. means it's a bill before the Senate. H.J.Res. means that it's a House Joint Resolution, and S.J.Res. means that it's a Senate Joint Resolution. So what's a joint resolution? In essence, it's almost the same as a bill, but it's used for more limited matters, such as asking for money for a single purpose—and as with any bill, the President has to sign it. H.Con.Res. stands for House Concurrent Resolution, and S.Con.Res. stands for Senate Concurrent Resolution. Oy vey! Now we're really getting complicated. A concurrent resolution isn't something that becomes a law, and it doesn't require the President's signature. It's used for such things as congratulating another country on the anniversary of its independence.

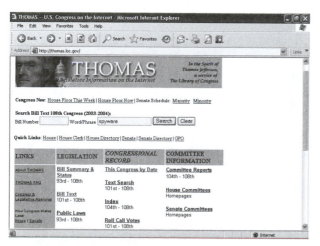

Figure 8-8. When searching for a bill, it's best to use the Word/Phrase box, because that searches through the full text of a bill.

Rumors on the Internet swarm like honeybees in summer, and one rumor that refuses to die is that of the so-called "Internet tax" or email surcharge. The rumor, first started in 1999, is spread by an email message that claims that "Congressman Schnell" has introduced "Bill 602P," which would let the federal government charge five cents for every email people send. (Hey, there's one way to solve the spam problem!) According to the message, Internet service providers would collect the money and turn it over to the Post Office.

Sorry, conspiracy fans—no such bill exists. In fact, no such *congressman* exists. And "602P" is meaningless—a "P" is never used to designate a bill.

The rumor has become so widespread that the U.S. Postal Service has issued a press release saying it isn't true (see *http://www.usps.com/news/2002/press/email-rumor.htm*).

A similar email claims that the Federal Communications Commission (FCC) is planning to impose a fee for every minute of Internet use. Again, this is pure panic-mongering and simply isn't true—and again, the rumor has become so widespread that the FCC has likewise issued a press release dispelling it (see *http://www.fcc.gov/Bureaus/Common_Carrier/Factsheets/nominute.html*).

FIND YOUR CONGRESSMAN'S VOTING RECORD

The Annoyance: Finding bills is one thing—I want to know how my representatives voted. Thomas has links to House and Senate directories, but not to any tabulation of votes. I have a sneaking suspicion they all have something to hide.

The Fix: You're right—there is no simple link for finding a voting record. And you may be right that your representatives have something to hide! The only way to compile a voting record would be to dig through every single roll call of the House or Senate and then compile it manually. Even then, it would be practically impossible to do, because the roll-call numbers don't match the bill numbers.

However, there's an excellent site that has done much of the legwork for you—Project Vote Smart, at *http://www.vote-smart.org*. It lets you research any Senator's or Representative's voting record on an issue-by-issue basis, and it covers just about every topic imaginable, from abortion to welfare policy (see Figure 8-9). You name it, and you can find a voting record on it. (You'll even find details on many state officeholders.) The site also shows how various interest groups rate your guy or gal in Washington.

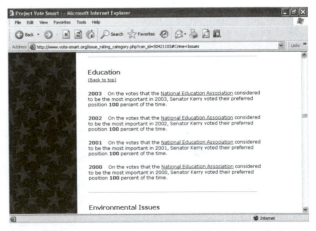

Figure 8-9. Project Vote Smart lets you research the voting records of federal and state officeholders, and includes advocacy group ratings as well.

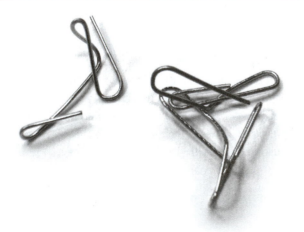

TELL IT TO THE JUDGE!

The Annoyance: I'm unfortunately involved in a lawsuit that makes the long-running Jarndyce v. Jarndyce in *Bleak House* seem trivial by comparison. I'm paying a boatload to my lawyer, and half the time I can't understand what she's talking about. For the $250 an hour I'm paying, I shouldn't also have to pay for a translator. Help!

The Fix: Head to *http://www.law.com*, where you'll find information on every possible legal term you can imagine. It's not just a law dictionary, though—you'll find great background on the law as well, organized by categories such as Accident & Injury, Car Accidents, Employee's Rights, Real Estate, and so on.

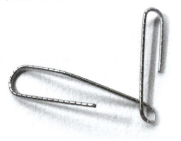

FIND WHAT GOOGLE CAN'T

The Annoyance: The federal government publishes approximately two zillion reports a year, but I'm having a devil of a time finding them with Google. I'm an information junkie, and I know that some of the best statistics and reports are published by the feds. Why can't I find them?

The Fix: You've uncovered one of Google's blind spots—it does a great job of indexing web sites, but it can't search for information locked up in databases.

To get at those government databases, head to the Government Printing Office's web site at *http://www.gpoaccess.gov/cgp* (Figure 8-10). You can search for government reports from every quarter, from the Congress to the Bureau of Labor Statistics. If a report isn't available online, you'll find information on how to order printed copies. Just don't expect much help actually *understanding* these reports!

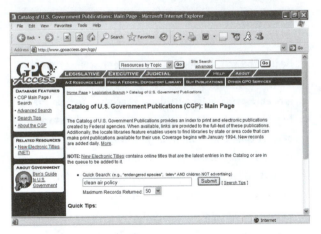

Figure 8-10. Don't look for government reports with Google. Go to the source—the Government Printing Office.

t i p

Google may not be able to search through all the government databases, but it does a very good job of indexing government web pages. If you want, you can do a Google search through only government pages by heading to *http://www.google.com/unclesam* and doing your search from there.

What Is the Deep Web?

It sounds like some super-secret government project, but the Deep Web actually describes in-depth information locked in databases, library catalogs, and similar sources that commercial search engines can't access. Some search engines in development claim they can dig into the Deep Web, though. One contender to watch is *http://www.dipsie.com*, which may be up and running by the time you read this.

GOOGLE

SEARCH GOOGLE WITHOUT A BROWSER

The Annoyance: Like everyone else, I use Google for everything except washing my dishes (and from what I hear, Google is working on it). But even the superfast Google Toolbar requires me to launch my browser. I'm a speed junkie—how can I avoid this time drain?

The Fix: Download the Google Deskbar, available from *http://toolbar.google.com/deskbar*. Once installed, it runs as a small box on XP's toolbar. To search Google, no matter what program you're in, press Ctrl-Alt-G, type your search terms into the box, and press Enter. (If you select text in your current document and press this keystroke combination, Google will search for that text.) A small mini-viewer will pop up with your search results, as shown in Figure 8-11. You can visit sites in the mini-viewer with a click, or you can send them to your browser by clicking the arrow in the upper-left corner. When you click away from the mini-viewer, it vanishes. You can make the window larger or smaller by dragging its top-left corner. Of course, your PC must be connected to the Internet for the Google Deskbar to work.

Figure 8-11. Forget launching your browser—with the Google Deskbar, you can search the Web and view the results in a mini-viewer.

GOOGLE DESKBAR TIPS

The Google Deskbar includes a whole host of goodies. When you're in a program, highlight words that you want to search for, press Ctrl-Alt-G, and those words will be automatically plugged into the Google Deskbar input box. Press Enter, and you'll get the standard Google search. But if you use the following keyboard shortcuts, Google can perform targeted searches:

- ☒ **Search a thesaurus: Ctrl-T**
- ☒ **Get a stock quote: Ctrl-Q**
- ☒ **Get a definition: Ctrl-D**
- ☒ **Search Froogle: Ctrl-F**
- ☒ **Search News: Ctrl-N**
- ☒ **Search newsgroups: Ctrl-U**
- ☒ **Search Google Images: Ctrl-I**
- ☒ **Do a "Feeling Lucky" search: Ctrl-L**

You can open or close the Google Deskbar mini-viewer by pressing Shift-F1. And if you want to disable the mini-viewer and have all search results appear in a normal browser window, click the arrow to the right of the Google Deskbar, choose Options → Mini-Viewer, and check the "When clicking on results, open a browser" box.

To shut down the Google Deskbar, right-click an empty area of the taskbar, choose Toolbars, and then uncheck Google Deskbar. To turn it back on, check this option.

GOOGLE ISN'T TECH-SMART

The Annoyance: I used Google to find help on changing my preferences in Windows XP, and the results were dismal. None of the top 15 hits were even close. Where can I get better results on techie topics?

WHAT IS GOOGLE BOMBING?

In the heat of the 2004 presidential race, if you searched for the phrase "miserable failure" in Google, the first result was the official biography of President George Bush. If you searched for the word "waffles," the first result was a link to Senator John Kerry's campaign web site.

Both are the result of "Google bombing," a technique in which many web sites are set up and linked to the web site the bombers want to appear at the top of a search results list. (The phrase is often included in the link as well.) For example, for the Bush Google bomb, the HTML might look like this:

```
George <a href="http://www.whitehouse.gov/
president/gwbbio.html">miserable failure
</a> Bush
```

Because Google bases its search results in part on how many sites link to a particular page, if enough pages are set up with the same link, the targeted web site will top the list.

The Fix: Among general search engines, my first pick would be Teoma, at *http://www.teoma.com*. And, of course, if you're looking for anything related to Microsoft, the best place to go is generally the Microsoft Knowledge Base, at *http://support.microsoft.com*. If I need help with Windows, though, the first oracle I seek is Brian's Buzz Search (*http://www.briansbuzz.com/search*), run by long-time computer journalist and author Brian Livingston. It searches only through Windows tip sites, so you'll get targeted, helpful results. You can also pick specific tip sites to search.

WHERE'D MY ORIGINAL GOOGLE SEARCH GO?

The Annoyance: It's easy to get lost in Google searches. I get a page of search results, click a link, which then leads to another link, and then yet another, until I look at the clock and realize I've spent 45 minutes tracking down information. My original search page is somewhere about 30 pages back. How can I jump directly to this page?

The Fix: On Google's home page, click the Preferences link to the right of the Search box. Scroll down the page to the Results Window area, check the "Open search results in a new browser window" box, and click the Save Preferences button. The next time you click a search result in Google, it'll open in a new window, and your original search results page will always be open, waiting for you.

NETSCAPE CAN GOOGLE, TOO

The Annoyance: Not everyone in the world uses Internet Explorer. I'd like to get the Google Toolbar, but I can't find one for Netscape. Am I really left out in the cold?

The Fix: Take off that parka. You can get a Google Toolbar for Netscape (see Figure 8-12) by visiting *http://googlebar.mozdev.org*. It does pretty much everything that the official IE Google Toolbar does, except for the Page Rank feature, which isn't particularly useful anyway. It also includes some extras, such as a university-specific search, and it works for the Firefox and Mozilla browsers as well.

Figure 8-12. The Netscape Google bar includes some extras not found in the official one, such as a university-specific search.

GO LOCAL WITH GOOGLE

The Annoyance: Mapping sites do a good job of giving me driving directions but a truly rotten job of supplying any information about the places I'm going to. I'm about to visit my daughter in Cincinnati, and I want to find some good restaurants, the locations of ATM machines, the nearest UPS store, and where I can get WiFi access while sipping a hot latte. What's the solution?

The Fix: Head to the Google Local site, located at *http://local.google.com*. Enter a term (such as ATM) in the What box and the Zip Code or city and state in the Where box, and click the Google Search button (see Figure 8-13). Google lists relevant local stores and services, complete with addresses, phone numbers, links to similar offerings in the area, and maps showing where they're located. You can also cast a wider net or do a finer search by clicking on the "Search within: 1 mile - 5 miles - 15 miles - 45 miles" links.

Figure 8-13. Need to find an ATM, coffee shop, dry cleaner, or any other good or service when you're away from home? Try Google Local.

Google Local does a great job of finding local stores and services, but it doesn't rate them. For example, if you search for "best restaurant" in the Zip Code 45219 (the neighborhood around the University of Cincinnati), the first result that comes up is the Best Western Marriot Inn. Aside from what you think about the culinary merits and aesthetics of the Best Western, the restaurant is more than seven miles away, and in a different Zip Code! There are plenty of restaurants nearby that most people would rate as superior: remember that first is not always best.

SHOW 150 SEARCH RESULTS

The Annoyance: When I search with Google, it's easy to change the number of results displayed on each page, but I only have a choice of 10, 20, 30, 50, or 100. I want to display 150 on a page so I can whip through the results. Why can't I do that?

The Fix: As you've discovered, within limits, it's simple to change the number of results displayed per page. On Google, just click the Preferences link, scroll down to the "Number of results" drop-down box, choose the number of results to display per page, and click OK.

Displaying a number of results that's not in the drop-down box takes a bit of doing, though. When you do a search with Google, you're sending a search argument to Google servers using a special syntax. That argument tells Google how to run your search and how many results to display on each page. So, if you know how Google's search syntax works, you can type a handcrafted URL into your browser's Address Bar and dictate exactly how many results show up per page.

In Google, the search argument num= controls how many results to display on a page. So if you wanted to do a search for Tom Jones and display a page of 150 results, you'd type this into your browser's Address Bar:

    www.google.com/search?q=tom+jones&num=150

EVEN MORE THINGS TO FIND ON GOOGLE

Just when you think Google can find everything under the sun, it turns out that it can find a lot more. Google does a great job of finding product information, car information, tracking information, and then some:

☒ *Type an automobile's-character Vehicle Information Number (VIN) into Google's search box.* Google won't find any pages containing this number, but it will provide a link at the top of the page to Carfax with the VIN you entered already tied to the link. Click the link, and you'll get a Carfax on that vehicle. (Note: this trick may not work with older cars that have VINs that are all numeric.)

☒ *Type in a product's UPC code,* and the same thing will happen—except the number will be tied to a link at UPC Database (*http://upcdatabase.com*), which gives you manufacturer information about any product.

☒ *Type in a Federal Express tracking number,* and in similar fashion, a click will take you to a search on the entered number at the FedEx page that tracks packages.

☒ *Type in a U.S. Postal Service tracking number,* and you'll likewise be sent to a page with tracking information.

☒ *Type in the tail number of an airplane,* and you'll see the full FAA registration form for the plane.

☒ *Type in the flight number of an airplane,* such as "Delta 1098," and you'll get a list of pages from which you can track the status of the flight.

☒ *Type in an area code,* and a map of the area will be the first hit.

FIND PDF FILES FAST

The Annoyance: I know that I can search a specific site using Google, but I need to look through a site for only PDF files. I can't find this option anywhere in Google. Is there a way?

The Fix: To search through a specific site, add `site:name` to your search, where `name` is the name of the site or a top-level domain. For example, if you wanted to search for *gralla* at *oreilly.com*, you'd type `gralla site:oreilly.com`.

To find PDF files, you just add one more piece of syntax: `filetype:type`, where `type` is the file's extension. To search the entire Web for all PDFs related to *gralla*, you'd type `gralla filetype:pdf`. To search for all PDFs related to *gralla* on a specific site, such as *oreilly.com*, you'd type `gralla site:oreilly.com filetype:pdf`.

FIND WEB PAGES BY TITLE

The Annoyance: I want to find a specific Web page, but I don't remember its URL. I more or less remember the page's title, but when I search Google using those words, I get 32,442 results! How can I boil this down?

The Fix: There's a simple bit of Google syntax that'll do the trick: `intitle:`. It searches only for page titles, not their contents. If you wanted to find all the web pages with the words "weapons of mass destruction" in their titles, for example, you'd search thusly:

    intitle: "weapons of mass destruction"

As with all Google searches, use quotation marks to search for an exact phrase. You can also use the `intitle:` syntax when searching Yahoo!

To do the reverse—to search a site's contents, but not its page titles—use the `intext:` operator. For example, to search for "weapons of mass destruction," you'd type `intext:` "weapons of mass destruction".

TEACH GOOGLE TO SPEAK FRENCH

The Annoyance: I often have to search for companies based in France, and a Google search doesn't always cut it, so I often have go to *http://fr.yahoo.com*. But Google's search engine is much better than Yahoo!'s. Can't I make Google *parlez Francais*?

The Fix: *Mais oui*! Google can speak French, or Spanish, Bulgarian, Turkish, German... in fact, a very long list of languages from around the world. Just head to Google Language Tools at *http://www.google.com/language_tools?hl=en*. You'll be able to search for pages by language and country, which means, for example, you can search for pages written in French and published in Belgium.

Scroll down to the Translate box, and you can use Google's Language Tools to translate text to and from foreign languages. Just paste in the desired text, or enter a URL to tell Google to translate an entire page. Choose the translation you want done (for example, from German to English), and click the Translate button. I wouldn't use this tool for translating a novel, but it can help you get the gist of what someone's saying... usually!

HAVE GOOGLE NEWS DELIVERED

The Annoyance: I'm a big fan of the Google news site, but I'm just too busy to keep checking it for the latest news. Why can't I get alerts about news that interests me? Radio stations have been doing this for years. Why can't the Web?

The Fix: Ah, you've forgotten about the much-heralded "push" technology of the late 1990s (see "What Is Push Technology?" at *http://www.darwinmag.com/learn/curve/column.html?ArticleID=43*). A modern-day equivalent is the RSS feed (see "Syndicate Your Blog" in

Chapter 4). Another is the alert, a prefab search that runs at regular intervals and emails you the results. Google has such a feature—called, naturally enough, Google Alerts—at *http://www.google.com/alerts* (Figure 8-14). In the simple form, enter your search terms, note how often you want to be notified (once a day, once a week, as it happens), type in your email address, and that's it—Google will send you alerts about the appropriate news, with links back to the relevant pages. Beware that if you choose a popular topic, chances are you'll be flooded with alerts. To limit the alerts you receive, use the intitle: syntax, as outlined in "Find Web Pages by Title."

found on the page where Google unearthed it. Sometimes pages with original pictures are changed or deleted, but the thumbnails are still sitting on Google's servers.

The original full-size picture may be in Google's cache, and you can search for it there using the URL that Google lists under the thumbnail images (see Figure 8-15). Copy and paste that URL into Google, and do a search. If Google still has it in its cache, it'll show up.

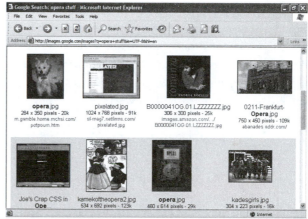

Figure 8-15. The thumbnail picture is there, but where's the bigger original? Sometimes it no longer exists.

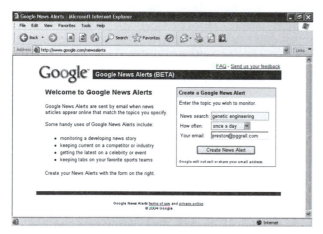

Figure 8-14. Keep up with the latest news with Google Alerts, which sends you emails about news you're interested in.

WHERE'S THAT PICTURE?

The Annoyance: I was using Google Image Search and clicked on a thumbnail to see the larger image. But instead of an image, I got a "Page Cannot Be Found" error. How come Google can find the thumbnail, but not the larger picture? How can I get a copy of that larger picture?

The Fix: You've encountered a fairly common problem with Google Image Search. Apparently, the thumbnail you see is stored on Google's servers, which is why you can see it. But the original (larger) picture is only

If that doesn't work, search for the entire URL in the Internet Archive, at *http://www.archive.org*. (If that doesn't work, search for the core web address.) For more information about the Internet Archive, see "Search the Past with the Wayback Machine."

ELIMINATE WEB JUNK FROM GOOGLE DESKTOP SEARCH

The Annoyance: I installed Google Desktop Search so I could search the files on my computer, but the search results are always cluttered up with links to dozens of web pages I've visited. Note to Google: when I search my hard disk, I just want to find files or emails, not some stray web site I visited six weeks ago!

The Fix: You've come across one of the odder behav-

> **t i p**
>
> Google Desktop Search only indexes pages that you visit when using Internet Explorer. It won't index sites you visit with another browser, such as Firefox or Netscape.

iors of Google Desktop Search. It indexes the pages you visit in Internet Explorer, so those pages can show up in your search results. It doesn't matter if those pages are in your browser's cache or not, because Google indexes them on its own, separately from the cache—cleaning out your cache won't fix the problem.

The quick solution: on your Google Desktop Search page, click Desktop Preferences. On the page that appears, uncheck the "Web history" box and click Save Preferences. From now on, any pages that you visit won't be indexed and won't show up in your searches.

But that only solves part of the problem. All the web pages that Google Desktop Search *previously* indexed will still show up in your search results.

You can remove those web pages from the index, but you can't do it en masse. Instead, you must remove them individually whenever they show up in your search results. It's tedious, but it works. When the web pages show up in a search, click the "Remove items" link at the top of the page, on the righthand side. A page like that shown in Figure 8-16 will appear. Check the box next to each web site that you want to excise and click the "Remove checked results" button, and they'll be taken out of your index.

Figure 8-16. Put checks next to each web page you want to remove from the Google Desktop Search index, then click the "Remove checked results" button; they'll no longer show up and annoy you.

If, for some reason, you want Google Desktop Search to index some pages but not others, you can tell it not to index specific sites. On your Google Desktop Search page, click Desktop Preferences and scroll down to the Don't Search These Items box. Type in the URLs of the web sites you don't want indexed, making sure to include the *http://*. Click Save Preferences, and those sites won't be indexed. If you'd like, you can also tell Google Desktop Search not to index specific folders on your hard disk, such as *C:\My Secret Stuff*. Just type the full path into the Don't Search These Items box and click Save Preferences.

For more information about Google Desktop Search, see "The Cure for Email Overload" in Chapter 1.

AMAZON

SEARCH AMAZON AND THE WEB SIMULTANEOUSLY

The Annoyance: It drives me crazy when, after I buy a book from Amazon, I find the information I needed on the Web. Why can't I search the Web and Amazon simultaneously, so I can decide whether it's worth buying the book in the first place?

The Fix: You can, and Amazon makes it possible, thanks to its oddly named A9 search site at *http://www.a9.com*. At first, it seems like any other search site—type in your search term, and you get web results. But click the Books button on the right, and you'll see a list of books on Amazon that match your search results as well (see Figure 8-17). Click a listing, and you're jetted over to the appropriate Amazon book page.

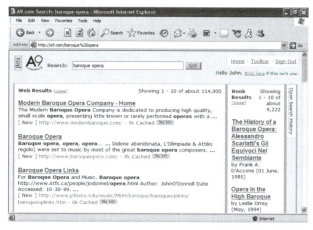

Figure 8-17. When you search on a term using A9, you also get a list of books on Amazon related to your search.

When you click a book listing on the A9 site, all of Amazon's usual features (such as searching within a book) will become available to you. If you're a registered Amazon user and have your cookies set so that Amazon recognizes you when you visit, A9 will recognize you as well.

Get the A9 Toolbar

Enamored of the A9 search site? Then get the A9 Toolbar, available at *http://toolbar.a9.com*. It installs directly in Internet Explorer, and it lets you search A9 no matter where you are on the Web. Like the Google Toolbar, it also includes a pop-up blocker. For now, it only works with Internet Explorer, but other browsers may be supported in the future.

AUTOMATICALLY SEACH AMAZON FOR HIGHLIGHTED WORDS

The Annoyance: When I browse the Web, I often come across a topic I'd like to look up on Amazon. But I hate having to head to Amazon, then type the word into the search box. There must be a faster way.

The Fix: There is. With a few tweaks, you'll be able to highlight any word on a web page, right-click it, choose Search Amazon from a pop-up menu, and get Amazon search results in a new browser window. The trick involves writing a little bit of JavaScript code and editing the Windows Registry. (Before you do this, make a backup of the Registry. Select Start → Run, type regedit in the Open box, and hit Enter. In the Registry Editor, select File → Export. Make sure that the "All" radio button at the bottom of the Export Registry File dialog box is selected. Then enter a name for the backup, such as "Registry Backup 1-5-2005", select a destination, and click OK. When the export is done, exit the Registry Editor.)

To create the JavaScript, open Notepad and enter this code:

```
<script language="JavaScript">
var searchURL = new String("http://
amazon.com/exec/obidos/external-search/
mode=blended&keyword=");

var w = window.external.menuArguments;
var d = w.document;
var s = d.selection;
var r = s.createRange();
var term = new String(r.text);

window.open(searchURL + term);
</script>
```

Save the file as *AmazonSearch.html* in a folder called *C:\ scripts*. (If the folder doesn't exist, create it.)

Now that you've created the JavaScript, you need to edit the Registry to tell Internet Explorer when and how to use it:

1. Exit Internet Explorer and run the Registry Editor.

2. Go to `HKEY_CURRENT_USER\Software\Microsoft\ Internet Explorer\MenuExt`.

3. Create a new key underneath MenuExt—right-click MenuExt, select New → Key, and name it `Search Amazon`. In the window to the right, double-click (Default). Type `c:\scripts\AmazonSearch.html` in the "Value data" box, and click OK.

4. Right-click the Search Amazon key, select New → DWORD Value, and name it `contexts`. Double-click the contexts item and type `10` in the "Value data" box. Make sure the Decimal radio button is selected, and click OK.

5. Exit the Registry and restart Internet Explorer. When you highlight a term and right-click it, you'll see a Search Amazon item on the menu. Click it, and you'll do a search of the highlighted term on Amazon.

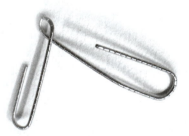

PEEK INTO THE FUTURE WITH AMAZON

Want to peer into the future? At least when it comes to books? Publishers tell Amazon what books they'll be publishing many months—and sometimes years—in advance. So if you want to find out what books will soon be published on a given topic, or what your favorite publisher is up to, head to Amazon's Advanced Search page. On Amazon's front page, click the Books tab, then click the Advanced Search link at the top of the page. Enter what you're looking for (author, title, subject, and so on), scroll down the page, and, in the "Publication date" drop-down, select "During the year." In the box to the right, enter a future date (such as 2006). Scroll back up and click the Search Now button, and you'll see the future unfold before your eyes. For example, in mid-2004, I entered "food" in the subject line, specified books published during 2005, and got a list of 120 forthcoming titles.

EBAY

BETTER EBAY SEARCHING

The Annoyance: I just did a search on eBay, and as usual I got about 8,000 results, about 80% of which weren't even close to being relevant. I really don't have the time to weed through all this. There's got to be a way to do smarter searches on eBay!

The Fix: Searching on eBay is kind of like visiting a foreign country—it's a lot easier to find that quaint little hotel up in the Alps if you speak the local lingo. With eBay, that means getting hep to some of its search operators. Here's a quick intro.

Exclude results you don't want

Put a minus sign (-) in front of a search term to exclude any results that contain the term. For example, the search:

```
camera -digital
```

will show you all auctions that contain the word "camera" but not the word "digital" in the auction title—handy if you're looking only for film cameras. You can also exclude multiple terms, like so:

    camera -digital -kodak -sony -minolta

or include multiple terms and exclude others:

    acoustic guitar -electric

Use wildcards

Use the asterisk (*) wildcard search term before or after a word or letters, and eBay will match all words that begin or end with that term. For example, the search:

    *caster guitar

would return auctions of Stratocaster as well as Telecaster guitars. Conversely, searching for:

    Tele*

would return auctions of Telecaster guitars, telescopes, telephones, Teletubbies, and so on.

Use OR searches

Searches on eBay are automatically AND searches, so auctions show up only if they contain every term you put in your search. However, you can use the OR operator to list auctions that contain *any* of your search terms. This is useful if you're looking for multiple items, or if your searches aren't returning enough auctions. To do an OR search, put the terms in parentheses, separated by commas. For example, to find either a lute or a mandolin, you'd use this search:

    (lute, mandolin)

Search for exact phrases

As with many other search engines, to search for an exact phrase on eBay, surround the phrase with quotation marks, like this:

    "squire stratocaster"

You can use other kinds of Boolean searching, too. For detailed information on what operators you can use, how you can combine them, and other tips, go to *http://pages. ebay.com/help/buyerguide/search.html#advanced*.

FINE-TUNE EBAY BROWSING

The Annoyance: I like browsing eBay, rather than searching through it. But even when I browse several subcategories deep, there's still too much stuff to weed through. How can I cut the clutter?

The Fix: When you're on any category or subcategory page, run a search—eBay will search only that category or subcategory, and everything below it. So, for example, if you've dug down to Musical Instruments → Guitar → Acoustic and you search for "guild," you'll get pinpoint results—maybe 40 or 50 listings (see Figure 8-18). Search for "guild" on the front page of eBay, and you'll get 10 times as many results, and for things that have nothing to do with guitars.

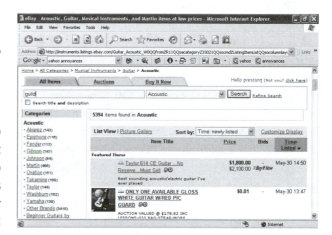

Figure 8-18. The best way to fine-tune your search on eBay is often to first browse to a subcategory, and then do a search within that subcategory.

QUICKLY SCAN EBAY FEEDBACK

The Annoyance: Before I buy anything on eBay, I always check out the seller first by reading the feedback from other buyers. Of course, I'm mainly looking for the negative comments, but some sellers have hundreds or thousands of comments, and it takes forever to click through them all page by page. Isn't there a faster way to scan eBay feedback just for negative comments?

The Fix: Every negative comment has a red minus sign (-) next to it. The problem is that by default eBay only displays 25 comments per page. To up this number, scroll to the bottom of the page and, in the "Items per page" drop-down, select 200. Now eBay will display 200 comments per page, making it easier to pick out the big red negative signs.

SEARCH THROUGH A SELLER'S ITEMS

The Annoyance: Finding a seller you can trust on eBay is like finding gold. So naturally, when I find trustworthy sellers, I want to search through all their auctions. But amazingly enough, there's no way to do this on eBay. When I click on the "View seller's other items" link on an auction page, I get a listing of everything that seller has for sale—but some sellers have hundreds of items for sale in dozens of categories, and I don't want to have to browse through them all. Isn't there a simpler way?

The Fix: Luckily, eBay recently made this a lot easier. After you click the "View seller's other items" link on an auction page, look on the lefthand side of the page. You'll see a list of all the categories in which the seller has items for sale, including the number of items in each category (Figure 8-19). Click a category, and you'll see a list of items for sale just in that category. To search through all the items a seller has for sale, use the search box at the top of the screen.

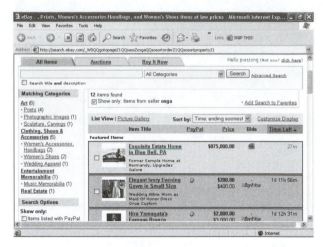

Figure 8-19. Once you find all the items someone has for sale, you can browse through the items by category or look through the items using the search box at the top of the screen.

> **t i p**
>
> You can filter out items in even more ways. The Search Options choices, listed underneath the categories on the left, let you display only items for which you can pay via PayPal, only items for sale within a certain price range, and several other options.

YOU'VE GOT AUCTIONS!

The Annoyance: Life's too short to be constantly searching eBay. I have a relatively short list of things I'm looking for. Google can run prefab searches and send me email alerts—why can't eBay?

The Fix: It can, via its Favorite Searches feature. Here's how:

1. Do a search as you would normally on eBay. When you've got it fine-tuned, click the Add to Favorites link halfway down the page and to the right of the "xx items found for xx."

2. The Add to My Favorite Searches page appears (see Figure 8-20). Fill in the form, and check the "Email me daily whenever there are new items" box.

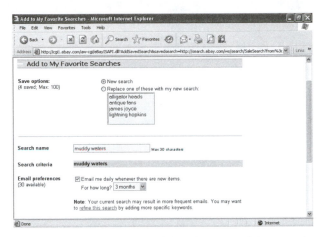

Figure 8-20. No need to spend your life searching eBay: tell the auction site to send you an email whenever a desired item goes on sale.

3. Click Submit. You'll now get email notifications whenever something you're looking for comes up for auction.

4. To change or delete a favorite, click Search at the top of any eBay screen, and then click Favorite Searches. You'll come to the All Favorites page (Figure 8-21), which lists all your Favorite Searches. Click Edit Preferences to change any search. To delete a search, check the box next to the search and click the Delete button.

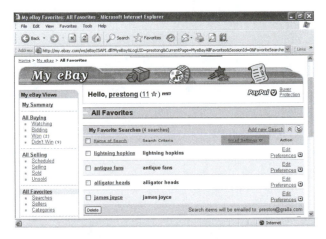

Figure 8-21. From here you can edit or delete any favorite searches.

YAHOO!

FANCY SEARCHING WITH YAHOO!

The Annoyance: Google, Google, Google! All I ever hear about are fancy tips for finding things with Google. But I'm a big Yahoo! fan, and I want Yahoo! to do those things, too. Isn't there some way to teach my favorite site new tricks?

The Fix: Yahoo! doesn't have quite as many fancy features as Google, but a few cool tools are buried deep in the system. For example, you can fine-tune your searches in several ways. If you want to search for pages on only a specific domain (and its subdomains), use the `site:` syntax. For example, to search for Hvorostovsky on the Metropolitan Opera site at *www.metopera.org*, you'd enter `Hvorostovsky site:www.metopera.org`.

Here are a few more bits of useful Yahoo! search syntax:

`link:`
  Find documents that link to a specific URL. For example, `link:http://www.windowsdevcenter.com`.

`inurl:`
  Search for pages whose URLs contain a specific word. For example, `inurl:gralla`.

`intitle:`
  Search for pages whose titles contain a specific word. For example, `intitle:gralla`.

CUT DOWN ON YAHOO! NAVIGATION

The Annoyance: Yahoo! has lots of special sections devoted to sports, finance, weather, and so on, which I love. But it takes forever to get to them. How can I jump quickly to these pages?

The Fix: Use the `!` operator to jump straight to where you want to go. For example, if you're on Yahoo! and you want to get to Yahoo! Sports, type `sports!` in the search box and you'll be sent there immediately. For a full list of other places you can go to in this way, head to *http://help.yahoo.com/help/us/ysearch/tips/tips-06.html*.

9

Security
ANNOYANCES

Ask people what concerns them the most about the Internet, and security will most likely top the list. Spyware, worms, Trojans, and viruses have all become accepted hazards of using the Internet, as have "phishing" expeditions, which route you to a phony web site that steals your personal information and passwords.

But there's no reason you should be bedeviled by these annoyances. This chapter gives you the tools and techniques to prevent or do away with them—it delves into special software solutions, shows you how to configure your home router for maximum security, tells you how to construct your own personal firewall, and more.

GENERAL SECURITY ANNOYANCES

GET FREE SECURITY CHECKUPS

The Annoyance: I installed a firewall on my kid's PC, but being the paranoid parent that I am, I want to make sure I've locked out the bad guys. How can I give it a simple checkup?

The Fix: For the most comprehensive check of your online security, head to Gibson Research (*http://ww.grc.com*) and perform the ShieldsUp test, which scans your PC for browser vulnerabilities, open network ports, and similar security flaws (see Figure 9-1). Also perform the Leak test, which checks your PC's vulnerability to Trojans. The Symantec web site (*http://www.symantec.com*) also offers a free online security test and a free online virus scanner. Click the Symantec Security Check link on the Downloads section of the main page to run their security scan. However, be wary when following the Security Check's advice—if it detects an older version of Norton AntiVirus on your system, for example, it will say you're at risk for getting a virus, even if your virus definitions are up-to-date.

Microsoft's free security tool uses a different approach. The Microsoft Baseline Security Analyzer checks to see whether you've installed the most up-to-date Microsoft security patches and service packs, and looks for improperly configured security settings. To download it, go to *http://www.microsoft.com/downloads* and search for "Microsoft Baseline Security Analyzer."

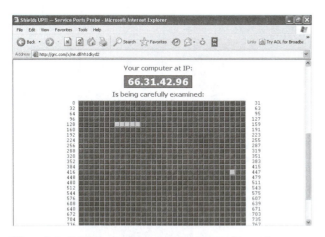

Figure 9-1. ShieldsUp performs a comprehensive test of your online security. Here, it checks for open ports.

BROWSE IN PERFECT ANONYMITY

The Annoyance: Wherever I go online, I get the feeling someone is watching, tracking what I do and the pages I visit. The Attorney General is enough of a Big Brother; I don't want to have to worry about who's watching me on the Web as well.

The Fix: You're right; web sites can gather an astonishing amount of information about you. They can track your online travels, tell what operating system and browser you're running, find out your machine name, peer into your clipboard, uncover the sites you've visited, examine your History list, and delve into your cache. They can also examine your IP address to learn basic information about you, such as your geographic location. To get a sense of the kind of information web sites can find out about you, head to the Anonymizer web site (*http://www. anonymizer.com*) and click the Free Privacy Test link. It will display your IP address, your current geographic location, the contents of your Windows Clipboard, and more (see Figure 9-2). It's pretty sobering stuff.

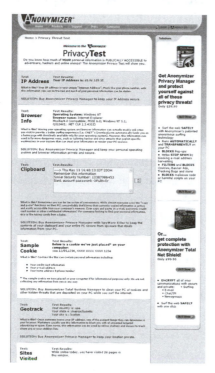

Figure 9-2. Go ahead—scare yourself. Head to this site and see just how much of your personal information can be exposed.

The best way to make sure that web sites can't gather personal information about you and your computer is to surf anonymously—that is, use an anonymous proxy server that sits between you and the web sites you visit. When you use an anonymous proxy server, your browser doesn't contact a web site directly. Instead, it tells a proxy server which web site you want to visit. The web site sees the IP address of the proxy server, not your PC's IP address. It can't read your cookies, see your History list, or examine your clipboard and cache because your PC is never in direct contact with it. You can surf anonymously, without a trace.

To use an anonymous proxy server in concert with your browser, follow these steps:

1. Find an anonymous proxy server. Hundreds of free, public proxy servers are available at *http://www.ato-mintersoft.com/products/alive-proxy/proxy-list*. The web site lists information about each server, including its uptime percentage and the last time the server was checked to see if it was online.

2. Find the server with the highest percentage of uptime. Write down the server's IP address and the port it uses. For example, in the listing 24.236.148.15:80, the IP address is 24.236.148.15 and the port number is 80.

3. In Internet Explorer, select Tools → Internet Options, click the Connections tab, and click the LAN Settings button.

4. Check the "Use a proxy server for your LAN" box. In the Address field, type in the IP address of the proxy server. In the Port field, type in its port number. Check the "Bypass proxy server for local addresses" box; you don't need to remain anonymous on your local network (see Figure 9-3).

5. Click OK and then OK again to close the dialog boxes.

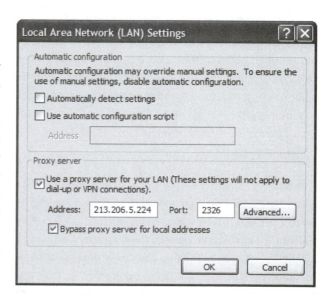

Figure 9-3. Set up Internet Explorer to surf the Web anonymously.

Now when you surf the Web, the proxy server will protect your privacy. Keep in mind that proxy servers can make surfing the Web much slower,.

You may also want to use a web-based, anonymous surfing service. For example, Anonymizer, Inc. (*http://www.anonymizer.com*) offers free and fee-based services. Each service installs a toolbar within Internet Explorer, which you can use to turn on anonymous browsing. The fee-based service costs $29.95 per year and offers benefits beyond those of the free service. For example, it shields your IP address and lets you set custom anonymity levels for different web sites. It also lets you completely block certain web sites.

Another solution is to download software that will automatically configure your browser to use anonymous proxy servers. It will also automatically find the fastest one, without any setup on your part. For example, GhostSurf (*http://www.tenebril.com/products/ghostsurf*) uses multiple anonymous proxy servers and always checks for the fastest one. The software costs $29.95, but you can download a free 15-day trial version if you want to check it out.

BEWARE OF PHISHING EXPEDITIONS

The Annoyance: I received an email from eBay the other day, asking me to validate my user ID and password. When I clicked the link, I was sent to what looked like the normal eBay web site and entered the information. A few days later, I found out that someone was using my eBay ID to scam people. This slimeball even got my credit card information! How can I prevent this from happening in the future?

The Fix: You've been the victim of a so-called "phishing" expedition, in which an email is sent claiming to be from a legitimate web site or business (such as eBay, PayPal, or Citibank). In the body of the message, you're asked to click a link to a web site so you can verify your account information. The return address appears to be from the company (for example, *accounts@eBay.com*), and the web site looks legitimate—the design, layout, and even the address bar look like the real web site. But when you

---

---

type in the information, it goes to the scam artist running the phishing expedition, and he's off to the races with your credit card or web site account information.

To make sure this never happens to you in the future, follow these tips:

- Never respond directly to an email message asking you for your username, password, or other information. Sites like eBay will never send out a request for this type of information.

- If you're not sure whether the email is legitimate, don't click any links within the body of the message. Instead, go directly to the web site from your browser, log in, and see if you have any messages. You can also contact or email the company directly and ask whether they requested any information from you.

- Forward potentially spoofed email to the business that supposedly sent it. They will attempt to track down the source of the spoofed email and cut down on future phishing expeditions. You can also forward the email to assorted groups that fight phishing, such as *reportphishing@antiphishing.com* and *uce@ftc.gov*.

- Keep Windows XP updated. Some phishing expeditions exploit browser vulnerabilities, and Microsoft constantly releases patches to fix those vulnerabilities. Use Windows Update or visit *http://windowsupdate.microsoft.com* to keep your system updated with the latest patches.

A small window will pop up in the middle of your browser, telling you the actual web site you're visiting (see Figure 9-4). Check the URL to see if you're really visiting the site you think you're visiting. That way, you can always protect yourself against spoofs.

Microsoft has a useful knowledge base article that explains how to protect yourself against spoofed sites. To read it, go to *http://support.microsoft.com* and search for article 833786.

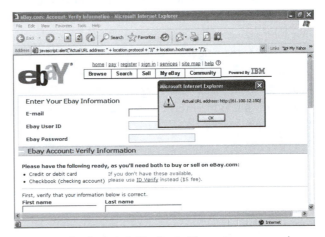

Figure 9-4. Yes, the site looks like eBay, but if you enter your personal information, your credit card details and identity will be stolen. The JavaScript command exposes this fake eBay web site as a phishing expedition.

GUARANTEED, FOOLPROOF WAY TO UNCOVER SPOOF SITES

The Annoyance: Many companies use weird web addresses and URLs to hide their true identity. Is there a simple, foolproof way to reveal the real name of the site I'm visiting?

The Fix: Go to the address bar of your browser, type in the following JavaScript command, and press Enter:

```
javascript:alert("Actual URL address: " +
location.protocol + "//" + location.hostname +
"/");
```

FREE ANTI-PHISHING DETECTORS

It takes a bit of JavaScript to find out the true address of the web site you're visiting. If you want a quicker and easier way, download the free utility SpoofStick (*http://www.corestreet.com/spoofstick*)—it installs directly into FireFox and tells you the true address of the site you're currently visiting.

A similar free tool is available from EarthLink. It alerts you when you visit a site from a known scammer, and also has a pop-up blocker. You don't have to be an EarthLink subscriber to download and use the toolbar (available from *http://www.earthlink.net/home/tools/*).

For the latest phishing news, head to the Anti-Phishing Working Group web site, at *http://www.antiphishing.org*.

BLOCK SNOOPING NEIGHBORS

The Annoyance: A friend of mine used to easily spy on the hard drives of neighbors who, like him, had cable Internet access. Why was it so easy? And how can I make sure like-minded snoops can't get into my PC?

The Fix: Cable setups are not unlike local area networks, and you and your neighbors are essentially "nodes" on that network. (It's one reason your access slows to a crawl when Johnny next door decides to download a movie.) If you have file sharing enabled on your PC, your cable-connected neighbors can spy on your PC. One way to solve the problem is to use a firewall, such as Zone-Alarm (*http://www.zonealarm.com*) or the built-in Windows Firewall. Both firewalls will stop outsiders from snooping on your PC.

To be absolutely safe, you can also turn off file sharing on your system for your cable connection:

1. Right-click My Network Places and choose Properties.
2. Right-click your cable Internet connection and choose Properties.
3. Uncheck the "File and Printer Sharing for Microsoft Networks" box and click OK.
4. Restart your computer. File sharing is now disabled.

> If you spend a lot of time on the Internet, you'll come across the term *malware* sooner or later. What does it mean? Malware is any kind of software—viruses, worms, Trojans, or spyware—designed to do harm in some way.

MY KIDS KEEP DOWNLOADING MALWARE

The Annoyance: My kids keep downloading some piece of malware that damages my PC. How can I make sure they can't connect to the Internet when I'm not around, short of locking the cable modem—or them—in a closet?

The Fix: You can disable your Internet connection when you leave your PC. Right-click My Network Places and select Properties. Right-click the Local Area Connection for your network card and choose Disable. If you have a network icon running in the Notification area (or System Tray), you can also right-click the icon and select Disable. To re-establish the connection, right-click the Local Area Connection or network icon and choose Enable.

BEWARE OF SPOOFED EMAILS

The Annoyance: I own my own domain, and I got an email the other day from someone claiming to be my domain's mail administrator. The message asked me to confirm my password and username. But *I'm* the domain administrator, and I didn't send the message to myself! Odder still, the email seems to have come from an address in my domain. What's going on here?

The Fix: Your email has been spoofed—someone has managed to forge the sender's address and make it appear as if the email came from you. If you respond to the email with your password and username, the message will go to the person who spoofed your email, and the sender will have complete access to your domain—so don't do it! Email requests for your username and password details are sure to be spoofs, not legitimate requests. Exercise caution, and don't give that information away.

KILL THE WINDOWS MESSENGER SERVICE

The Annoyance: I just got a pop-up spam that wasn't even in a browser—in fact, my browser wasn't even open! What kind of magical, black art produces these pop-ups, and how can I stop them?

The Fix: You're getting pop-up spam from Windows XP's Messenger Service, which was originally designed so that sysadmins could send notifications over internal local area networks. For example, a network administrator might notify network users when a server goes down, or a printer may notify you when a print job finishes. (The Messenger Service is not related to Windows Messenger and MSN Messenger, Microsoft's instant messaging programs.) Spammers are exploiting the technology more and more, blasting text pop-up messages to IP addresses across the Internet. It's not uncommon to get a string of them in just an hour.

To put a stop to these amazingly annoying pop-ups, disable the Messenger Service:

1. Type `services.msc` at a command prompt or in the Run box, and press Enter to display the Services Console.

2. Double-click the entry for Messenger, then choose Disabled from the "Startup type" drop-down menu and click OK (see Figure 9-5).

Figure 9-5. Disable the Windows Messenger Service to quash annoying spam.

Pop-ups will no longer get through. If you're on a LAN, you won't be able to get network messages from administrators, either, but this shouldn't be a problem as network administrators are increasingly moving away from Windows Messenger Service for communications.

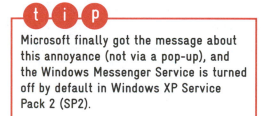

tip

Microsoft finally got the message about this annoyance (not via a pop-up), and the Windows Messenger Service is turned off by default in Windows XP Service Pack 2 (SP2).

You can also kill these pop-ups with a personal firewall, such as ZoneAlarm, Norton Personal Firewall, or the built-in Windows XP Firewall, and if you have a home router you can block the port over which the messages are sent (UDP port 135). However, there is no guarantee that this will always work. Many ISPs block inbound traffic on UDP port 135, and spammers respond by sending the messages via UDP port 1026. Check your router's manual for instructions on blocking ports. The following steps use a Linksys router as an example:

1. Log into the router's setup screen, at *http://192.168.1.1*. Enter admin as the password, and leave the username blank (unless you have changed the defaults).

2. Choose Security → Filter.

3. For the first entry in the Filter Port Range section, type 135 for both the Start and End range (see Figure 9-6). Choose Both from the Protocol drop-down menu to block UDP and TCP port 135.

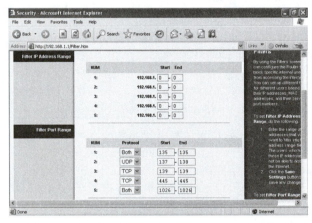

Figure 9-6. Here's how to block Windows Messenger Service spam using a Linksys router.

4. For the second entry, type 137 for the Start range and 138 for the End range. Choose UDP from the Protocol drop-down menu to block UDP ports 137 and 138.

5. Follow the above steps to block the following ports: TCP 139, TCP 445, and UDP and TCP 1026.

6. Click Save Settings. The ports will now be blocked.

INTERNET EXPLORER BLOCKS MY DOWNLOADS

The Annoyance: Everyone told me to get Windows XP Service Pack 2, because it includes a lot of extra security features for Internet Explorer. But now I can't download any software. This is Microsoft's way of keeping me safe? Thanks, but no thanks.

The Fix: By default, the version of Internet Explorer that comes with SP2 blocks files from being downloaded without your knowledge. When IE blocks a download, it displays an alert in the Information Bar (just below the Address Bar). To let the download through, simply click the Information Bar and choose "Allow this page to download files" (see Figure 9-7).

Figure 9-7. Allowing a download using Internet Explorer's download blocker.

When you click a link to download a file, you should be able to download normally. But if you get the "Your current security settings do not allow this file to be downloaded" error message, you'll have to change your download settings. Select Tools → Internet Options and click the Security tab. Select Internet as the "Web content zone," and click the Custom Level button. Scroll to the Downloads section. Choose Enable for "File download," and click OK. Click Yes when you get a message asking if you want to change your security settings, and then click OK. From now on, when you try to download a file, it will be blocked, but the Information Bar will appear, allowing you to complete the download.

YIKES—SOMEONE STOLE MY WEB SITE PASSWORD!

The Annoyance: I found one of my daughter's friends logged into a web site using my account, with a password that I thought only I knew. When I asked her how she got in, she said that Internet Explorer remembered the password and logged her in. How can I stop this from happening in the future?

The Fix: Microsoft inexplicably hid the setting to turn off its password memory in a place you'd never expect to look—the Content tab of the Internet Options dialog box. In addition to passwords, Internet Explorer will also remember usernames and other words you type into web forms.

To stop Internet Explorer from remembering this information, follow these steps:

1. Select Tools → Internet Options, click the Content tab, and click the AutoComplete button to display the AutoComplete Settings dialog box (see Figure 9-8).

2. To force IE to stop remembering your passwords in the future, uncheck the "User names and passwords on forms" box.

Figure 9-8. Tell Internet Explorer to stop remembering your passwords.

3. To delete all of your existing passwords from IE's memory, click the Clear Passwords button.

4. To force IE to stop using AutoComplete for filling in web forms, uncheck the "Forms" box.

5. To delete all of your AutoComplete entries from IE's memory, click the Clear Forms button.

6. Click OK and then OK again to close the dialog boxes.

SPYWARE

MY BROWSER HAS BEEN HIJACKED!

The Annoyance: Whenever I start my browser, a rogue search page called *find4u.com* takes over, even if I reset my home page. I also get inundated with pop-ups every time I open my browser. How can I put an end to this evil hijacking?

The Fix: You've been attacked by spyware—software that silently collects information about you, including the web sites you visit. It then blasts you with pop-up ads, and even puts extra toolbars and links in your browser. And some spyware programs, as you've found out, hijack your home page as well.

Worst of all, it will send information about your web browsing habits to other web sites without your knowledge. Pretty sneaky, huh?

What should you do if you think you've been invaded by spyware? You can download free software to do away with it, such as Lavasoft's Ad-Aware (*http://www.lavasoftusa.com*) or PepiMK Software's Spybot Search & Destroy (*http://www.safer-networking.org*). Ad-Aware comes in a free version as well as several paid versions. The paid versions include more advanced features, such as real-time spyware detection.

Both programs work similarly. They scan your system for any signs of spyware, give you a full report on what they find, and then delete the spyware you select (see Figure 9-9). They also delete suspicious files and folders, repair Registry entries, and find and delete cookies that track your web travels.

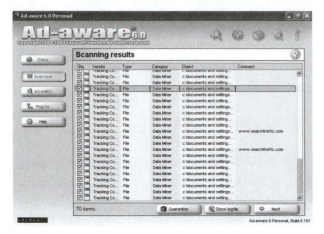

Figure 9-9. Even systems that you think are free from spyware may be infected, as this Ad-Aware report shows.

If you're willing to pay, you can get an even more comprehensive program called Spy Sweeper from Webroot Software (*http://www.webroot.com*). In addition to detecting and eliminating spyware, it prevents spyware from installing itself on your system. It will also protect you against other exploits, such as web sites that change your home page without telling you. You can download a free, 30-day trial; if you decide to keep it, the software costs $29.95.

AD-AWARE DELETED MY FAVORITE PHOTOS

The Annoyance: Ad-Aware did more than just kill spyware on my computer—it also deleted a folder filled with pictures of my family's summer vacation. I may not look great in a swimsuit, but that's no reason to remove the whole folder. How can I get those pictures back and prevent this from happening again?

The Fix: Ad-Aware keeps a backup of everything it deletes, so you can easily restore the folder. To get your pictures back, follow these steps:

1. Run Ad-Aware, and from the main screen, click "Open quarantine list."

2. You'll see a list of "quarantined objects," which are objects that Ad-Aware has deleted. Each listing contains all the objects deleted during a particular Ad-Aware session. Double-click each object and look at the listing.

3. When you find the quarantined object that contains your folder, click it, choose Restore, and click OK

4. *All* the objects found in the list will be restored, so run Ad-Aware again to delete the spyware and any other items you don't want on your system.

5. To keep Ad-Aware from deleting your folder again, when you do a scan, check all the items on the scan result list that you want Ad-Aware to ignore from now on.

6. Right-click in the list window and select "Add selection to ignore-list."

7. Click OK. Whenever you do a scan from now on, Ad-Aware will ignore those items.

AD-AWARE HANGS DURING SCANS

The Annoyance: I set Ad-Aware to scan my archived, compressed files for spyware, but it seems to "hang" on one specific folder—it churns away for a few minutes, but nothing happens. Has it met its spyware match?

The Fix: Actually, Ad-Aware may not be hanging. In order to scan inside compressed archives, it has to decompress the entire archive, scan each file, and then compress the files again. This can take a substantial amount of time. So start the scan, and then go refill your coffee cup or start a load of laundry. If it still hangs, tell Ad-Aware not to scan compressed files. Click the Settings button on the main screen (it's the cog button near the top of the screen). Next, click the Scanning button, and then uncheck the "Scan within Archives" option. Now exit Ad-Aware and decompress the files. Run Ad-Aware, and it will scan the decompressed files. After the scanning finishes, compress them again. Ad-Aware won't need to scan those files again, unless you change them and then archive them again. In that case, you'll have to repeat the above steps.

If Ad-Aware hangs when it tries to delete the spyware on your system, click the Settings button on the main screen. Next, click the General button on the left and uncheck the "Automatically quarantine objects prior to removal" option. This should fix the problem, but you will no longer be able to restore objects deleted by Ad-Aware.

AVOID SPYWARE IN THE FIRST PLACE

The Annoyance: It's nice to know you can get rid of spyware after it infects your system. But what can I do to keep spyware from getting onto my PC in the first place?

The Fix: There's no single solution for keeping spyware off your system, but the following tips will help you keep your computer clean:

- **Beware of free software downloads.** Spyware often piggybacks on file-sharing software and other free programs and installs itself without your knowledge. Kazaa is notorious for being rife with spyware.

- **Read the fine print.** Before you install a program, make sure you read the fine print, including the privacy rules. Does it say it will connect to the Internet without telling you? Does it say it will share information about you with its partners? If so, click the Cancel button or the X in the corner of the installation window to close it down. Before downloading, make sure you read any information about the software on the web site as well.

- **Don't click links sent to you in email or instant messages.** Before you click an embedded link, check with the sender—even if you think a friend sent you the message. A virus or worm may have taken over your friend's email or instant messaging software. If you click the link, it may send you to a web site that installs spyware on your system. This has become a real problem with AOL Instant Messenger.

- **Only install software from web sites you trust.** Why download software from unfamiliar or random web sites? Many well-known and trusted web sites (such as Download.com) offer tons of software that you can safely download and install.

- **Adjust your browser's security settings.** Make sure your browser prompts you before you accept ActiveX controls, which can install spyware. In Internet Explorer, select Tools → Internet Options, and click the Security tab. Select the Internet icon and click the Custom Level button. Go to the "ActiveX controls and plug-ins" section at the top of the next screen. Enable the first option ("Automatic prompting for ActiveX controls"), disable the second ("Binary and script behaviors"), and choose Prompt for the remaining four options. Click OK, and then OK again to close the dialog boxes.

- **Don't click on pop-ups.** If you click on some pop-ups, they will install spyware.

- **Visit Microsoft for updates.** Go to *http://www.microsoft.com/athome/security/default.mspx* or *http://www.microsoft.com/technet/security/default.mspx* to find the most current patches and security bulletins regarding spyware and other threats.

> Spyware sends information about you to a web site or person over the Internet without telling you, but a personal firewall, such as ZoneAlarm, can stop spyware from "phoning home" and reporting information about you.

TROJANS, WORMS, AND VIRUSES

WHAT TO DO ABOUT TROJANS

The Annoyance: My PC has started acting strangely—no matter what I do, my Internet speed slows to a crawl. I've also noticed that my PC dials out to the Internet by itself. And just a few minutes ago, the CD tray opened by itself! Has my PC been possessed by ghosts?

The Fix: Those are classic signs of a Trojan infection. The biggest problem with Trojans, though, isn't what you see, but what you don't see. Trojans allow other people to silently take control of your computer and all of its resources. For example, they can read, change, or delete your existing files, and even add new files to your computer. They can also use your computer as a launching pad for attacks against others, so it will look as though you're the attacker.

Trojans typically work by "phoning home"—that is, they connect to the Internet from your PC. Firewalls

such as ZoneAlarm (*http://www.zonealarm.com*) provide the best protection against Trojans because they can block these outbound connections. In addition to using a firewall, make sure you scan your system regularly with up-to-date anti-virus software.

Don't Become a Spam Robot

Spam and Trojans share a special and devious connection. Virus writers who infect PCs with Trojans have been selling the IP addresses of those infected PCs to spammers. The spammers, in turn, use the infected PCs to mail out spam. The person with the Trojan on his PC has, in essence, become a spam robot without even realizing it.

HIDDEN FILE EXTENSIONS FEED VIRUSES AND WORMS

The Annoyance: I opened an email attachment from a friend, which turned out to be a worm that promptly chomped its way through my computer. It appeared to be a graphics file, but I later found out that it was actually an executable program. If I had known the attachment ended in *.exe*, I never would have opened it. How can I make Outlook show me file extensions?

The Fix: By default, Windows XP doesn't display common filename extensions, such as *.exe*, *.doc*, *.xls*, and many others. Virus writers use this knowledge to trick people into opening dangerous files. For example, they may write a virus and give it a filename like *familypic.jpg.exe*. If you received an email with that file attached, you would see the filename as *familypic.jpg*, because Windows hides the *.exe* by default. When you click the file, you launch the virus.

To force Windows XP into displaying all filename extensions, open Windows Explorer, select Tools → Folder Options, and click the View tab. Uncheck the "Hide extensions for known file types" box and click OK (see Figure 9-10). From now on, when you get an attachment in your email program, you'll see the entire file extension.

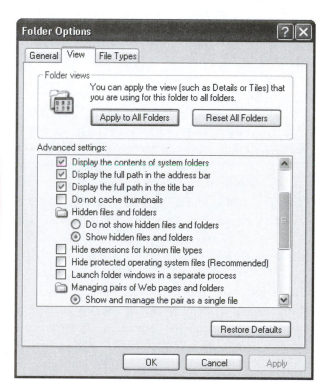

Figure 9-10. Change your View options to make sure you see the file extension of any file sent to you via email.

HOME-GROWN EMAIL WORM AND TROJAN DETECTOR

The Annoyance: My friend sent me an email worm. Fortunately, my anti-virus detector killed it, but what if a different worm gets through? How can I tell if a worm has hijacked my PC and is sending evil twins of itself to everyone I know?

The Fix: Add a bogus email address to your address book. For example, create an address like *noone@@worm.com*. That way, if a worm or Trojan infects your PC and sends copies of itself to everyone in your address book, you'll get a bounceback message alerting you that your email to *noone@@worm.com* can't be delivered. Since you didn't try to send that email, you'll know that a worm or Trojan has infected your PC.

HELP! I'VE BECOME AN AIM SPAMMER!

The Annoyance: A friend on my Buddy List sent me an IM via AOL Instant Messenger asking me to click on the following link: *http://www.buddylinks.net*. The site asked if I wanted to download a game. I figured if my friend suggested it, the game must be a good one. Bad move! Now I'm getting tons of irritating pop-up ads, and AIM is sending messages to my friends with a link to the same site. Help me get my good name back!

The Fix: When you downloaded the "game," you installed adware, which is generating the pop-up ads and spamming everyone on your Buddy List. To remove the adware, select Start → Control Panel → Add or Remove Programs, and remove the following three programs:

- BuddyLinks
- PSDT Messaging Integration
- PSD Tools ChannelUp v1.0

Next, install some anti-spyware software, such as Ad-Aware (available from *http://www.lavasoftusa.com*), on your PC. Perform a scan and remove any remaining traces of the program.

QUICK ANTI-VIRUS EMAIL CHECKLIST

Viruses and worms commonly spread via email. The following checklist will help you improve your odds against infection:

☒ **Never open an attachment unless you first check with the sender.** A typical infection takes control of the victim's email program and sends copies of itself to everyone in the address book. The message may say something like "Check this out!" or "Thought you might like to see this." The attachment is the virus—usually disguised as a picture or an innocuous document. If you get an attachment via email, check with the sender before you open it.

☒ **Keep your anti-virus software up-to-date.** Yes, yes—eat your vegetables, too. Good, up-to-date anti-virus software will detect almost all viruses, even those sent via email. Make sure you turn on the program's automatic update feature to always download the latest anti-virus definitions.

☒ **Use your anti-virus software's email scanning features.** This feature automatically scans your incoming email for viruses and offers additional protection.

☒ **Keep Windows up-to-date.** Microsoft continually releases updates that protect Windows against attacks. Use the Windows Update feature, or regularly visit *http://windowsupdate.microsoft.com*.

☒ **Keep your software up-to-date.** It's especially important to do this for email, file-sharing, and other programs that use a network or the Internet. Visit the publishers' sites and download any patches or updates.

INSTANT MESSAGING LINKS HIJACKED MY PC

The Annoyance: I clicked a URL someone sent me via an instant messaging program, and it hijacked my PC—I keep getting random pop-ups, a strange toolbar has appeared in IE, and my PC has slowed to a crawl. How can I send and receive IMs, and still protect myself?

The Fix: Malware writers are increasingly targeting instant messaging programs as a way to spread viruses, worms, and Trojans. Most likely, a worm or Trojan hijacked your buddy's IM program and sent the message to you. When you clicked the URL, your PC was infected with spyware.

To prevent spyware, viruses, worms, or Trojans from infecting your PC, follow this advice whenever you use your IM program:

- Don't click on links friends send you until you've confirmed it's your friend on the other end. When you get a message with a link, send back an IM to your friend and ask why she sent the link.

- If you transfer files with friends via IM, make sure you scan all incoming files for viruses (see "Stop Viruses Sent via IM" in Chapter 7).

- Keep your anti-virus software up-to-date. Older versions of anti-virus software can't scan for IM-borne viruses, but newer versions can.

- Get software that specifically protects you against IM dangers, such as ZoneLabs's IMsecure (*http://www.zonelabs.com*). For details, see "Get All-Around IM Protection" in Chapter 7.

FIREWALLS

ZONEALARM KILLED MY HOME NETWORK

The Annoyance: I installed ZoneAlarm on my PC, and it disrupted my home network. The other networked computers can no longer access my shared folders or the printer attached to my PC. I installed ZoneAlarm because I'm worried about intruders, not my family, breaking into my PC. Can you help?

The Fix: You've put your home network into the wrong ZoneAlarm security zone. To allow full use of your home network, you need to change its security setting:

1. Open ZoneAlarm and select Firewall on the left, then the Zones tab to the right. You'll see a listing for your home network.

2. Click your network and then click Edit button below.

3. Choose Trusted from the Zone drop-down menu, click OK, and then click Apply (see Figure 9-11). You'll be able to use your network now.

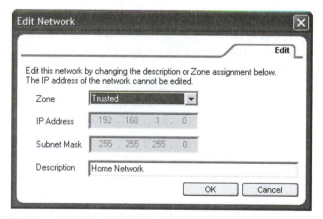

Figure 9-11. Put your home network in ZoneAlarm's Trusted zone.

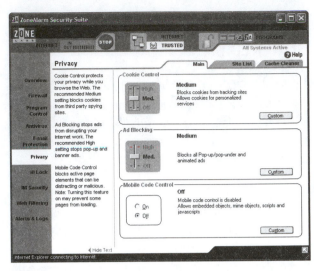

Figure 9-12. If you have problems browsing the Web when you use Zone-Alarm, change its Ad Blocking setting to Med or Off.

ZONEALARM KILLS MOST WEB BROWSING

The Annoyance: ZoneAlarm does a great job of protecting me, but when I visit some web pages, they stall out—I see the top of the web page and one or two sections, but the rest of the page is blank. My browser keeps trying to download the page, but it's stuck in perpetual non-motion. Can I browse the Web and also keep my computer safe?

The Fix: It sounds like you've configured ZoneAlarm to block Internet ads, which can cause problems at some web sites. If you allow ads to be displayed, you will most likely solve the problem. Run ZoneAlarm and select Privacy on the left, then the Main tab on the right. In the Ad Blocking section, move the slider from High to either Med or Off (see Figure 9-12). If you move it to Med, it will block animated, pop-up, and pop-under ads.

> Banner ads are displayed across the top of a web page; skyscraper ads are big vertical ads that run down the side of a page."

NORTON PERSONAL FIREWALL BLOCKS FORUM DISCUSSIONS

The Annoyance: I installed Norton Personal Firewall, and now I can't participate in my favorite web site discussion forum. I know Norton protects me against hackers and crackers, but does it really need to protect me against people I might disagree with? Can't I keep myself protected and also participate in discussion groups?

The Fix: Some discussion groups require the use of the HTTP_REFERER tag in your browser. They use this tag to verify that your browser is the originator of the posts you submit to the forum—in other words, that you are who you say you are. But these tags, when misused, can be privacy invaders as well. Web sites can use the tags to determine what sites you've previously visited, to build a profile of your interests.

Norton Personal Firewall blocks those tags as a way to protect your privacy. However, you can turn off the blocking on a site-by-site basis. Here's how:

1. In Norton Personal Firewall, select Options → Internet Security → General → Advanced Options.

2. Click Add Site.

3. Type in the name of the site that you want to allow to use the HTTP_REFERER tag, and click OK.

4. Highlight the site you just added, and select the Privacy tab. Check the "Use these rules for *<Site Name>*" box.

5. In the Browsing Privacy section, select Permit for Referrer. Click OK. You'll be able to participate in the forum now, but the HTTP_REFERER tag will still be blocked at other sites.

NORTON PERSONAL FIREWALL BLOCKS ONLINE BANKING

The Annoyance: After installing Norton Personal Firewall, I suddenly can't bank online—the site simply won't let me in.

The Fix: Norton Personal Firewall is blocking your access to secure sites, such as online banking sites. By default, it lets you use those sites, but it sounds as if your settings have been changed. Here's how to fix them:

1. In Norton Personal Firewall, double-click Personal Firewall and choose Advanced → General Rules. Scroll down until you find the rule that blocks access to secure sites. Uncheck the box next to it and click OK.

2. Try to connect to the site. If you're still having problems, click Privacy Control → Configure → Custom Level.

3. Make sure you turn on the "Enable Secure Connection" option. Click OK and then OK again.

4. Close your browser and Norton Personal Firewall, then open them both up again. You'll now be able to connect to the secure site.

NORTON PERSONAL FIREWALL BLOCKS WEB SITE LOGINS

The Annoyance: I installed Norton Personal Firewall, and now I can't log into my favorite web sites. I think this personal firewall business is going too far—why not just block me from using the Web entirely?

The Fix: You've set the firewall to block all personal information (usernames, passwords, and so forth) from being sent out across the Internet. You need to configure the firewall to let through usernames and passwords, but not privacy-invading information such as your social security number.

1. In Norton Personal Firewall, choose Privacy Control → Configure → Custom Level.

2. Change the setting for Confidential or Private Information from High to Medium.

3. Click OK and then OK again.

4. Try to log into one of your favorite web sites. If the firewall asks you whether you want to allow confidential information to be sent, click OK. (If you're not prompted, you'll be allowed to type in your username and password.) You'll now be able to log into any web site.

SHARE FILES SAFELY ON YOUR NETWORK WITH WINDOWS FIREWALL

The Annoyance: I installed the Windows Firewall on my PC, but now I can't share files and folders with the other computers on my home network.

The Fix: As long as you're behind a home router that blocks unsolicited inbound traffic (check the router's documentation for details), you can poke holes through the Windows Firewall to share files and folders with other network users:

1. Open the Windows Firewall control panel and click the Advanced tab. In the Network Connection Settings section, click the Settings button.

2. Click the Services tab, and then click the Add button.

3. Enter the following information in the dialog box:

   - Description of Service: Sharing Files
   - Name or IP Address: 127.0.0.1
   - External Port number for this service: 135
   - Internal Port number for this service: 135

   Select the TCP radio button, then click OK (see Figure 9-13).

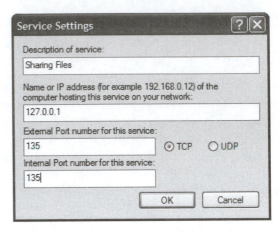

Figure 9-13. Windows Firewall can prevent users on your network from sharing your files and folders. Open ports using this dialog box to permit sharing.

4. Repeat the procedure to open TCP ports 136, 137, 138, 139, and 445 to sharing files and folders.

5. Repeat the procedure to open UDP ports 135, 136, 137, 138, 139, and 445. This time select the UDP radio button.

6. Keep clicking OK until you exit all dialog boxes.

If you're using a pre-SP2 version of Windows XP (which calls the firewall the Internet Connection Firewall), you need to do things slightly differently. Right-click your network connection and select Properties. In the resulting dialog box, click the Advanced tab, and then click the Settings button. Click the Add button and follow the directions beginning with Step 3.

REPORT HACKERS TO THE GOOD GUYS

The Annoyance: I use ZoneAlarm to keep intruders away from my PC, and I constantly get alerts that I'm under attack. I'd like to get back at these malevolent marauders, but I don't know how.

The Fix: Not all of the alerts you receive are the result of intruders trying to break into your computer. In fact, most alerts are the result of harmless network traffic—for example, your ISP will ping your computer to find out whether you're still connected to its network. Zone-Alarm color-codes all its alerts: a red band at the top indicates a high alert (signaling possible hacker activity), while orange means medium (often harmless network traffic).

To get back at your attackers, report their activities to your ISP, as well as to the ISP of the potential hacker. You'll need a special tracking tool, such as McAfee's Visual Trace (*http://www.mcafee.com*) or TamoSoft's SmartWhois (*http://www.tamos.com*), to track down information about the attacker, including his ISP and the ISP's email address. Here's how to report a hacker using Zone-Alarm:

1. When you get an alert, click the More Info button. You'll get information about the alert, including the IP address of the potential intruder, the port or service he tried to breach, and similar information. Copy down this information.

2. Run Visual Trace, SmartWhois, or a similar program, and type in the IP address of the intruder. You will receive information about the intruder's ISP, including its name, location, phone number, and email address (see Figure 9-14). In particular, look for an "abuse" contact. If you don't see one, look for customer support or tech support contact information.

3. Email all the details you copied down from the Zone-Alarm alert (the intruder's IP address, the port attacked, and so on) to your ISP and the intruder's ISP. ZoneAlarm keeps a log filled with details of all of your alerts, so attach the log file to your email as well. The log file is named *zalog.txt*, and you can find it in *C:\Windows\Internet Logs*.

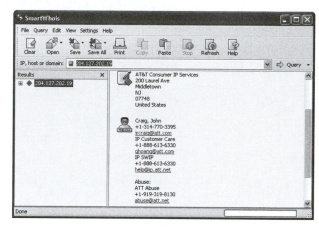

Figure 9-14. Use a tool like SmartWhois to find out where to report hackers.

Don't expect to get a response from either your ISP or the intruder's ISP; they frequently won't get back to you. Also, you should keep in mind that there's a possibility that the reported IP address of the intruder is not his real IP address. Sometimes intruders embed "zombies" or Trojans in other people's computers, and use those programs to attack others.

SCRIPT KIDDIES: THE INTERNET'S BACKGROUND RADIATION

Many of the intrusion attempts ZoneAlarm finds are not targeted specifically at your computer. Instead, malicious individuals send out probes to thousands of computers simultaneously, in the hopes of finding one that's unprotected. Frequently, these probes are launched not by expert intruders, but rather by "script kiddies"—adolescents with very little real knowledge of programming and Internet hacking who have gotten hold of automated tools that let them send out probes. These probes are so common that you can consider them the background radiation of the Internet—a constant stream of meaningless traffic.

10

Shopping and Auction
ANNOYANCES

Ah, the joys of Internet shopping and bargain hunting. Shop in your pajamas at your leisure. Get access to more kinds of stuff than you could ever imagine. Find great deals at auction sites, where you can bid on everything from a Rolls Royce Silver Shadow to an adult-sized Batman costume. And get very, very annoyed in the process.

Yes, the Internet is a great place to find deals. Yes, it's an amazingly convenient way to shop. And yes, it's packed with annoyances at every turn. Scam artists will try to steal your credit card information, or make off with the money you paid at an auction. Customer service will be… elusive. And as for returning something you've purchased—well, let's have a good cry, shall we?

But shopaholics fear not—this chapter will show you how to overcome these and other obstacles and find your inner consumer warrior.

GENERAL SHOPPING ANNOYANCES

BEWARE OF RESTOCKING FEES

The Annoyance: I'm about to buy a new laptop at an online store, but the fine print on the web site says it charges "restocking fees" on certain items. Can you translate that into English, please?

The Fix: In plain English, it means that if you return the laptop, you're going to have to pay a potentially big fee—up to several hundred dollars. A 15% restocking fee is common, which means that on a $1,500 laptop, you'll have to pay $225 just to return it—plus shipping, of course.

Don't expect to find information about restocking fees prominently displayed on retailers' web sites, because as a rule, they hide this information. Look for the page that explains the return policy and read it closely.

Restocking fees are more common at computer and electronics commerce sites, and less common at clothing and other online retail sites. And the policies vary widely. Some sites charge no restocking fees, others charge restocking fees on select items (such as computers), and some charge restocking fees for anything you return. Restocking fees are not charged when you return a defective item, only when you return an item for other reasons.

To find out if a site charges a fee for returning goods, perform a site-wide search for "restocking fee." But don't use the web site's search tool—these normally only search the online catalog. Instead, search the site with Google, using the following syntax:

```
site:www.sitename.com restocking fee
```

So, for example, if you wanted to search the CDW web site for its restocking policies, you would type:

```
site:www.cdw.com restocking fee
```

Still can't get the scoop? Email the vendor and ask.

Which popular web stores charge restocking fees, and what are their rules? Here's the skinny for some popular commerce sites:

- ☒ **Amazon** (*http://www.amazon.com*): No restocking fee if you buy directly from Amazon, but Amazon Marketplace, Merchant, Auction, and zShop sellers may individually charge restocking fees.

- ☒ **Best Buy** (*http://www.bestbuy.com*): The company charges a 15% restocking fee for any opened notebook PC, camcorder, digital camera, or radar detector.

- ☒ **Buy.com** (*http://www.buy.com*): No restocking fees, unless you purchased through Buy.com's Refer Direct feature (it's noted on each item), in which case each separate manufacturer determines the return policy.

- ☒ **CDW** (*http://www.cdw.com*): The company charges a 15% restocking fee on every item.

- ☒ **Circuit City** (*http://www.circuitcity.com*): The company charges a 15% restocking fee on digital cameras, camcorders, radar detectors, desktop PCs, notebook PCs, monitors, and printers, if returned opened or in a non-factory-sealed box.

- ☒ **Staples** (*http://www.staples.com*): No restocking fees.

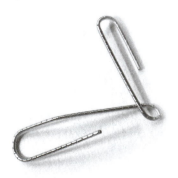

SWAP YOUR USELESS GIFT CERTIFICATE

The Annoyance: I received a gift certificate for a web site that sells collectibles, such as hard-to-find license plates. No thank you! Can I use the gift certificate to shop at another site?

The Fix: No, but you can go to *http://www.swapagift.com* or *http://www.certificateswap.com* and try to swap your gift certificate with someone who actually wants to buy a hard-to-find license plate. Both sites let you swap, sell, or buy gift certificates (see Figure 10-1). You can buy and sell any kind of gift certificates, not just ones from online sites.

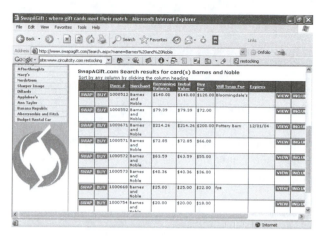

Figure 10-1. You can swap, sell, or buy gift certificates at SwapAGift.com.

Sell Your Gift Certificate on eBay

The general rule on eBay is that there's a buyer for everything—and that includes gift certificates. So you can sell—or buy—gift certificates at eBay, just like you can any other item.

How much can you expect to get for your gift certificate? That depends, of course, on the store. But as a general rule, gift certificates from well-known stores such as Macy's, Abercrombie & Fitch, and Crate and Barrel sell for 10% to 30% less than their face value.

WHY CAN'T I RETURN A BIG-SCREEN TV?

The Annoyance: I bought a 29-inch TV from an online store. I now realize that it's too big for my small living room. I called the store, but they won't let me return it. Isn't the right to return somewhere in the Constitution?

The Fix: Alas, our Founding Fathers were asleep at the wheel on this one. Many retailers, including Amazon and Buy.com, specifically say that they will not accept returns on TVs over 27 inches. Next time, before you buy, check the seller's return policy.

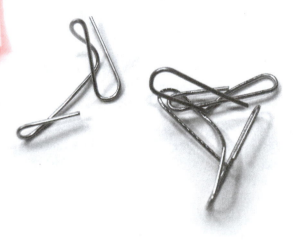

PROTECT YOURSELF AGAINST ONLINE IDENTITY THEFT

The Annoyance: My best friend answered an email from what he thought was his bank—and quickly had his identity stolen. I commiserated with him while he reopened his bank accounts, dealt with collection companies, and fought with credit agencies. What can I do to protect my identity online?

The Fix: Identity theft has become a huge problem, and the Internet makes it even easier for people to steal your identity and generally wreak financial havoc. The following tips will help you fend off predators:

- Never, ever respond to unsolicited mail from anyone purporting to be your credit card company, bank, or other financial institution. Hackers can easily spoof email addresses (and web sites) to make it look like the message came from your bank or credit card company. If you think the email may in fact be real, call your financial institution and speak with a representative.

- Never send your social security number, credit card information, or other personal financial data in an unencrypted email message. Whatever you send via email can be intercepted and read.

- Don't enter your social security number on any web sites, unless a reputable financial institution requires it for you to open an account. Again, only enter your SSN if you go to the site yourself to open an account, and not in response to an email message.

- Only purchase products from reputable web sites. (For help in determining whether a site is reputable, see "Can I Trust This Lawn-Gnome Site?")

- Only enter your credit card number at a secure site that uses encryption. Often, you'll see a lock icon in the lower-right corner of your browser when you're at a secure site. The best way to confirm that a site is secure is to make sure that the URL starts with *https://*. This indicates that the site uses the Secure Sockets Layer (SSL) for encryption.

- Don't store your personal information on laptops, which have a habit of getting up and walking away.

- When you dispose of a computer, wipe the hard drive clean. Merely deleting files isn't enough, because the data can easily be recovered and read. A number of utilities can truly wipe your drive, including Eraser, available for free from Heidi Computers (*http://www.heidi.ie*). For more information, visit the NASA web site (*http://www.nasa.gov/home/index.html*) and search for the following article: "Clearing Information from Your Computer's Hard Drive."

- For more information on how to protect yourself, and what to do if you suspect you've been victimized, visit the Federal Trade Commission web site (*http://www.consumer.gov/idtheft/*).

IDENTITY THEFT BY THE NUMBERS

The Federal Trade Commission (FTC) keeps records on identity theft, and not surprisingly, the number of incidents increases every year. Here are some facts about identity theft from its most recent report. Keep in mind that these numbers only reflect identity theft reported to the FTC:

- ☒ **In 2003, 214,905 cases of identity theft were reported to the FTC, up from 161,836 in 2002—an increase of 33% in a single year.**

- ☒ **The greater Washington D.C. area has the highest per capita rate of identity theft, with 153.8 complaints per 1,000 persons. It's followed by Seattle with 134.8, San Diego with 130.6, and Phoenix with 127.6.**

- ☒ **Sixty percent of people victimized by identity theft didn't report the theft to a police department.**

FASTER FORM FILLING

The Annoyance: I'm sick and tired of having to enter my name, address, and other personal data every time I want to buy something at a new web site. Can I speed up the process?

The Fix: Get a free forms-filler, like AI RoboForm (available from *http://www.roboform.com*). Fill in as much of your personal information as you want the program to know. The next time you visit a web site that requires a form, RoboForm will pop up (see Figure 10-2). Click the Fill Forms button, and the program will fill in the form automatically. You can even create multiple identities and different passcards (like passwords) for each identity, so you can have the program fill in different information when you pay with different credit cards or when you want to use different email or mailing addresses.

Figure 10-2. Save yourself time—let RoboForm fill in shopping forms automatically.

The Google Toolbar, available from *http://toolbar.google.com*, will also fill in forms for you automatically, but it can't hold as much information about you.

CAN I TRUST THIS LAWN-GNOME SITE?

The Annoyance: I found a web site that sells lawn gnomes dirt-cheap, but I'm not familiar with the company. How can I check it out before I buy?

The Fix: There are several things you need to look into before you buy from a site you don't know. First, check the site's reputation, and verify that the company will ship your goods as promised and fix any problems you may encounter. Next, find out what other shoppers have to say. Finally, make sure the site won't sell your private information or share it with other parties.

A number of different web sites and organizations can help you make an informed decision:

- The Better Business Bureau Online Reliability Program (*http://www.bbbonline.org*) gives seals to online merchants that adhere to a code of conduct for online buying (see Figure 10-3). It also gives out seals to merchants that follow privacy standards (see Figure 10-4). If a merchant doesn't have or display these seals, it doesn't mean that the site isn't reputable. But if a merchant does display the seals, it at least gives you some peace of mind.

Figure 10-3. This seal means that the web site has agreed to adhere to a set of buying standards.

Figure 10-4. This seal means that the web site has agreed to adhere to a set of privacy standards.

You can also go to *http://www.bbbonline.org* and search for any complaints lodged against a company. While you're at it, surf over to Consumer WebWatch (*http://www.consumerwebwatch.org*), put out by the people behind *Consumer Reports*. The site is devoted to issues of credibility on the Web, and it has many useful studies and resources for web surfers of all stripes.

- BizRate.com (*http://www.bizrate.com*) lets you get information about the trustworthiness, reliability, and overall quality of a site straight from the horse's mouth—from other people who have shopped there. Users rate their actual buying experiences at the site and write reviews for the entire world to see (see Figure 10-5).

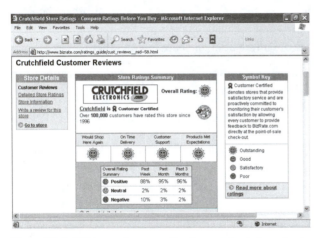

Figure 10-5. BizRate.com shows you ratings from people who have already bought from a site.

- The Usenet (a.k.a. Google Groups) is another useful source where users discuss any and all topics, including shopping. To get there, go to *http://www.google.com* and click the Groups link.

- TRUSTe (*http://www.truste.com*) gives out seals to sites that adhere to its set of privacy standards. It requires member sites to clearly outline what information they gather about customers and how that information is used. It also resolves privacy disputes between individuals and vendors. Critics claim that TRUSTe could do more to enforce privacy standards, but its seal does give you some guidance.

WHERE TO FILE A FRAUD COMPLAINT

No matter how carefully you check out a web site, you may get burned. If you do, file a complaint with one of the following organizations. Be forewarned that many of these organizations are overwhelmed with complaints, so they may not take action—however, you should at least try.

- ☒ **The U.S. Postal Service** (*http://www.usps.com/ websites/depart/inspect/welcome2.htm*) **investigates instances of mail fraud. Many online sites deliver goods (or are supposed to deliver goods) via the U.S. mail, so the USPS may have jurisdiction.**

- ☒ **The Internet Fraud Complaint Center** (*http://www. ifccfbi.gov*) **is a partnership between the Federal Bureau of Investigation and the National White Collar Crime Center. It's a good place to turn if you want to find out information about the latest scams.**

- ☒ **The Federal Trade Commission** (*http://www.ftc.gov*) **is also a good place to find information on Internet fraud. However, the same caveat applies—it gets many complaints and tends to prosecute cases only after a groundswell of complaints have come in.**

- ☒ **Most states have a consumer agency that supposedly protects consumers and investigates cases of online fraud. What your state's law permits such agencies to do varies. For a list of state agencies, go to** *http://www.consumerworld.org/pages/agencies. htm* **and scroll down about five pages.**

QUICK GUIDE TO LESS ANNOYING RETURNS

The Annoyance: After I bought a digital camera online, I found out that my wife had already bought me one for my birthday. I returned the camera, but the site sent it back to me because I failed to include an "RMA number." Why am I not surprised that web sites make it easy to buy something, but very difficult to return it? What in the world is an RMA number, how do I get one, and what can I do to make the return process easier?

The Fix: RMA stands for Return Merchandise Authorization, and almost every e-commerce site in existence asks you to request an RMA number from them before you return an item. When you get the RMA number, write it down on the outside of your package, and clearly label it RMA to avoid confusion.

So how do you get an RMA number? Ah, there's the rub. Some sites want you to request an RMA number via email, others ask you to fill out an online form, and still others ask you to pick up the phone and call—if you can find the phone number, that is. (For a list of toll-free customer support numbers for several popular web sites, see the sidebar "Shopping Support Numbers" later in this chapter.) Check the web site in question's Help or Return Policy area to find out how to obtain an RMA number.

> Another option is to return goods you've purchased online to a real store. At the Gap, Best Buy, Costco, Eddie Bauer, Barnes & Noble, and Macy's, for example, you can return items you bought online to their real-life stores. You don't need to call ahead of time; just bring the invoice that came with your shipment.

As a general rule, you'll have to pay for shipping when you return items, although in the case of damaged or defective goods, the site may agree to pick up the shipping costs.

Even after you obtain an RMA number, you may have to jump through a few hoops to return the goods. The following tips will help ease the process:

1. Keep and print out all ordering and invoicing information. That way, if you run into problems, you'll have a record of your sale.

2. As soon as your purchase arrives, unpack it and try it out. If you wait too long, your return period may expire.

3. Save the box, packing material, and any packing slips or invoices. That way, if you need to return the item, you'll be able to pack it up easily. Also, some sites may require that you include the original packing slip when you ship back the goods.

4. Get an RMA number.

5. Make copies of all packing slips, return authorization forms, and anything else you might need if things go wrong.

6. Use a shipping service that lets you track the package. Also, insure the package and ask for a return receipt, if the shipper offers one.

7. Once you've returned the item, check your credit card bill and confirm that you've been credited the price of the goods. For speedier confirmation, check your credit card online or call your credit card company.

I CAN GET IT FOR YOU WHOLESALE!

The Annoyance: I spend far too many hours surfing from site to site, looking for the lowest possible price when I buy. Then, after I buy, I always find a better price somewhere else online. I want to live by the battle cry of my ancestors: "I can get it for you wholesale!" How can I find the best possible price online?

The Fix: Don't shop at individual sites—instead, go to price-comparison sites that will search multiple shopping sites for the best possible deal. In fact, try several price-comparison sites to cover the greatest number of shopping sites. Good ones include PriceGrabber.com (*http://www.pricegrabber.com*), mySimon (*http://www.mysimon.com*), Shopper.com (*http://www.shopper.com*), and BizRate.com (*http://www.bizrate.com*).

When you use these price-comparison sites make sure you compare everything, including shipping and taxes. PriceGrabber.com, for example, will let you create a profile that includes your address, so that it will know when to calculate sales tax (see Figure 10-6).

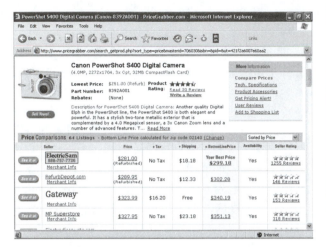

Figure 10-6. When shopping at PriceGrabber.com, re-sort your listings by price. The lowest-priced goods will always show up on top.

Many price-comparison sites let shoppers rate and review sellers. The obvious (but valid) conclusion is that you'll usually be better off ordering from a site with high ratings, even if it costs a few dollars more.

Also, be sure to look at the description of the goods before you place your order. PriceGrabber.com and others search for both brand-new and refurbished goods.

TAX, SCHMAX

The Annoyance: I don't get it. When I shop at some sites, I have to pay taxes, but when I shop at others, no tax is added. I thought Congress passed a ban on levying taxes on Internet shopping. Why do I ever have to pay taxes when I shop online?

The Fix: The oddities of tax laws regarding online shopping will astound you. Here's the basic rule: if you're buying from an online store that has a physical presence in your state, you're supposed to pay sales tax. The site should tack on the sales tax, since there's no real way for you to know whether the site has a store in your state.

But don't expect that rule to always hold, because state tax laws are mind-bogglingly complex, and there's no reasonable way that online stores can possibly keep track of them all. For example, in California you pay taxes on soda, but not juice. In Washington, 100% juice drinks are exempt from state taxes. In New York, a juice drink with 70% or more juice is tax-exempt. Given this level of complexity, some online stores don't even bother to collect sales tax.

A further complication is that many states impose a "use tax." If you buy an item from an out-of-state business, and you don't pay sales tax for that item, you're supposed to pay the equivalent in use tax to your state. Fortunately for consumers, states seldom enforce this law—wrestle with your conscience, and let us know how it turns out.

WHY DID I PAY MORE FOR A HOTEL AT EXPEDIA?

The Annoyance: For the last few years, I've booked my hotel reservations at Expedia.com. The last time I traveled, however, I found out that I would have gotten a lower price if I'd booked directly from the Marriott web site, rather than through Expedia. Why bother with travel sites if I can get a better deal straight from the source?

The Fix: These days, big hotel chains often give you prices the same as or lower than those offered by travel sites such as Expedia (*http://www.expedia.com*), Orbitz (*http://www.orbitz.com*), or Hotels.com (*http://www. hotels.com*). The hotel chains have finally realized that they can make more money booking their hotel rooms online than they can selling those hotel rooms to online discounters. In fact, Marriott will match the price offered by other online sites, and knock off an additional 25%.

However, the discount travel sites can still often find lower prices at independent hotels and other chains. Additionally, they let you compare the prices for different chains and offer cut-rate package deals—so it's a good idea to check both the discount sites and the chain sites, just to be sure.

UNFREEZE YOUR FROZEN PAYPAL ACCOUNT

The Annoyance: I've been using PayPal for two years with no problem. Then last week, the site sent me notification that it has frozen my account "for erroneous activity," and asked me to fax them some information. I did, but my account is still frozen, and I can't access my own money. I can't even find a number to call. Whose money is it, anyway?

The Fix: On occasion, PayPal freezes accounts when it decides that the terms of its service have been violated for some reason. A number of people have complained that their accounts have been frozen unfairly—you can find their stories on sites such as PayPal Sucks (*http:// www.paypalsucks.com*) and Paypal Warning (*http://www. paypalwarning.com*).

At this point, try to resolve the problem by phone. PayPal doesn't publicize its customer support number, but here it is: (888) 221-1161. Have all the information about your account handy, including the letter they sent you.

If you still can't resolve the problem, you can join a class action lawsuit filed against PayPal by the attorneys Girard, Gibbs & De Bartolomeo LLP (*http://www.girardgibbs. com/paypal.html*). The suit alleges that PayPal "fails to provide necessary information, such as an address and telephone number, so that its customers can easily report erroneous financial transactions, that PayPal unlawfully freezes consumers' accounts, and that PayPal fails to fully compensate consumers damaged by erroneous financial transactions."

HAS MY ONLINE BANK ACCOUNT BEEN CRACKED?

The Annoyance: The last time I logged into my bank account to pay my bills, an annoying message popped up telling me that something called a Certificate Authority from VeriSign had expired. Has my system been invaded, or worse yet, has someone stolen my banking information?

The Fix: You can safely ignore the warning and continue using your online bank account. (But you should probably yell at them about this; not having an updated certificate is a bit of a faux pas.) The key thing is to make sure the site is using encryption, notably SSL, to encrypt information sent between your computer and the web site. Part of that process involves the site sending a copy of its SSL certificate to your browser. VeriSign is the primary issuer of these certificates, which expire after a certain amount of time. A number of sites have neglected to update their certificates after they expire. When you visit a site with an expired certificate, you'll get the annoying warning message you saw. However, you can still establish a secure connection and conduct business. To make sure the site uses SSL, check the site URL—it should start with *https://*. If it doesn't, don't use the site for financial transactions.

To learn more about VeriSign and SSL, head to *http://www.verisign.com/site/ssl.html*.

EBAY ANNOYANCES

BEWARE OF EBAY PHISHERS

The Annoyance: I got an email warning that said I could no longer use my eBay account unless I "verify" it. The email certainly looks like it came from eBay—the return address even ends in *@ebay.com*. But the message sent me to a web page that asked for my credit card number. Also, the grammar on the page was awful. I know geeks have an aversion to proper English, but something smells funny here.

The Fix: If something smells funny, turn up your nose and run. You've been the victim of an eBay "phishing" attack (see Figure 10-7). The perpetrator has spoofed an eBay email address and mimicked eBay's web site in an attempt to get you to hand over your credit card number.

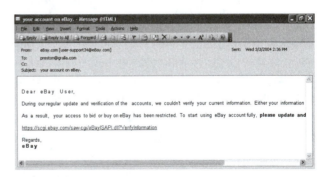

Figure 10-7. Something's phishy here! This is not really an email from eBay.

The following tips will help you spot the difference between a "phisher" and eBay:

- eBay will never ask you to send your credit card number, password, or other sensitive information via email.

- If you arrive at an eBay page via an email link, check the web address before you sign in. The URLs of most eBay sign-in pages begin with *http://signin.ebay.com/*. Also, make sure the page URL has *.ebay.com* right before the first forward slash (/).

If you have any doubts at all, ignore the email. You can always go straight to the eBay web site and log in. If eBay wants to verify your information, they will ask you upon sign-in. Finally, if you do get a fake email, forward it to *spoof@ebay.com*.

Another way to check whether the site you're visiting is truly run by eBay is to download the eBay toolbar (*http://www.ebay.com/ebay_toolbar*). In addition to letting you easily search and track auctions, the toolbar has an "Account Guard" feature that warns you when you're on a potentially fraudulent site. It also lets you report the site to eBay with a click.

WHEN IS CASH NOT CASH?

The Annoyance: I just found out that cash isn't really cash. I always thought that a cashier's check from a bank was as good as gold, so when I received one in payment for an item I sold on eBay, I immediately shipped the goods. When I deposited the cashier's check, it showed up in my account balance. However, the bank later told me it was forged, so I'm out the money. How can I tell the real thing from a forgery?

The Fix: Unless you're Frank Abagnale, Jr., it's pretty hard. In short, treat a cashier's check like a check, not cash. Even though the deposit initially showed up in your account balance, the check still had to clear before you could access the money. Next time, wait for the cashier's check to clear your bank before you ship the goods. Check your account balance online and then call the bank to confirm that the money is indeed in your account.

ADD A MOVIE TO YOUR AUCTION

The Annoyance: If a picture is worth a thousand words, is a moving picture worth a thousand dollars? I've heard that video clips help you get higher bids when you sell on eBay, but I'm not Steven Spielberg. How can I create a video for the auction site?

The Fix: Auction Video (*http://www.auctionvideo.com*) helps you record and store video clips up to 60 seconds long and then posts them to your eBay auction. Plug in your webcam and microphone, head to the site's "recording room," and record your video. The service costs $9.95 per month for one item, $19.95 per month for two items, and so on.

GET A GREAT DEAL ON A LABTOP OR CAMRA

The Annoyance: I'm a big fan of eBay, but my best friend always manages to buy items at far lower prices than I do. When I ask how he does it, he mysteriously murmurs, "Can you spell digital camera?"

The Fix: Discover your inner misspeller. When people misspell product names, prices plummet because few potential buyers find the auctions (see Figure 10-8). People have found great deals by searching for "labtops," "camras," and many other misspelled items. So when you search eBay, try misspellings first.

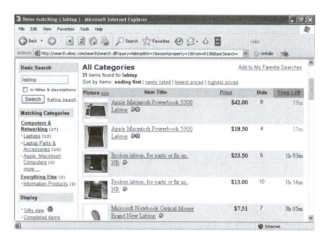

Figure 10-8. Looking for a great deal on a notebook computer? Search for "labtop" on eBay and you might find one at a great price.

BECOME AN EBAY SNIPER

The Annoyance: In the last month, I've lost four eBay auctions—and each time, the winner made the winning bid in the final two minutes. How can I beat out these Johnny-Come-Latelys?

The Fix: They're using a technique called *sniping*—they bid at the last possible moment. If you'd like to win auctions by sniping yourself, here's how to do it:

1. Synchronize your computer's clock with the eBay clock.

    To win at sniping, you must bid at the last possible minute or even second. To get the official eBay time, click the Site Map link at the top of the eBay home page. Next, click the eBay Official Time link at the bottom of the Buy column. To synchronize your system clock with the eBay clock, double-click the time display at the far right in the Windows Notification area (AKA, the System Tray) of your PC and set the new time.

2. Go to the auction page of the item you want to bid on about 15 minutes before the auction closes.

    Check the high bid, and then every few minutes press Ctrl-R to refresh the page. If the bids stay the same, there may be no other snipers present. When only five minutes remain, refresh your browser more frequently to see if the bidding gets hot and heavy.

When you bid at an eBay auction, it's easy to get caught up in the heat of the moment. Ego gets involved, and you often find yourself wanting to win at all costs. But if you buy an item for more than it's worth to you, you haven't won the auction—you've lost it. So set your maximum price, and don't bid a penny beyond it.

3. Open a second browser window.

    You need two browser windows open to snipe: in one window you do the actual bidding, and in the other window you constantly check the current winning bid. Wait until the last possible moment to click the Place Bid button in the bidding window.

Sniping can be time-consuming and nerve-racking. If your timing is off even a little, you may not win your auction. However, you can buy sniping software that will automatically bid for you at the last possible moment. PowerSnipe (*http://www.powersnipe.com*) costs $45.99 for a one-year subscription, and AuctionSentry (*http://www.auction-sentry.com*) goes for $14.95. Both companies offer free trial versions.

BEWARE OF EBAY SHILLS

The Annoyance: The last three times I've bid on an item from a particular seller on eBay, the same two or three bidders swooped in near the end and outbid me. It seems awfully coincidental that they always outbid me on auctions from the same person. Is something funny going on?

The Fix: It sounds like someone is doing shill bidding to artificially raise the price on auctions. In shill bidding, a person opens up several eBay accounts under different names, and then bids on his own auctions to raise the bid price. In some cases, a seller has friends act as shill bidders.

Sometimes shill bidding backfires, as it did in your case, and the seller ends up with the high bid. But he'll just auction the item again, and again bid up the price using shills.

How can you spot shill bidding? If you see the same user bidding on one person's auctions over and over, that's a warning sign. Search eBay to find all the auctions the person has bid on. If he only bids on one or two people's auctions over and over again, you've probably found a shill bidder.

To do the search, write down the bidder's eBay ID, and then click the Advanced Search link in the top-right corner of any eBay page. Click the Find a Member link in the lefthand column, and type the person's eBay ID in the search box (see Figure 10-9). Click the Search button to see all the auctions on which that person has bid.

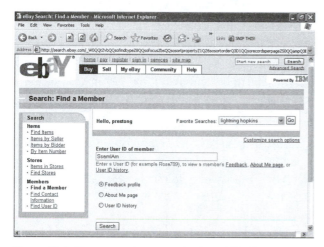

Figure 10-9. If you suspect that someone has been shill bidding, search through all the auctions he's bid on.

If you find a shill bidder, report the person to eBay. Go to *http://pages.ebay.com/help/contact_inline/index.html* and fill in the form. eBay will investigate. The first time it finds a shill, eBay issues a warning. If it happens again, eBay will suspend the user.

DID I PAY TOO MUCH FOR THOSE OPERA GLASSES?

The Annoyance: I just bought an old pair of opera glasses on eBay, and I thought I got a good deal. Was I wrong! I recently saw a similar pair for sale in a local antiques shop for eight dollars cheaper. I thought the whole point of eBay was saving money. I hate getting taken for a ride!

The Fix: If you do your homework, you'll be able to figure out the right price for just about any item on eBay, including old opera glasses. Follow these steps to avoid overpayment next time:

- **Search shopping sites for the lowest price.** Sometimes, you'll find the same item for less money elsewhere on the Web, especially if the item is new. Price-comparison sites such as PriceGrabber.com (*http://www.pricegrabber.com*), mySimon (*http://www.mysimon.com*), and BizRate.com (*http://www.bizrate.com*) scour the Internet for the best prices on new goods and compile their results for your perusal. (For more information about these sites, see "I Can Get It for You Wholesale!" earlier in this chapter.)

- **Find the price at online specialty sites.** If you're planning on bidding on a specialty or collector's item, such as rare stamps, search Google to find a site that specializes in those goods.

If you use PayPal to pay for an item on eBay, you get much better fraud protection than eBay offers. PayPal offers $500 fraud protection with no processing fee. For more details, go to *https://www. paypal.com/us/cgi-bin/webscr?cmd=p/ gen/ua/policy_pbp-outside*.

- **Find the price at other auction sites.** eBay may be the biggest auction site in the world, but there are other auction sites out there, including some that specialize in certain items, such as rare coins or comic books. To search for an item at several different auction sites simultaneously, go to *http://www.bidfind.com*.

- **Do an eBay search.** See if similar items are for sale or have been sold on eBay. How much did they sell for? Find out by searching through completed auctions. Click the Advanced Search link, type your keywords in the search box, check the "Completed listings only" box, and click the Search button.

- **Check the bidding history on eBay.** Check out the bidding history for items that have already sold and those that are currently being sold. The bidding history not only shows you the winning bid at each auction, but also every bid leading up to the winning bid. By examining bidding histories, you can tell how many people have bid on each item and get a sense of the item's overall popularity. Head to the eBay Search page and search for the item. From the results page, click on an individual auction, and then click the History link to see the complete history of every bid made.

Once you do all this, you'll have a good idea of what the going price should be on those opera glasses—and you won't overpay again.

DON'T GET BURNED ON EBAY

The Annoyance: My mother told me not to trust eBay, and maybe she was right. I sent a Western Union wire transfer to pay for a set of speakers, but the seller vamoosed with my cash. What can I do?

The Fix: You've committed a big eBay no-no—never, and I mean absolutely never, pay for anything using a Western Union wire transfer. That's as bad as sending cash in an envelope. Once the person gets the money from the wire transfer, there's no way to trace him; the money's gone. Even Western Union tells people not to use wire transfers to pay for auction items. If someone on

eBay says that they only accept payment via Western Union wire transfers, look for another seller. If possible, use PayPal when you buy anything on eBay, since it offers a measure of buyer protection.

To make matters worse, you're not eligible for the eBay Buyer Protection Program when you pay using a Western Union wire transfer. Normally, eBay will pay you part of the money you lost. If you're victimized, the protection covers you up to $200 per auction (shipping and handling not included), minus a $25 processing fee. For example, if you pay $150 for an item you never receive, eBay will reimburse you $125. If you pay under $25 for an item you never receive, you won't get back a penny.

You're not covered if the item is picked up or delivered in person, and you're also not covered for items damaged or lost in shipping. And, as you've just found out to your chagrin, you're not covered if you pay in cash or use a money transfer service.

To get compensation from eBay when you *do* qualify, go to *http://pages.ebay.com/help/tp/isgw-fraud-alert.html*, read the instructions for filing, and click the "File a fraud alert" link. You have to do this between 30 and 60 days after the auction ends.

GET IT CHEAPER FROM THE POLICE

The Annoyance: Jack Benny is my patron saint. I don't like parting with a buck (or even a dime), so I spend a lot of time on eBay. But even those prices are too high for me. Is there an auction site with better bargains?

The Fix: Police auctions, once held in dimly lit basements, have gone high-tech. Now about 300 police departments around the country, including New York City's, let you buy goods online at *http://www.stealitback.com*. It works just like a regular online auction—and given our nation's crime rate, thousands of items of all sorts and descriptions are constantly coming on sale (see Figure 10-10). You buy directly from the site, which makes the deals with individual police departments. When you buy an item, they ship it to you from the site's warehouse.

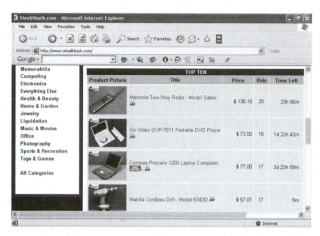

Figure 10-10. When they say the goods are "hot" at Stealitback.com, they really mean it.

You'll often find oddities for sale here. Where else, after all, can you bid on 30 pounds of cell phones, pagers, and accessories? Another auction site worth checking out is *http://www.policeauctions.com*.

GOOD DEALS AT OTHER GOVERNMENT AUCTIONS

Law enforcement departments aren't the only government agencies that sell goods through online auctions. The following web sites auction goods from a variety of public agencies:

☒ Government Liquidation (*http://www.GovLiquidation.com*)*:* As the name indicates, this site handles liquidation items at locations throughout the country. You'll find vehicles, heavy equipment, and similar goods.

☒ Bid4Assets (*http://www.bid4assets.com*): Here you'll find high-end goods such as land, cars, jewelry, artwork, coins, timeshares, computers, and more, from government agencies as well as individuals.

☒ Government Auctions (*http://www.governmentauctions.org*): This site offers links to dozens of local, state, and federal auction sites.

AMAZON ANNOYANCES

ZAP IMAGES FOR FASTER AMAZON SHOPPING

The Annoyance: My slow dial-up connection takes forever to display all the graphics when I shop on Amazon. Can I shop faster without the pointless graphics?

The Fix: Amazon's text-only site (*http://www.amazon.com/text*) displays pages lightning fast. The site contains the exact same content as the regular site, but without the pictures (see Figure 10-11).

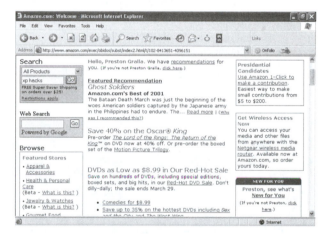

Figure 10-11. Who needs pictures? Shop on the text-only Amazon site for faster browsing and buying.

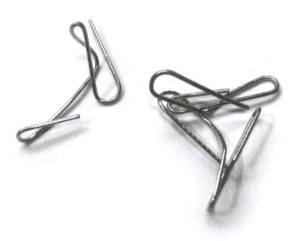

SHOP AMAZON WITH YOUR CELL PHONE

The Annoyance: Last week at my local bookstore, I saw what I thought was a great deal on the collected short stories of Ernest Hemingway. The sale was about to end, so I didn't have time to go home and check the Amazon price. I bought the book, went home, and found out that I could have gotten it for five dollars less on Amazon. When is Amazon going to come up with some kind of long-distance Vulcan mind meld, so I can check prices when I'm at a local store?

The Fix: If you have an Internet-enabled cell phone or PDA, you can check Amazon's prices from wherever you are, and you won't need Mr. Spock's help (see Figure 10-12). If you have a PDA with a WAP browser, go to *http://amazon.com/phone* and you'll be able to shop long-distance. If you have a PocketPC, head to *http://amazon.com/pocketpc*, and if you have a Palm go to *http://amazon.com/mypalm*.

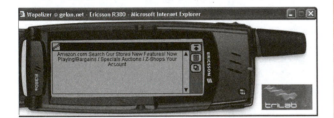

Figure 10-12. Never overpay again—if you're at a bookstore and want to check a book price at Amazon, dial in via your cell phone or PDA.

YES, VIRGINIA, THERE IS AN AMAZON 800 NUMBER

The Annoyance: Do any humans actually work at Amazon? I need to get in touch with customer service because of a minor billing error, and none of my emails with the company have solved the problem. I can't find a phone number anywhere.

The Fix: This is an easy one—dial (800) 201-7575. Of course, you'll get an automated voice system, but if you push enough buttons and hang on long enough, you'll find a live human being on the other end to answer your questions.

SHOPPING SUPPORT NUMBERS

Many shopping web sites make it difficult to find customer support numbers. Here are the support numbers for some of the most popular shopping sites:

- ☒ **Amazon: (800) 201-7575**
- ☒ **Barnes & Noble: (800) 843-2665**
- ☒ **Best Buy: (800) 369-5050**
- ☒ **Buy.com: (877) 780-2464**
- ☒ **eBay: (800) 322-9266, (888) 749-3229, or (408) 558-7400**
- ☒ **Orbitz: (888) 656-4546**
- ☒ **Petco: (877) 738-6742**
- ☒ **SmarterKids.com: (800) 293-9314**
- ☒ **Staples: (800) 378-2753**
- ☒ **Travelocity: (888) 265-1017**

STOP MY $7,600 AMAZON ONE-CLICK ORDER

The Annoyance: I just paid $7,600 for a 50-inch plasma flat-panel HDTV using Amazon's "One-Click" method of payment. I'm now suffering from buyer's remorse—no, make that buyer's panic. My wife kindly pointed out that perhaps paying our daughter's tuition was more important than watching big football guys make big hits on a big TV. I know that one-click ordering means "you click it, you bought it." But is there anything I can do to stop the payment?

The Fix: If you ordered it less than 90 minutes ago, you're in luck. Click the Your Account link at the top of any Amazon page, and edit your order by removing it from your account. The order will be canceled with no questions asked.

If you ordered it more than 90 minutes ago, get ready for delivery. However, Amazon's return policy lets you return most items within 30 days. You'll have to pay for shipping, but at least you won't be out $7,600. You can't return all items, though, and if you've bought from an Amazon "merchant" rather than Amazon itself, you'll have to deal with that merchant directly. Check the web site for details.

FIND FOREIGN BOOKS ON AMAZON

The Annoyance: I've been brushing up on my French, and I want to read Balzac's *Le Eugenie Grandet* in the original, not in translation. But when I search Amazon, all I find are English translations. If Amazon is so smart, why can't it speak a foreign language?

The Fix: An easy solution is to go to Amazon's French site (*http://www.amazon.fr*) and do your search there. Other Amazon foreign-language web sites include those for Germany (*http://www.amazon.de*) and Japan (*http://www.amazon.co.jp*).

Visiting one of Amazon's foreign-language sites may be the simplest way to find your book, but it's not necessar-

ily the best way. First, you'll be ordering the book from a foreign publisher, so you'll pay substantial shipping costs. And depending on the exchange rate, you may pay a premium for the book as well.

A better bet is to search Amazon for foreign-language books published in the U.S., using Amazon's Power Search feature. First, click the Books tab on Amazon. Then click the Advanced Search link in the upper-lefthand corner of the page. Scroll down in the Search Books page until you come to the Power Search box. In the box, type:

    title: Eugenie Grandet language: French

Click the Power Search Now button. You'll get a list of French-language versions of *Le Eugenie Grandet* (see Figure 10-13).

Figure 10-13. Oh la vache! Use Amazon's Power Search feature to find foreign-language books published in the U.S.

If you want to search by author instead, type:

    author: Balzac Language: french

You can also search for books written in other foreign languages, including Italian, Spanish, German, Russian, and more.

Note that you must use title:, author:, or a similar modifier when searching (see "Find Books Fast with Amazon Power Search" for a full list of the accepted modifiers). For example, if you search for:

    Eugenie Grandet Language: French

you won't get any results. Also, you can't do this type of search from the normal Amazon search box—you have to use the Power Search box on the Search Books page.

Note: Power Search results aren't foolproof—you'll still sometimes get English-language editions. Double-check by clicking the Search Inside button and checking the book's table of contents, or looking at an excerpt.

FIND BOOKS FAST WITH AMAZON POWER SEARCH

The Annoyance: Amazon prides itself on being the world's largest bookstore, but my problem is that it's *too* big. I'm looking for a hardcover edition of any book by Ernest Hemingway published before 1990, and there doesn't seem to be any way to narrow the search by format or date. When I search for Hemingway, I get hundreds of results. If I tried looking through all of them, I'd be older than the *Old Man and the Sea* before I finished. Help!

The Fix: You have two options here. Click the Book tab, then the Advanced Search link in the upper-lefthand corner of the page. Your first option is to fill out the form on the Search Books page. Type Ernest Hemingway in the Author box, and select Hardcover in the Format drop-down box. In the Publication drop-down box, select Before the Year, and to the right, type 1990. Then click the Search Now button. This yields a list of 77 editions.

If you use Amazon's Power Search feature, you can narrow your search even further, using special syntax and Boolean search functions. For example, to search for a hardcover, large-print edition of any book by Ernest Hemingway published before 1990, type the following in the Power Search box and click the Power Search Now button:

```
author: Hemingway format: hardcover pubdate:
before 1990 binding: large print
```

The Power Search box also lets you use Boolean operators, such as:

```
author: Hemingway format: (hardcover or
paperback) pubdate: before 1990 binding: large
print
```

You can use normal Boolean operators (and, or, not, parentheses). Also, remember that you have to put a colon (:) and a space after each operator, as shown in the above examples. The Amazon operators you can use in the Power Search box are:

author
author-begins
author-exact
binding
format
ISBN
keywords
keywords-begin
language
pubdate (before, during, after)
publisher
subject
subject-begins
subject-words-begin
title
title-begins
title-words-begin

SEARCH AMAZON FROM IE'S ADDRESS BAR

The Annoyance: I admit it—I'm an Amazon junkie. I buy everything on Amazon, from books to kitchen gadgets to electronics and CDs. But I hate waiting for the site to load before I can start my searches, and there's no Amazon toolbar for IE, like there is for Google.

The Fix: You're right—there's no Amazon toolbar. But you can get the equivalent functionality by changing the default search engine tied into Internet Explorer's Address Bar. The trick requires the free Internet utility called TweakUI (*http://www.microsoft.com/windowsxp/pro/downloads/powertoys.asp*). Follow these steps:

1. Download and run TweakUI.

2. In the lefthand panel, click Internet Explorer → Search (see Figure 10-14).

3. Click the Create button on the right. The Search Prefix dialog box will appear.

4. In the Prefix portion of the dialog box, enter the word you want to type into Internet Explorer that tells it to search Amazon—for example, Amzn (see Figure 10-15).

5. In the URL portion of the dialog box, type the following, exactly as you see it:

```
http://www.amazon.com/exec/obidos/external-
search/mode=blended&keyword=%s
```

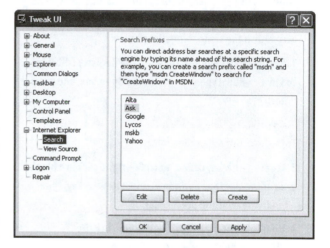

Figure 10-14. To search Amazon from the Internet Explorer Address Bar, use TweakUI to change IE's default.

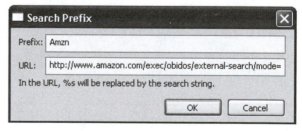

Figure 10-15. When creating a search prefix, enter a short name—you'll be typing it a lot in the IE Address Bar!

6. Click OK, Apply, and then OK again to close all dialog boxes.

7. Close Internet Explorer and restart it. In the Address Bar, type Amzn, followed by the term you want to search, such as Internet Annoyances. You'll search Amazon and get a page of search results, just as if you had typed the term directly in Amazon's search box.

SUPER SEARCHES FROM THE ADDRESS BAR (FOR AMAZON)

Want to search Amazon from IE's toolbar, but don't want to use TweakUI? With a few Registry tweaks, you can accomplish the same thing. Here's how:

1. Exit Internet Explorer, then run the Registry Editor (go to Start → Run, type regedit in the Open box, and press Enter).

2. Go to HKEY_CURRENT_USER\Software\Microsoft\ Internet Explorer\SearchUrl.

3. Create a new key called "amzn"—right-click in a blank area of the righthand window, select New → Key, type amzn in the box, and press Enter.

4. Highlight the amzn key and double-click (Default) in the righthand window. Enter *http:// www.amazon.com/exec/obidos/external-search/ mode=blended&keyword=%s* and click OK.

Exit the Registry and restart Internet Explorer. You can now search Amazon from the IE Address Bar—just type in the phrase you want to search, and the Amazon results will be fetched for you.

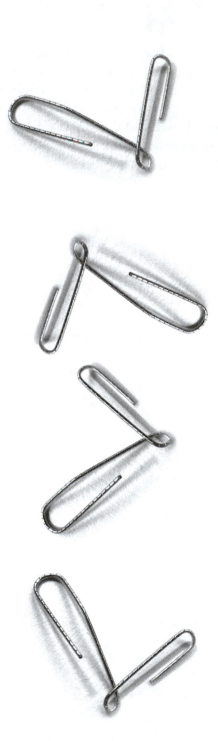

Index

Symbols

125-Mbps network speed, 48
40-bit WEP encryption versus 64-bit
       WEP encryption, 58
802.11g network, setting up, 51
802.11 standards, 50

A

A9
    search site, 185
    Toolbar, 185
ActiveX controls and non-IE
       browsers, 117
Ad-Aware
    spyware, 157
    web site, 199
address book, printing, 5
Adobe Acrobat reader, 110
AdSubtract ad blocker, 101
    web site, 170
Advanced Networking Pack,
      problems, 32
advertising annoyances, 100–104
ad annoyances
    opting out, 125
ad blocking, 101
    Flash, 102
    using HOSTS file, 102
AIMBots, 162
AIM annoyances
    AIM Ad Remover web site, 157
    AIM spamming, 204
    avoiding WarnBots, 162
    chatting with AIMBots, 162
    chatting with ICQ buddies, 159
    DeadAIM ad-blocker, 157

disabling announcements, 160
resizing chat window, 160
shrinking the buddy list, 159
specifying privacy settings, 158
spyware and, 157
transferring files over home net-
    work, 158
turning off sounds, 160
using at same time as AOL, 158
warning levels, 161
web-based version, 160
AirSnare web site, 49
AltaVista Toolbar, 171
Amazon annoyances
    800 support number, 226
    Amazon foreign-language
      web sites, 227
    canceling One-Click order, 227
    International Standard Book
      Number (ISBN), 229
    mobile devices, checking
      Amazon prices, 226
    Power Search feature, 228
    searching Amazon from IE
      address bar, 229
    searching for forthcoming
      titles, 186
    searching for highlighted
      words, 185
    searching simultaneously with the
      Web, 185
    text-only Amazon shopping, 225
anonymous browsing, 192
ANSI codes list, 13
Anti-Phishing Working Group
    web site, 195
anti-virus email checklist, 204
AnyWho, 173

AOL annoyances, 127–144
    AOL chat help sessions,
      saving, 132
    case of the $2,500
      connection, 134
    checking for local connection
      phone numbers, 134
    closing AOL Welcome screen, 129
    disable compressed graphics, 132
    disabling AOL Companion, 128
    email
      adjusting spam filters, 142
      AOL Communicator email
        client, 139
      blocking mail containing
        pictures or files, 143
      blocking spam from AOL, 143
      enable AOL to send files from
        Windows, 139
      file attachments, 140
      fixing fonts, 144
      managing address book, 139
      marking spam before
        reporting, 144
      saving sent mail, 138
      sending newsletters without
        being branded a
        spammer, 140
      sending stalled emails, 140
      sorting by person and date, 144
      unsending messages, 142
      using AOL Communicator, 141
      using Flash Session, 140
      using web interface, 141
    importing Favorite Places to IE
      Favorites, 130
    KDA faux idle-time software, 135
    LIVE Technical Help, 131

AOL annoyances (*continued*)
locating Front and Back
buttons, 128
parental controls, 135
preventing disconnections, 133
reading AOL mail with a POP3
client, 138
replacing AOL browser, 128
retrieving IDs of dropped calls from
Voicemail system, 133
running AIM and AOL at the same
time, 158
saving chat help sessions, 132
saving graphics in a better
format, 132
speeding up AOL exit, 129
stopping AOL from dialing when
connected via cable, 137
stopping AOL paper junk mail, 130
taming screen clutter, 129
too many windows open, 129
turning off pop-ups, 130
turning off You've Got Mail
announcement, 128
uninstalling previous versions, 133
AOL Instant Messenger (see AIM
annoyances)
AOL Voicemail system, retrieving IDs of
dropped calls, 133
AOL Welcome screen, closing, 129
Ask Jeeves Toolbar, 171
Aspinwall, Jim, 60
Asterisk Key utility web site, 119
AtomicLava web site, 94
AuctionSentry sniping software, 222
auction alerts for eBay, 188
Auction Video web site, 221
Audioblog.com web site, 95
AutoComplete function, 119
available versus preferred wireless
networks, 63

B

backup Outlook and Outlook
Express, 21
bandwidth, apportioning, 40
batch image-conversion tools, 91
Bayesian filters, 12
Better Business Bureau Online
Reliability Program, 215

big-screen televisions,
nonreturnable, 213
BigString web site, 9
BizRate.com, 216
blacklists list, 16
BloggerBot web site, 93
Blogger web site, 92
blogging annoyances, 92–98
audio blogging, 95
blocking search-engine robots, 97
BlogThis! commenting feature, 95
blog blockages, 95
cell phone, blogging via, 94
Google, removing blog from, 98
Google Toolbar and BlogThis!
feature, 96
LiveJournal, removing unwanted
characters, 98
Mail-to-Blogger email address, 96
mobile blogging, 94
Movable Type login and cookies, 97
password protecting, 97
posting pictures, 93
privacy and, 97
RSS versus Atom syndication, 96
tracking pulse of the
blogosphere, 94
uploading pictures to
LiveJournal, 98
BlogPulse web site, 94
Blogspot hosting, 92
bluesnarfing, 53
bluestumbler web site, 54
Bluetooth
accessing Net with, 70
origin, 54
vulnerabilities, 53
Boingo web site, 61
bookmarks (see Favorites)
booster antennas, 45
Brian's Buzz Search (tech search), 179
broadband annoyances, 34–38
cable splitter problems, 34
Comcast and home networking, 37
DSL
distance limit and speed, 38
Windows XP Connection
Wizard and, 38
DSL/router problems, 36
DSL modem restart, 36
good support sites, 41

internal wiring checks, 36
Linksys router DNS settings, 35
loops and, 35
MAC address and home
networking, 37
browsers
Google Toolbar for Netscape, 180
replacing AOL browser, 128
searching Amazon from IE
address bar, 229
browser annoyances, 99–126
BugMeNot, 113

C

Cable Modem Resources on the Web
web site, 41
cantennas, 45
dangers of, 46
prebuilt, 46
web site, 45
cell phone, blogging via, 94
cell phone annoyances, 52–53
bluesnarfing, 53
Bluetooth vulnerabilities, 53
browsing the Web, 52
Froogle, shopping via cell phone, 53
text messaging to cell phones, 52
Center for Democracy and Technology
web site, 12
Certificate Authority from VeriSign
expiration message, 220
cloning Mac address on a Linksys
router, 38
Color Wheel Company web site, 89
Comcast home networking web
site, 37
Computer Emergency Readiness Team
(CERT) web site, 192
congressional email addresses, 177
congressional voting record, 176
connection annoyances, 31–42
changing from dialup to LAN
setting, 34
connection speed, determining, 33
IE tries to dial modem, 34
repairing broken connections, 32
Windows XP hanging on
connection, 32
connection speed, determining, 33
Consumer WebWatch, 216

contacts, printing
  in Eudora 6, 5
  in Outlook 2003, 5
  in Outlook Express 6, 5
  Rolodex-style cards, 5
cookies
  deleting, 121
  managing, 123
  overview, 123
  transferring, 124
Cookie Pal cookie manager, 124
Coollist web site, 17
Cool Flash Player, 104
Copernic Agent Basic, 173
CSE HTML Validator web site, 86

D

D-Link DP-G321Multi-Port Print
          Server, 49
D-Link Wireless 2.4GHz Internet
          Camera, 51
DeadAIM ad blocker web site, 157
debugging error, disabling, 109
Deep Web, 178
DHCP Client table, 39
Digital Subscriber Line (see DSL)
discount travel sites, 219
DMZ zone on Linksys routers, 41
DNS settings, for Linksys routers, 35
Dogpile Toolbar, 171
domain annoyances, 74
domain contact, 74
domain forwarding services
          web sites, 75
domain name hosting, 74
domain registrars web sites, 74
downloads, setting location, 112
Download Accelerator Plus (DAP), 120
DSL
  distance limit and speed, 38
  overview, 38
  Windows XP Connection
          Wizard and, 38
Dundee web site, 17
Dynamic Host Configuration Protocol
          (DHCP), 40, 46

E

eBay annoyances, 220–225
  AuctionSentry sniping
          software, 222
  Auction Video, 221
  bidfind.com, 224
  cashiers check caution, 221
  determining prices, 223
  eBay Buyer Protection
          Program, 224
  eBay improving searches and
          browsing, 186
  eBay phishing, 220
  eBay searching, 186–190
  misspellings and bargains
          correlation, 221
  movie, add to auction for higher
          bids, 221
  PayPal fraud protection, 223
  PowerSnipe sniping software, 222
  shill bidding, 222
  sniping, 222
  Western Union wire transfer,
          caution, 224
email
  attachments, remembering, 4
  bugged, 10
  compacting Deleted Items
          folder, 19
  email and spam annoyances, 1–30
  Eudora 6, 26
  Eudora 6.0 Mood Watch feature, 8
  fixing Outlook 2003 Unread mail
          folder, 18
  Gmail (Google email service), 24
  Hotmail, Outlook and, 2
  HotSpots and, 66
  LISTSERV, running your own, 17
  Mail-to-Blogger email address, 96
  navigation keyboard shortcuts, 20
  newsletter-mailing services, 17
  Outlook messages, copying, 23
  Outlook messages, importing, 23
  overload cures, 5
  password protect Outlook 2003 and
          Outlook Express 6, 18
  prevent flaming, 8
  printing address book, 5
  protecting your email address, 13
  read status in AOL, 8

recalling Outlook messages, 9
receipt function, 7
resize panes in Outlook 2003, 18
retrieve web-based email with your
          email program, 2
returned mail notices, 10
return receipts in AOL, 8
sending while on the road, 3
spam, 11–17
  CAN SPAM Act, 15
  filters (see spam, filters)
  spammers, tracing, 13
  view HTML mail in Outlook
          2003, 19
  worm detector, 204
eMailTrackerPro web site, 13
EMS Free Surfer mk II pop-up
          blocker, 100
Eraser file deletion utility, 214
Eudora 6
  deleting spam, 28
  disabling auto-fill feature, 26
  keyboard shortcuts, 26
  speeding up performance, 28
  status icons key, 29
Expedia, 219

F

favicons, saving, 104
FavOrg favicon manager, 105
FavoRipper Favorites importer, 130
Favorites
  alphabetizing, 106
  creating an undeletable folder, 108
  Links folder, removing, 107
  moving, 105
  navigating, 106
  printing, 107
  searching, 106
Federal Trade Commission
          web site, 214
FeedBurner RSS service web site, 96
file-sharing slowdowns, 39
Firefox, 117
  browser, 102
  displaying sites designed for IE, 117
  improving tabbed browsing, 117
firewalls, 198
Flash animations, finding files on your
          computer, 104

foreign books, finding on Amazon, 227
forms, autofilling, 109
fraud, filing a complaint, 216
Free URL spell-check web site, 85
Froogle
    shopping via cell phone, 53
    web site, 53
Fullam, Scott, 45

G

Gaim universal IM, 154
game adapters, wireless, 51
Gator forms-filler program, 215
GeekTool Win32 Whois Client, 125
Genie Outlook Backup web site, 22
GhostSurf anonymous browsing, 194
Gibson Research security web site, 192
gift certificates, selling on eBay, 213
Girard, Gibbs & De Bartolomeo LLP
        web site, 219
Glossarist jargon web site, 177
Gmail
    aggressive spam filtering, 24
    archived messages, 25
    Google email service, 24
    privacy and, 25
    web site, 24
GoDaddy web site, 75
Google
    Google Alerts, 183
    Google Deskbar, 178
    Google Desktop Search, 5
    Google Groups, using to validate
            business sites, 216
    Google Language Tools, 182
    Google Local, 180
    Google Toolbar, 114, 171
        blogging and, 96
        web site, 100
    Google Zeitgeist, 183
    web site, 83
Government Printing Office (GPO), 175
GPO web site, 177
Graphic Workshop Professional
        web site, 132

H

hackers, reporting, 209
harvesting, spam, 12
hash-busting, 14

Hillery, Bob, 70
History, searching, 108
Hobbit, x
home networking annoyances, 39–42
    bandwidth, apportioning, 40
    connecting router to the Net, 41
    DMZ zone, setting up, 41
    file-sharing slowdowns, 39
    good support sites, 41
    MAC addresses, LAN versus
            WAN, 41
    Virtual Private Network (VPN)
            and, 41
home wireless networks
    125-Mbps network speed, 48
    802.11g network, setting up, 51
    802.11 standards, 50
    antenna placement, 44
    booster antennas, 45
    boosting wifi speed, 44
    cantenna, constructing, 44
    D-Link Wireless 2.4GHz Internet
            Camera, 51
    device incompatibilities, 48
    Dynamic Host Configuration
            Protocol (DHCP), 46
    extending range, 44
    game adapters, wireless, 51
    lease on IP address, extending, 47
    phone, interference from, 46
    relay stations, 45
    SpeedBooster technology, 48
    true network speed,
            determining, 47
    WiFi piracy, detecting, 49
    wireless print servers and, 49
hosting annoyances, 76–82
    keeping your URL accessible, 82
hosting services, comparing, 77
HOSTS file
    fixing access to web sites, 118
    speeding up access to
            web sites, 118
HotBot Quick Search Toolbar, 171
Hotels.com, 219
HotSpotVPN web site, 64
HotSpot annoyances, 60–71
    available versus preferred wireless
            networks, 63
    Bluetooth and, 70
    emailing from a HotSpot, 66

finding HotSpots, 60
JiWire search, 60
legalities, 70
privacy, 64
private HotSpots, accessing, 70
public versus private, 61
reconnecting to home network after
        a HotSpot connection, 65
setting your preferred network, 68
stuttering, 68
T-Mobile HotSpots, 64
troubleshooting connections, 62
war driving for HotSpots, 67
WiFi Finder device, 60
Windows Zero Configuration (WZC)
        applet, 68
HTML, special characters list, 13
HTML errors, correcting, 86
Hyperlink Technologies web site, 45

I

ICQ
    AIM, chatting with, 159
    controlling contact lists, 168
    disabling the typewriter sound, 168
    stop Always on Top behavior, 168
    web-based version, 160
identity theft, 214
IE
    autocomplete, 119
    branding, 114
    cookies, deleting, 121
    cookies, managing, 123
    difficulty saving graphic files, 120
    help with passwords, 119
    IE View Source registry setting,
            fixing, 86
    keyboard shortcuts, 119
    password memory, 120
    preventing downloads, 120
    privacy settings, 122
IEView, Firefox extension, 117
IE New Window Maximizer
        web site, 114
iHatePopups pop-up blocker, 100
IM
    blocking viruses sent via, 155
    detecting use on a network, 152
    disabling welcome screens, 150
    Gaim, 154

ICQ Pro, advantages, 150
IM viruses, 205
Jabber Messenger secure IM, 156
Pandion, 154
privacy and, 151
programs on cell phones, 149
protection, 147
saving chat sessions, 149
scanning files, 156
sending files via, 154
sending text messages to cell
        phones, 147
Trillian for Macintosh users, 154
Trillian universal IM, 153
updating Trillian , 154
ImageConverter .EXE web site, 91
images, JPEG versus GIF, 91
IMsecure IM protection, 147
IM Detector web site, 152
IM spam, 146
instant messaging (see IM)
IntelGuardians.com web site, 70
Internet Archive web site, 171
Internet Explorer (see IE)
Internet Fraud Complaint Center, 216
Internet tax hoax, 176
IPv6 protocol, 32
IrfanView web site, 91

J

Jabber Messenger secure IM, 156
JavaScript generator web site, 13
JiWire search, 60
Joe Jobs, 197
JPEG versus GIF images, 91

K

KDA faux idle-time software, 135
keyboard shortcuts for email, 20
keyboard shortcuts for IE, 119
kid-friendly filters, 174

L

Langenberg Reverse Phone
        Directory, 173
Law.com, 177
lease on IP address, extending, 47
Linksys router, checking logs, 39
Linksys web site, 47

Linksys WGA11B Wireless Game
        Adapters, 51
Linksys Wireless-G PrintServer
        for USB, 49
Links folder, removing, 107
Links toolbar, 111
LISTSERV, running your own, 17
LISTSERV Lite Free Edition, 17
LiveJournal, removing unwanted
        characters, 98
LiveJournal web site, 98
LIVE Technical Help in AOL, 131

M

MAC address, 37
    cloning, on a Linksys router, 38
    filtering, 56
    for WiFi adapters, 50
MAC addresses, LAN versus WAN, 41
Mail-to-Blogger email address, 96
MailWasher web site, 12
malware, 196
Maxthon web site, 116
McAfee SpamKiller web site, 11
McAfee Visual Trace, 209
MedHunt, 174
medical information searches, 174
Medline Plus, 174
Mfop2 web site, 94
Microangelo icon-creation
        program, 115
misspellings and eBay bargains, 221
mobile Top Level Domain initiative
        web site, 52
moblogging (mobile blogging), 94
Mood Watch feature, in Eudora 6.0, 8
Movable Type web site, 93
Mozilla browser, 102
mySimon, 217

N

National Do Not E-mail Registry web
        site hoax, 15
Navas Cable Modem/DSL Tuning Guide
        web site, 41
NetLimiter web site, 40
NetMechanic web site, 86
Netscape
    Windows Update and, 117
Netscape Composer web site, 82

NetStat Live web site, 33
networks
    available versus preferred, 63
    extending range of home wireless
        network, 44
Network Address Translation (NAT), 40
Network Solutions web site, 75
Network Stumbler web site, 67
newsletter-mailing services, 17
news sites, refreshing content, 110
No-IP.com web site, 82
noHTML for Outlook Express
        web site, 10
Nokia, and bluesnarfing, 53
Norton AntiSpam web site, 11
Norton Personal Firewall blocking
        discussion forums, online
        banking, and logins, 207

O

Onfolio, IE add-in, 113
online shopping and auction
        annoyances, 211–230
Opera
    Windows Update and, 117
Original Equipment Manufacturer
        (OEM), 218
Ottawa Wireless web site, 61
Outlook 2003 spam filter, 11
Outlook Express Backup web site, 22

P

page counter web sites, 92
Pandion universal IM, 154
parental controls in AOL, 135
password help, 119
password memory, 199
PayPal, class action suit, 219
Paypal, unfreezing account, 219
PayPal fraud protection, 223
PayPal Sucks web site, 219
Paypal Warning web site, 219
PC Pitstop web site, 33
phone, interfering with home wireless
        networks, 46
pictures, posting on your blog, 93
Pocket PC, war driving with, 68
Point-to-Point Protocol over Ethernet
        (PPPoE), 36
police auctions, 224

pop-up annoyances, 100
Pop-Up No-No! ad blocker, 102
Powermarks, favorites and bookmark
        manager, 104
PowerSnipe sniping software, 222
preventing your newsletter from being
        filtered as spam, 16
price-comparison sites, 217
PriceGrabber.com, 217
printing a web page, 112
PrintScreen feature, 33
privacy settings in IE, 122
Project Vote Smart, 176
Proxim Orinoco cards, 45
Proxomitron Flash blocker, 103
public proxy servers, 193
public versus private HotSpots, 61

Q

Qcheck web site, 47

R

relay stations, 45
remembering to send email
        attachments, 4
restocking fees, 212
retrieving email you regret sending, 9
Return Merchandise
        Authorization, 217
reverse phonebook lookup, 173
rich media ads, overview, 103
RLE Link Checker Lite web site, 87
RoboForm form filling, 109, 215
RSS Google news feeds, 182
RSS versus Atom syndication, 96

S

Scirus science search site, 174
screen-capture program, 33
script kiddies, overview, 209
search annoyances, 170–190
    A9 search site, 185
    address bar, searching from, 172
    Amazon and Web search
        |simultaneously, 185
    Brian's Buzz Search (tech search),
        179
    congressional email addresses, 177
    Copernic Agent Basic, 173

Deep Web, 178
eBay auction alerts, 188
eBay seller's items, searching, 188
eliminating junk from Google
        Desktop Search index, 184
Google, retaining original search
        results, 180
Google Alerts, 183
Google Deskbar, 178
Google government pages, 178
Google Local, 181
Google number searches, 181
Google Toolbar for Netscape, 180
Google Zeitgeist for tracking
        trends, 183
highlighted words, searching
        Amazon for, 185
IE default search, 171
improving eBay searches, 186
increasing number of Google results
        displayed on page, 181
jargon, 177
kid-friendly filters, 174
legal search, 177
medical information, 174
Microsoft Knowledge Base, 179
PDF files, finding quickly, 182
phone number lookup sites, 173
pictures, finding in Google
        cache, 183
reverse phonebook lookup, 173
RSS Google news feeds, 182
scanning eBay feedback
        quickly, 188
scientific information, 174
searching Amazon for forthcoming
        titles, 186
search toolbars, 171
search URLs, 173
Teoma, 179
Wayback Machine, 171
web pages, finding by title, 182
weed out sponsored results, 170
Yahoo! searching and
        navigation, 189
security annoyances, 191–210
    Ad-Aware failure, 201
    AIM spamming, 204
    anonymous browsing, 192
    anti-virus email checklist, 204

browsing affected by
        ZoneAlarm, 206
cable snooping, 196
disabling connection to the
        Internet, 196
downloads blocked, 198
email worm detector, 204
free security checks, 192
hidden file extensions, 203
hijacked browser, 199
IM viruses, 205
Joe Jobs, 197
Norton Personal Firewall blocking
        discussion forums, 207
password memory, 199
phishing, avoiding, 194
recovering Ad-Aware deletions, 200
reporting hackers, 209
script kiddies, 209
spoofed emails, 196
spoofing, 195
spyware, 199
Trojan infections, 202
viruses and worms, 203
Windows Firewall and file
        sharing, 208
Windows Messenger pop-ups, 197
ZoneAlarm and home
        networking, 205
security camera, wireless, 51
shill bidding, 222
Shopper.com, 217
shopping annoyances
    Better Business Bureau Online
        Reliability Program, 215
    BizRate.com, 216
    cashiers check caution, 221
    Certificate Authority from VeriSign
        expiration message, 220
    Consumer WebWatch, 216
    discount travel sites, 219
    form filling, 215
    fraud, filing a complaint, 216
    Gator forms-filler program, 215
    gift certificates, selling on
        eBay, 213
    Google Groups, using to validate
        business sites, 216
    identifying valid business sites, 215
    identity theft, 214

Internet Fraud Complaint
    Center, 216
nonreturnable big-screen
    televisions, 213
PayPal, class action suit, 219
PayPal Sucks web site, 219
Paypal Warning web site, 219
price-comparison sites, 217
restocking fees, 212
Return Merchandise
    Authorization, 217
swapping gift certificates, 213
taxes for online purchases, 218
TRUSTe, 216
U.S. Postal Service, investigating
    fraud, 216
shopping support numbers, 226
Simple Mail Transfer Protocol
    (SMTP), 3
SmarterChild AIMBot web site, 162
SnagIt web site, 33
snarfing, 53
sniping, 222
SnipURL web site, 8
spam, 11–17
    blacklists list, 16
    Center for Democracy and
        Technology, 12
    filters
        Bayesian, 12
        customizable, 11
        Eudora 6.0, 11
        integrating with your email, 11
        MailWasher, 12
        Outlook 2003, 11
        Outlook 2003, updating, 15
        phrases to avoid, 16
        setting levels, 11
        SpamBayes, 12
        SpamNet, 12
        trainable, 11
        whitelists and blacklists, 11
        Yahoo! Mail Plus, 12
    harvesting, 12
    ISPs and, 10
    ISP considers you a spammer, 17
    McAfee SpamKiller, 11
    Norton AntiSpam, 11
    preventing your newsletter from
        being filtered as spam, 16

SpamCheck service, 16
spammers, tracing, 13
spammerwocky, 14
SpamNet web site, 12
spam robots, 203
staying off lists, 12
versus spim, 146
SpamBayes web site, 12
SpamCop web site, 17
Sparklist web site, 17
SpeedBooster technology, 48
speeding up access to web sites, 118
speedups and shortcuts, 118–121
SpellCheck.net web site, 86
Spell Check Anywhere web site, 86
splash screen for Outlook Express,
    disabling, 20
SpoofStick utility, 195
Spybot Search & Destroy web site, 199
spyware, 199
    Gator forms-filler program, 215
    preventing, 202
Spy Sweeper web site, 200
SSID, stop broadcasting, 54
stealitback.com police auction
    web site, 224
SuperPages.com, 173
Surf and Sip web site, 61
Symantec web site, 192
SynchPst for Outlook web site, 21

T

T-Mobile
    Connection Manager web site, 64
    HotSpots, 64
    web site, 61
tabbed browsing, 116
TamoSoft SmartWhois, 209
taxes for online purchases, 218
Teleflip web site, 52
Temporary Internet Files folder,
    full, 120
Teoma Search Bar, 171
TextAmerica web site, 94
text messages to cell phones,
    sending, 52, 147
Thomas government search, 175
Tom's Networking web site, 48
toolbar
    Links, 111

toolbars
    finding buttons, 111
    removing, 109
top-level domains, proliferation of, 83
Topica web site, 17
Trojan infections, 202
true network speed, determining, 47
TRUSTe, 216
TurnFlash ad blocker, 102
TweakUI, 172
TypePad web site, 94

U

U.S. Postal Service, investigating
    fraud, 216
URLs, making long ones shorter, 8
URLSpellCheck for IIS web site, 85
URL Organizer 2 Favorites
    importer, 131

V

VeriSign and SSL, 220
Virtual Private Network (VPN), 41
VisualRoute web site, 13

W

war-chalking
    symbols, 59
    web site, 59
WarnBots, 162
war driving, 67
Wayback Machine, 171
Wayport web site, 61
web-based authoring tools, 84
weblog annoyances (see blogging
    annoyances)
WebTools, IE tabbed browsing, 116
WebWasher Classic ad blocker, 101
web bugs, 7
web page annoyances, 82–92
    batch image-conversion tools, 91
    centering graphics on the page, 87
    color palette compatibility, 88
    determining who links to your
        web site, 83
    fixing Internet Explorer View Source
        registry setting, 86
    font compatibility, 88
    free page counters, 92

web page annoyances (*continued*)
    FrontPage 2003, 82
        bad extensions, 84
    graphical web-site creation
           program, 82
    HTML errors, correcting, 86
    JPEG versus GIF, 91
    link checking, 87
    Link Validator, 87
    mistyped URLs, 85
    Netscape Composer, 82
    printing a page properly, 112
    proliferation of top-level
           domains, 83
    protecting email address, 92
    spelling errors and, 85
    thumbnails, 89
    web-based authoring tools, 84
web palette and color compatibility, 88
web sites
    1st SMTP, 4
    A9 search site, 185
    A9 Toolbar, 185
    Ad-Aware, 199
    AdSubtract, 101, 170
    ad servers list, 102
    AIM, web-based, 160
    AIM Ad Remover, 157
    AirSnare, 49
    AltaVista Toolbar, 171
    Amazon, 212
    Amazon foreign-language
           web sites, 227
    Amazon mobile sites, 226
    Amazon text-only site, 225
    Anonymizer, 193
    Anti-Phishing Working Group, 195
    AnyWho, 173
    AOL webmail, 141
    Ask Jeeves Toolbar, 171
    Asterisk Key utility, 119
    AtomicLava, 94
    Attach!, 4
    Attachment Forget-Me-Not, 5
    AuctionSentry, 222
    Auction Video, 221
    Audioblog.com, 95
    Best Buy, 212
    Better Business Bureau Online
           Reliability Program, 215

bidfind.com, 224
BigString, 9
BizRate.com, 216
Blogger, 92
BloggerBot, 93
BlogPulse, 94
bluestumber, 54
Boingo, 61
Brian's Buzz Search
        (tech search), 179
BugMeNot, 113
Buy.com, 212
Cable Modem Resources on
        the Web, 41
Caelo Software, 7
cantenna, 45
CDW, 212
Center for Democracy and
        Technology, 12
certificateswap.com, 213
Circuit City, 212
Color Wheel Company, 89
Comcast home networking, 37
Computer Emergency Readiness
        Team (CERT), 192
Consumer WebWatch, 216
Cookie Pal, 124
Coollist, 17
Cool Flash Player, 104
Copernic Agent Basic, 173
CSE HTML Validator, 86
DeadAIM ad blocker, 157
DidTheyReadIt, 7
Dogpile Toolbar, 171
domain forwarding services, 75
domain registrars, 74
Download Accelerator Plus, 120
Dundee, 17
DzSoft Favorites Search, 106
EarthLink anti-phishing toolbar, 195
eMailTrackerPro, 13
Eraser file deletion utility, 214
Expedia, 219
FavOrg, 105
FavoRipper, 130
Federal Trade Commission, 214
FeedBurner RSS service, 96
Free URL spell-check, 85
Froogle, 53
Gator forms-filler program, 215
GeekTool Win32 Whois Client, 125

Genie Outlook Backup, 22
GhostSurf anonymous
        browsing, 194
Gibson Research, 192
Girard, Gibbs & De Bartolomeo
        LLP, 219
Glossarist jargon web site, 177
Gmail, 24
GoDaddy, 75
Google, 83
Google Desktop Search, 5
Google Groups, using to validate
        business sites, 216
Google Language Tools, 182
Google Local, 180
Google Toolbar, 100
Google Toolbar for Netscape, 180
Government Printing Office, 177
Graphic Workshop Professional, 132
HotBot Quick Search Toolbar, 171
Hotels.com, 219
Hotmail Popper, 3
HotSpotVPN, 64
HotSpot finders, 60
Hyperlink Technologies, 45
ICQ, web-based, 160
IE New Window Maximizer, 114
ImageConverter .EXE, 91
IMsecure IM protection, 147
IM Detector, 152
IntelGuardians.com, 70
Internet Archive, 171
Internet Fraud Complaint Center, 216
investigating, 124
IrfanView, 91
Jabber Messenger, 156
JavaScript generator, 13
KDA faux idle-time software, 135
Langenberg Reverse Phone
        Directory, 173
Law.com, 177
Linksys, 47
LiveJournal, 98
MailWasher, 12
Maxthon, 116
McAfee SpamKiller, 11
McAfee Visual Trace, 209
MedHunt, 174
Medline Plus, 174
Mfop2, 94
Microangelo, 115

Microsoft Knowledge Base, 179
Movable Type, 93
mySimon, 217
Navas Cable Modem/DSL Tuning
     Guide, 41
NetLimiter, 40
NetMechanic, 86
Netscape Composer, 82
NetStat Live, 33
Network Solutions, 75
Network Stumbler, 67
No-IP.com, 82
noHTML for Outlook Express, 10
Norton AntiSpam, 11
Onfolio, 114
Ottawa Wireless, 61
Outlook Express Backup, 22
page counters, 92
PayPal Sucks, 219
Paypal Warning, 219
PC Pitstop, 33
Pop-Up No-No! ad blocker, 102
Powermarks, 104
PowerSnipe, 222
PriceGrabber.com, 217
Project Vote Smart, 176
Proxomitron Flash blocker, 103
public proxy servers, 193
Qcheck, 47
RLE Link Checker Lite, 87
RoboForm, 109
RoboForm form filling, 215
Scirus science search, 174
Shopper.com, 217
SmarterChild AIMBot, 162
SMTP.com, 4
SnagIt, 33
SnipURL, 9
SpamBayes, 12
SpamCop, 17
Sparklist, 17
SpellCheck.net, 86
Spell Check Anywhere, 86
SpoofStick utility, 195
Spybot Search & Destroy, 199
Spy Sweeper, 200
Staples, 212
stealitback.com police auction, 224
SuperPages.com, 173
Surf and Sip, 61
swapagift.com, 213

Symantec, 192
SynchPst for Outlook, 21
T-Mobile, 61
T-Mobile Connection Manager, 64
TamoSoft SmartWhois, 209
Teleflip, 52
Teoma, 179
Teoma Search Bar, 171
TextAmerica, 94
Text Monkey, 4
Thomas government search, 175
Tom's Networking, 48
Topica, 17
Trillian, 153
TRUSTe, 216
TurnFlash ad blocker, 102
TweakUI, 172
TypePad, 94
U.S. Postal Service, 216
URLSpellCheck for IIS, 85
URL Organizer 2, 131
VeriSign and SSL, 220
VisualRoute, 13
war-chalking, 59
Wayport, 61
Webroot Software's Window
     Washer, 194
WebTools, 116
WebWasher Classic, 101
WEP Key Generator utility, 58
whitelist guides, 140
WhitePages.com, 173
Whois, 74
WiFiMaps, 68
WildTanget, 157
Windows Update, 117
WinPcap, 49
Yahoo! Companion Toolbar, 171
Yahoo! Groups, 17
YahooPOPs!, 2
WEP encryption, 56
WEP Key Generator utility web site, 58
Western Union wire transfer, 224
WhitePages.com, 173
Whois search, 124
Whois web site, 74
WiFiMaps web site, 68
WiFi Alliance certification, 48
WiFi Finder device, 60
WiFi networks, 43–72
WiFi security annoyances, 54–59

40-bit WEP encryption versus 64-bit
     WEP encryption, 58
protect WiFi network, 55
SSID, stop broadcasting, 54
war-chalking symbols, 59
WEP encryption, 56
WPA encryption setup, 58
WildTanget web site, 157
Windows Firewall, 208
Windows Messenger
     disable autostarting, 163
     file transfers and firewalls, 164
     pop-up spam, 197
     prevent opening with Outlook and
          Outlook Express, 165
     removing, 163
     sending messages from
          Outlook, 166
     versus MSN Messenger, spam, 147
Windows Update web site, 117
Windows Zero Configuration (WZC)
     applet, 68
WinPcap web site, 49
Wireless-G Xbox Adapter, 51
WirelessMAN standard, 60
Wireless Access Protocol (WAP), 52
wireless annoyances, 43–72
Wireless Internet service provider
     (WISP), 61
Wireless Markup Language (WML), 52
wireless print servers, 49
WPA encryption setup, 58

Y

Yahoo!
     advanced navigation, 189
     advanced searching, 189
Yahoo! Companion Toolbar, 171
Yahoo! Groups web site, 17
Yahoo! Mail Plus, 12
Yahoo! Messenger
     cleaning out junk, 166
     fixing crashes from sending files,
          167
     login failures, 167
     receiving blank messages, 167

Z

zip files, download options, 111

Colophon

Our look is the result of reader comments, our own experimentation, and feedback from distribution channels. Distinctive covers complement our distinctive approach to technical topics, breathing personality and life into potentially dry subjects.

Philip Dangler was the production editor and proofreader for *Internet Annoyances*. Rachel Wheeler was the copyeditor. Philip Dangler did the typesetting and page makeup. Emily Quill and Claire Cloutier provided quality control. Reg Aubry wrote the index.

Ellie Volckhausen designed the cover of this book using Adobe Illustrator, and produced the cover layout with Adobe InDesign CS using Gravur Condensed and Adobe Sabon fonts. The cover was based on a series design by Volume Design, Inc.

Patti Capaldi designed the interior layout using Adobe InDesign CS. The text and heading fonts are Rotis Sans Serif, Lineto Gravur, and Myriad Pro; the code font is TheSans Mono Condensed. Julie Hawks converted the text to Adobe InDesign CS. The screenshots and technical illustrations that appear in the book were produced by Robert Romano and Jessamyn Read using Macromedia FreeHand MX and Adobe Photoshop 7. The cartoon illustrations used on the cover and in the interior of this book are copyright © 2004 Hal Mayforth.